10 THINGS

EVERY MINISTER'S WIFE NEEDS TO KNOW

10 THINGS

EVERY MINISTER'S WIFE NEEDS TO KNOW

JEANA FLOYD

First printing: January 2010

ISBN-13: 978-0-89221-698-7
ISBN-10: 0-89221-698-0
Library of Congress Number: 2009943788

All Scripture quotations in this book, unless otherwise noted, are from the New Living Translation of the Bible.

Printed in the United States of America

For information regarding author interviews, please contact the publicity department at (870) 438-5288.

Please visit our website for other great titles:
www.newleafpress.net

New Leaf Press
A Division of New Leaf Publishing Group

DEDICATION

There have been many women who have influenced
my life as a minister's wife, but one in particular
immediately comes to my mind — Barbara O'Chester.
Barbara greatly influenced my life as a young pastor's
wife — along with thousands of others through her
retreat ministry and personal example. Barbara has
been a blessing to my life for a number of years, and I
am grateful to call her friend and mentor. Thank you,
Barbara, for living out the model of a godly pastor's wife
before many others and me all these years.

Also, I would like to dedicate this book to all ministry
wives who have ever served with Ronnie and me on our
staff. You have made ministry life richer and I consider
it one of God's greatest blessings in my life to be called
your pastor's wife. May you be blessed as you continue
in service to our Lord.

I WANT TO THANK . . .

MY HUSBAND, RONNIE, IS ALWAYS the one who gently nudges me to go beyond my comfort zone — and once again, he's encouraged me to share some of our experience in ministry life through this book. It was his encouragement that led me to write this companion book to his *10 Things Every Minister Needs to Know* from the minister's wife lens. Thanks for the "nudge," Ronnie.

I am appreciative to Tim Dudley and Laura Welch from New Leaf Press for believing this is a needed voice for ministers' wives. Thanks to my friend for over 23 years, Debby Thompson, for helping me frame the chapters and giving me a "starting place." The ministers' wives that I chose to help with the interactive testimonies are living examples of what I share in the book. These are special women who I love dearly, and I respect their walks as ministers' wives.

I am grateful for those ministers' wives who so willingly shared their wisdom in the interactive testimonies at the end of each chapter. Thanks to Susie Hawkins, Kathy Ferguson-Litton, Barbara O'Chester, Donna Gaines, Leigh Lowery, Janice Thomas, Carol Young, Jennifer Landrith, Meredith Floyd, Charlotte Akin, and Tracey Smith. Their words added real life experience to each chapter.

I couldn't fail to mention my mom — a pastor's wife for over 40 years. Thanks, Mom, for being an example of a quiet and gentle spirit before me. Ten ladies committed to pray for me through this project. They prayed me through schedule challenges, word counts, deadlines, and the many highs and lows of writing a book. I am grateful for their prayer support and encouragement along the way. Thanks to Dana Tanner, Mona Elliott, Kate Floyd, Meredith Floyd, Kathy Ferguson-Litton, Susie Hawkins, Tracey Smith, Vickie White, Cheyrl Lyall, and Becky Wilson.

Last but not least, I want to thank my precious staff wives of the church that I have the privilege of being their pastors' wife — the staff wives of the First Baptist Church and the Church at Pinnacle Hills. You gave great input and a fresh look at ministry through young eyes!

CONTENTS

FOREWORD

KNOWING THAT THE BIBLE IS the best handbook by which a minister's wife should model her life, it is also important and beneficial to seek wise counsel from one who has already exerienced some of the joys and pitfalls of this most treasured position.

I have personally known Jeana for more than 15 years as the wife of a godly pastor and as a good friend. In this book, she has pinpointed what I believe are key elements that can be a tremendous help for the wife of a minister.

Throughout the last 18 years of mentoring ministers' wives, many doors of discussion have been opened and many questions have been asked that only another minister's wife can answer with confidence.

From my experiences, I believe Jeana has chosen the topics that are of greatest concern among ministers' wives and addressed them with biblical insight, personal experience, and practical advice.

Thank you, Jeana, for providing an official handbook for the helpmeet of the minister. I could not have said it better myself!

— Janet Hunt (wife of Dr. Johnny Hunt, current president of the Southern Baptist Convention, and pastor at First Baptist Church of Woodstock, Georgia)

INTRODUCTION

AFTER SERVING BY MY husband's side in ministry now for over 30 years, I can still say that I love being in ministry and love being a pastor's wife. It would be a blessing for me to know that this book has encouraged other wives to make ministry life not just tolerable and bearable but enjoyable and fulfilling.

We are always wise to learn from others — gleaning from their mistakes as well as the things done "right." I've tried to take a practical, authentic, transparent, and realistic view of my life as a pastor's wife and many of the issues we face. Maybe something I say will save another from grief or heartache. Maybe it will encourage someone to continue in faithfulness when they are weary in the ministry God has called them to. Maybe it will resonate with a resounding, "I've felt that way before, too!"

Regardless, my desire for this book would be that after serving many years in ministry — amidst the joys and sorrows, the challenges and triumphs — one could say as I do after all these years, "I love my job as pastor's wife and consider it a high calling and privilege to walk by my husband's side in ministry." May you be blessed and encouraged as you read this journey of mine.

1

THE "SECRET" TO SURVIVAL

I WAS JUST TRYING TO SURVIVE. What once seemed so easy was now difficult. How could that be? As a pastor's wife, how could I be struggling with something so basic? I burdened myself with guilt, personal expectations, and other emotions, wondering what people in my congregation would think of me if they knew how I struggled.

With two small boys, a busy schedule, and a very busy husband leading a growing, thriving ministry, I definitely felt overwhelmed. I certainly didn't feel like I "had it all together."

However, as the years have passed, my children have grown up, and other situations of my life have changed, I have learned that there will always be a reason *not* to spend time every day with our Father. Distractions don't end with the age of your children, the dynamics of your church, or your personal obligations. But what must be realized above all else is that daily time with the Lord is the secret to "survival," regardless of the circumstances of your life.

In ministry, survival can mean a lot of things. It can be every-thing from not being fired to spending many gratifying years of ministry in one location. Survival can mean the difference between "existing" and "thriving" in a place of ministry. It can mean you enduring your husband's job joyfully or grudgingly. The definition of survival in ministry can be relative — depending on where you are and how you feel about ministry. One thing is for sure: your survival and the way you feel about ministry are critical to your husband's success. After 30-plus years in ministry, I have observed that rarely is a minister successful in ministry when his wife is miserable.

Survival in ministry is easier when you remember what it is and what it is not. It's not a numbers game, and it's not about total expenditure of yourself in an unhealthy way. It's not about serving in positions that you may or may not feel called to or be-ing available to every person who has a critical need. It's not about being the perfect pastor's wife to the perfect pastor with perfect children. Survival in ministry to me is knowing that I have a per-sonal relationship with Christ, who knows every detail of my life, and gives me the awesome privilege of coming before Him — in the "secret place."

WHERE DO YOU LEARN TO SURVIVE?

Psalm 91:1 says, "He who dwells in the secret place of the Most High shall abide under the shadow of the Almighty" (NKJV). The psalm goes on to list the things God will do for you when you dwell in that secret place: He will be your refuge and your fortress; He will deliver you; He will cover you with His feathers and keep you under His wings; He will keep you from being afraid; He will let no evil befall you or any plague come near your dwelling; He will give His angels charge over you, to keep you in all your ways; He will set you on high; He will answer you; He will be with you in trouble; He will satisfy you with long life and show you His salvation.

Understanding the meaning of two phrases gives tremendous insight into this passage. The phrase "in the secret place" is the Hebrew word *sether,* which means "in the secret," "a covering," "a hiding place," or "a protective place." Then the words "to dwell" are the Hebrew word *yashab*, meaning "to sit down, remain, settle, even to be a constant guest of God." Therefore, when we remain in and settle in the secret place, we will experience the covering and the protective care of God. What great words of promise, comfort, and peace!

The secret to your survival is your "secret place," where you learn how to practice the presence of God and rely on Him alone, every moment of every day. It is learning to "abide under His shadow." If you learn to do that, you will be a survivor — a woman who pleases and honors God, a woman God cares for and protects as He promised in Psalm 91.

THE SECRET PLACE

How do you practice the presence of God? You find your "secret place" with Him every day. For years, time with God has been referred to as "quiet time," but I would like for you to think of it as your "secret place." The secret place is not so much a physical location as it is a place in your heart and spirit where you spend time with God. Time in your secret place is the secret to survival in ministry. This secret place is your personal private sanctuary with God. It is where you study the Word of God and listen to what He is saying to you in His Word. It is where you pour out your heart to your Father. You alone with God — that's the secret place. No husband, no children, no extended family, no friends, no distractions of any kind — just you and God.

WHY THE SECRET PLACE?

Today's world affords all of us many opportunities and distractions. You have opportunities to serve in your church in various roles, to get involved in community activities and the activities of your children, and the list goes on and on. In order to keep all of life's challenges and opportunities in perspective, it is crucial that you spend time with Christ.

In my personal life, I go to my secret place early in my day, before I get heavily involved in anything else. That is not to say that my way is the best or only way, it is just what works best for me. I know if I waited until the end of the day to visit the secret place, it just wouldn't happen. I need to begin my day in the secret place, armed with God's Word in my heart and mind. Only then am I ready to face the challenges of the day, both known and unknown.

Overwhelmed is a word I often use in my times with the Lord. Life can be busy, demanding, and uncertain. When I have that feeling, I ask the Lord to multiply my hours, to set my feet on level ground, and to guide my steps. I ask Him to help me not to fear the "what if's" in life. I need His direction in my life before I do anything else — before I talk to others, read e-mails, make appointments, or leave for the day. As the Scripture says, "I cry to you for help when my heart is overwhelmed. . . . Let me live forever in your sanctuary, safe beneath the shelter of your wings!" (Ps. 61:2–4).

When you commit your daily plans to Him, He promises to make your plans successful (Prov. 16:3). I just cannot overemphasize the importance of spending time in the secret place. It is crucial to your survival, and success, in ministry.

IN YOUR SECRET PLACE

Basically, the secret place is where you talk to God and He talks to you. Ask the Holy Spirit to lead in your time with the Father, and I suggest you include the following things.

Read God's Word

Reading the Word is one way you can really know God and hear His voice. He speaks to us through His Word — that's His method of communication with us. Don't get caught up in the amount of Scripture you read each day. I would encourage you, however, to give yourself as much time as you can to "soak up" the truth He has for you each day. When you meditate or think about what you have read, ask God to bring it to life for you. Maybe God has spoken audibly to you, but I'll tell you how God speaks to me — it's through His Word, and sometimes it's so profound to my life that it seems audible.

Spend Time Talking to God

There is no one, including your husband, who is *always* available, and who wants to hear from you and listen to your cares like the Lord Jesus. Prayer simply means talking to God, and it is our privilege to do so because of what Christ did for us on the Cross. This is your opportunity to praise Him for who He is and to thank Him for every blessing and circumstance in your life. He wants to hear your heart's cry. He's pleased to hear your intercession for others and your personal requests. Don't you love it when your husband or your children share their hearts with you? Our Heavenly Father loves it when we share our hearts with Him.

How to Dwell in the Secret Place

There is no right or wrong way to spend time with the Lord. The elements of reading the Word, meditating on the Word, and talking to God should all be included, but how you go about that is up to you and the Lord. However, in the event that my "plan" might help you enhance or improve your secret place, I want to share some ways I spend my time with the Lord. Let me add, also, that I do not always do the same thing. It depends on what is happening in my life, but I am consistent in going to my secret place on a daily basis. Be careful not to impose undue guilt on yourself about your methods, and don't compare your secret place with others' time with the Lord. The most important thing is that you are faithful every day to meet God in your secret place.

I have followed different plans of reading God's Word in my secret place. Some years, I have incorporated reading the Bible through in one year — something my husband does every year. Other times, I may focus on a single Bible verse that I read that day or the Scripture given to me in a devotional book. When I am involved in a Bible study group at church, I include that as part of my time in the secret place. As I am reading the Word and after I have finished reading it, I think about how it applies to my life, what it means for me that day, and how I can incorporate it into my day. That process may take more time on some days than others, but I consider that to be God's message to me on that day.

As part of my prayer time, I write in a journal a one-page prayer to God each day. That prayer usually includes the urgent prayer needs in my life and the lives of those close to me for that day.

In addition to the above, I keep a three-ring notebook that includes specific ongoing prayer requests, Scriptures I claim for individuals, and recorded answered prayers. I have sections for family, our staff and their families, friends, church members, our country and its leaders, and any ministry I am involved in. I break these up into days of the week so that I am not actually praying for everyone or everything every day.

I have shared with you the plan I use and the tools that help me to accomplish my time in the secret place. Here are those simple steps that might help guide you in your time with the Lord.

1. Pause and ask the Holy Spirit to fill you and give you an understanding of His Word and its application to your life for that day.
2. Read and meditate on Scripture, as He leads you, whether it is a single verse, a chapter, or a passage in His Word.
3. Write a one-page letter to God in a journal, thanking and praising Him for who He is and what He has done for you, confessing your sins to Him, and sharing your concerns for that particular day with Him.
4. Talk to God about your needs and the needs of others. (Here you might want to use the three-ring notebook binder.)
5. Give your day to God.

The key to your secret place is finding out what works best for you and practicing it habitually. I cannot dictate to you a set amount of time to spend in the secret place. At this stage of my life, I spend about an hour daily — sometimes more, sometimes less. A preschool mom may be fortunate to grab ten minutes. The focus should not be the amount of time you spend. The focus should be the attitude of your heart to recognize that strength for the day will come only through spending time in the secret place.

I Found the Secret

I found the secret to survival in the secret place. It is only when I enter into that secret place that I find the peace, the joy, and the strength to meet the demands of daily life and ministry. What I have learned is that every time I abide in that secret place I gain perspective, find joy in the blessings and strength for the difficulties, knowing that I am not alone. Every uncertainty, every heartache, every personal or ministry concern always leads me back to the same place — dwelling in the secret place, on my knees before the Father. For a number of years now, I have practiced pouring out my heart to God. I take extreme comfort in knowing that God knows *all* the details of the concerns of my life — those injustices, real or imagined. I can tell Him how I feel when I am sad or hurt or lonely or any number of other emotions! He is always available. He hears all my requests, and He will never repeat anything I tell Him. When you consider all the benefits to being a minister's wife, why wouldn't you want to "dwell" there? Also, when my heart is full of praise and thanksgiving — and giving God all the glory knowing He alone is worthy of all my praise — that, too, is entering the secret place! I do praise Him for the honor of being a minister's wife — and the privilege to walk by my husband's side in ministry.

Are You . . .

Overwhelmed?
Discouraged?

Fearful of the future?

Depressed?

Worried?

Experiencing other emotions I may not have mentioned?

The secret to your survival in ministry is found in the secret place. God is waiting on you right now. One of my favorite devotional books is *Nearer to Jesus* by Sarah Young. I love the following quote; it states so well how important our time in the secret place is — definitely a wise investment of our time daily.

> Time with Me cannot be rushed. When you are in a hurry, your mind flitters back and forth between Me and the tasks ahead of you. Push back the demands pressing in on you; create a safe space around you, a haven in which you can rest with Me. I also desire this time of focused attention and I use it to bless you, strengthening and equipping you for the day ahead. Thus, spending time with Me is a wise investment. Bring Me the sacrifice of your precious time. This creates sacred space around you — space permeated with My Presence and My Peace.[1]

Another powerful quote from Vance Pittman, senior pastor of Hope Baptist Church in Las Vegas, Nevada, so adequately states what our motive should be in our call to Christ and His ministry:

> The primary call on my life is not a call to ministry, it is a call to intimacy. Ministry is what He does out of the overflow of intimacy. Everything Jesus desires to do through my life He will do as the overflow of His love relationship with me."[2]

May we dwell in the secret place — having "intimacy" with the Father so that ministry will flow through our lives as a result of our relationship with Him. That is the secret to survival.

He who dwells in the secret place of the Most High shall abide under the shadow of the Almighty (Ps. 91:1; NKJV).

INTERACTIVE TESTMONY

Donna Gaines is married to Dr. Steve Gaines, pastor of the Bellevue Baptist Church in Cordova, Tennessee. In addition to her roles as wife and pastor's wife, she's also a mother, grandmother, and author. Donna is a woman of the Word, prayer, and great faith to see God move in all areas of her life. I believe that whatever conversation Donna and I have had through the years, on many different subjects, Donna always seems to bring the conversation back to God's working in her life — whether it's a son coming back to God after a season of rebellion, the blessing of the birth of a grandchild, or struggles in ministry that we all experience. In Donna's book *There's Gotta Be More!*[3] she shares about the Spirit-filled life. Without a doubt, the reason that Donna is able to walk in ministry not only surviving, but thriving, is because of her personal walk with Christ. Donna has been a blessing to my life for a number of years now, and I can't think of a better woman of God to share her thoughts on "dwelling in the secret place."

Jeana: When did you realize the importance of "dwelling in the secret place"?

Donna: In college the Lord ignited a passion in my heart to know Him. I began to search the Scriptures and observe people. In our first pastorate there were two women who walked with God at a level I had never experienced. It was through their vibrant prayer lives that I began to understand not only the significance of communing with God through prayer, but that prayer and God's Word were the lifelines for living the Christian life.

Jeana: What brought you to know that without that personal designated daily time with God, you wouldn't survive?

Donna: You don't have to be in ministry very long before you realize how inadequate you are for the task. As I continued to grow in my relationship with the Lord, I realized the significance of living life "in the Spirit." I also realized that it was impossible to be filled with the Spirit and the flesh at the same time. I had to take the words of Christ seriously and die daily to my flesh. It is in offering myself to the Lord as a living sacrifice on a daily basis that He is able to fill me and use me for His glory. Then as I spend time sitting at the feet of my Lord, He gives life and wisdom. I long to be like Mary of Bethany, who chose to sit at the feet of Jesus and listen to His words. Jesus said she had chosen the "good part, which will not be taken away from her" (Luke 10:42; NKJV).

Jeana: How has your personal walk with Christ (habitually residing in the "secret place") benefitted your husband's ministry?

Donna: It is through daily deposits into your spirit that you are strengthened in your inner man. God's ways are not our ways, nor are His thoughts our thoughts. The only way I can be in tune with Him is through spending time with Him in His Word and prayer. Then when the crisis hits, or the difficulty in ministry arises, your stronghold is the Lord. You find that He truly is your refuge and that He will sustain you as you walk through any valley. During a dark time in our own ministry, the Lord used His Word to enable me to encourage my husband. Immersing yourself in the Word of God by systematically reading, memorizing, and meditating upon it is what grants you God's perspective. It is a constant reminder that this life is not about us — it is His story — and in His grace and mercy He has chosen to write us in. I am to simply "dwell in the land and cultivate faithfulness" (Ps. 37:3; NASB) wherever He places me.

Jeana: As a minister's wife, what advice would you give other ministers' wives about making their time in the "secret place" a priority in their lives?

Donna: As ministers' wives we are called upon to care for, pray with, and counsel many in our congregations. We are woefully inadequate apart from the Lord. We must rely upon His wisdom that is imparted through His Word and prayer. My advice would be to have a place and a time that you meet with the Lord every day. Prepare the place. None of us would think about going to an appointment late or unprepared. Do not miss your appointment with the Almighty. It will initially be a choice of the will that will turn into a relationship that you will value above all others! Your special place will become a holy place. From that place you will go out filled with His Spirit, having had your perspective adjusted and able to more accurately reflect Christ to your family and a lost world.

Endnotes

1. Sarah Young, *Nearer to Jesus* (Nashville, TN: Thomas Nelson Inc., 2008), p. 30.
2. This impressive quote was made in my presence, and I asked him to write it down exactly as he said it.
3. Donna Gaines, *There's Gotta Be More!* (Nashville, TN: B&H Pub. Group, 2008).

2

REMEMBER
WHO YOU ARE

HAVE YOU EVER THOUGHT OF HOW your life would be different if you were no longer the pastor's or minister's wife? I have a very good friend who was forced to come to grips with that question of "Who are you?" Her husband was the pastor of a large church in Denver, and on a family vacation she lost him suddenly in a tragic automobile accident. Suddenly she was no longer a pastor's wife. That loss drastically changed her life and stripped her of some of her most beloved titles, but it did not change her identity in Christ or His purpose for her life. This is a part of Kathy Ferguson's story:

> The day I lost Rick Ferguson, life as I knew it was changed in an instant. In the midst of deep grief I began to face life-altering changes of epic proportion. Among those changes was the loss of the role as pastor's wife. Few vocations involve and include a wife as much as the ministry.

Suddenly upon my widowhood I was forced to look at "who would I be." It was clear I would no longer stand in the foyer and receive guests each Sunday, but now I was forced to look at how I would play out the spiritual values I claimed to believe. What had my motives been in my life as "minister's wife"?

Much of the way I exercised my faith, my calling, my gifts, and my service to the Kingdom of God was intertwined in my husband's position and our place in the local church to which we were called together. Clearly I would continue to be a woman who wanted to invest in the Kingdom of God in a local church but no longer beside my pastor husband. Less clear to me in those early days was how I would now walk it all out. Yet the loss of the title "pastor's wife" in no way meant that I would cease to have callings and responsibilities as a woman of faith.

Being a pastor's wife had identified my life. Yes, I was often identified as "Dr. Rick Ferguson's wife." I mourned the loss of being identified with the man I loved and loved serving beside. Yet, I discovered that role did not have to be my entire identity. My core identity was in Christ and in the way *He* called me and empowered me to serve in His Kingdom. For 26 years I had done that in a local church serving alongside my husband. That role provided me a venue to work out my faith and serve the Kingdom of God. Upon the loss of that role, in time I discovered that I would work out my faith and service in other venues — immediately in the unwanted venue of widowed, single parent, then in the corporate world in a major city center and then later on a church staff. While the venue changed, these things did not: depending on God, walking in obedience, yielding to the Spirit, loving and serving people, looking for opportunities to share Christ, engaging a local church, and being warm and encouraging to those around you. Those features ought to mark our lives in whatever venue God places us. And He expects that of His children who are serious about glorifying Him with their lives. Ministry is *not* the motive; glorifying His name is the motive.

In the months and years to come God would give me grace in grief as well as give me surprising clarity of purpose despite the dramatic lifestyle changes. Those changes even served to purify my motives concerning ministry and work in the Kingdom of God. Yes, my roles changed. Nothing in my life looked the same. Instead of leading and teaching a large Sunday morning Bible study opportunity, I found myself in a small group of mostly working single women, not teaching or leading but attending. My place in corporate worship services was no longer at the front supporting my husband in the pulpit but now alone, single and anonymously tucked away in a crowd. As painful as these changes were, I slowly began to discover that God still had great purposes in my life and He still expected me to serve and lead, just no longer as Rick Ferguson's wife.

God in no way meant for me to be sidelined because I was no longer a pastor's wife. The landscape would be entirely different, but my purpose as a believer to help advance the gospel was not changed. In fact, I suspect because of purified motives, a more tender heart, and a faith made more precious by trials, God may have allowed me to become more useful for the sake of the gospel. I understood that I was alone going to be responsible for the stewardship of my life — no matter what the landscape God allowed for me either as pastor's wife or widowed single mom. The last message Rick relayed in an email to our eldest son ended with this admonition: "Stay faithful no matter what." I want to live that no matter what role He chooses for me.

Kathy Ferguson's life was changed in an instant, but Kathy's life has recently led her back to being a pastor's wife again, as she married Ed Litton, who had also lost his spouse tragically. As Kathy re-enters the world of being the "pastor's wife," here are some of her thoughts:

Just as unexpectedly as my role ended as a pastor's wife to Rick Ferguson, God unexpectedly brought another pastor husband into my life. After seven years of singleness I find myself today fulfilling the familiar role as pastor's wife once again in marrying Ed Litton. My season spent in widowhood and serving God alone not tied to the title "pastor's wife" gives me greater understanding that my identity will always remain grounded in Christ and His purpose for my life. Whether married or not, wherever God's pathway may take me I am responsible to serve Him and glorify His name. And in *God's* chosen pathway for our lives His grace is sufficient for that calling . . . no matter what the calling is.

For many minsters' wives, it can be hard to separate the issue of who you are in Christ and who you are married to and what he does for a living.

In 30-plus years of ministry with my husband Ronnie, I have had the opportunity to observe many wives of ministers. Some of these have been on our staff and others have served elsewhere. These women have come from different backgrounds, some religious, others from completely non-religious roots. Some felt called to marry a minister while others married men already in the business world, later called to ministry life. They are young, old, and middle-aged. They come in all sizes and shapes with different personalities and gift mixes. But there remains a common thread among these women: they are all married to a man in ministry.

Who are you? Are you comfortable in your "ministry-induced skin"? It has been a personal challenge of mine to love unconditionally the uniqueness of the ministry staff wives who have served with us through the years, appreciating the differences, but always challenging them toward a common goal — loving God, loving His Church, and loving His man in ministry.

After all these years of observation and experience, I have come to a conclusion about men and women in ministry: unhappy men are usually married to unhappy women. And many times, ministry tenure is short. I believe much unhappiness in ministry, especially on the wives' part, comes from "spiritual identity recognition."

Who do you think you are? We've all asked that question when we've perceived another person as being haughty or arrogant, but I want you to stop for a moment and answer that question completely and honestly. Who are you? Who do you think you are?

In addition to being a minister's wife, you wear many titles or labels. You may be mother, teacher, hostess, administrator, nurse, counselor, taxi driver, financial expert, maintenance engineer, and home manager. All of these things are a part of your identity, but none of them, including minister's wife, defines who you are.

Does your role as a minister's wife consume you to the point where you can't even imagine being separate from that identity? I recently heard someone in a business setting propose this question: "Who would you be if you left your position tomorrow?" If that question were proposed to you as a minister's wife, how would you answer it?

In order for you to be the best and most effective minister's wife you can be, you must grasp who you are — separate from anyone else and complete in Christ. While your role as a minister's wife is an important part of your identity, it is only a part your identity.

More important than who you *think* you are is how God sees you. Who does God say you are?

YOU ARE GOD'S UNIQUE CREATION

There is no one in the universe exactly like you. You have unique talents and gifts bestowed on you by God, and no one can fulfill His purpose for you except you. Psalm 33:15 says, "He made their hearts, so he understands everything they do." The New King James translation says, "He fashions their hearts individually." You can't get much more individual attention from the *Creator* than that! So why would we question or doubt being a special and unique creation of God? And how can that not influence the way we see ourselves as HIS creation? Consider this: What is unique about you that makes you the perfect companion to your husband? To answer that is not vanity but searching your soul and recognizing how truly unique God has made you even down to the spouse He has chosen for you to spend your life with. In God's sovereignty, He has chosen *you* to be your husband's helpmeet and walk beside him in ministry!

I have been blessed these many years in ministry by the uniqueness of the couples on our staff team. I am amazed to see God work at bringing two people together here on earth to fulfill His will in their lives. I've seen couples that come from diverse backgrounds marry and be very effective for the Kingdom. I've seen couples who were saved later in life have enormous influence for Christ. I've seen couples enter ministry life after spending years in a secular profession. I've seen young couples surrender their lives totally, and older couples who have given all of their lives to ministry. In each of these situations, there is a very unique wife in that couple situation, a wife that is God's unique creation, intended to walk by the side of her man in ministry.

One of the most fun things about taking our staff on an annual retreat is that we get to spend concentrated time together — we really get to know one another — and I am always amazed, challenged, and encouraged to spend time with those precious ladies and learn about their "uniqueness." As I see these women devote time and energy to ministry life, I have seen how God's unique design is so "customized" in who He has led them to marry, the children He chooses to give them, the specific areas of ministry that He calls them to, and even the challenges that come to each of us from time to time. Truly being one of God's unique creations should liberate us and cause us to "know ourselves" and become all that God wants us to be! What a beautiful plan from God for our benefit — if we will just wholly submit our wills and lives to His plan. God only wants us to be what He's equipped us for — each with unique gifts and talents.

Recognize that God didn't just do that for Ronnie and Jeana Floyd. God did that for *you*, His unique creation, and *your spouse*, His unique couple! What an awesome recognition of God working on our lives. I believe if you will look at your life in ministry and your life with your spouse in this way, it will give you a fresh look at being God's unique creation and how He can use this in your lives together as you serve Him.

You Are God's Chosen Creation

Jesus said, "You did not choose me, but I chose you . . ." (John 15:16; HCSB). God chose you to be His child, and He chose you to walk alongside your husband in ministry. You are not in the position you are in by chance. You are who you are and where you are because God ordained it to be so. He could have chosen someone else to gift with your talents. He could have called another woman to be your husband's helpmate, but He, in His divine wisdom, chose you.

I feel very blessed to have been called by God. I know that within that calling to salvation, He also chose Ronnie to be my husband and for me to be a part of his life and ministry. I would encourage you to think of yourself as blessed to be a minister's wife — you are chosen and special in the eyes of God. "You saw me before I was born. Every day of my life was recorded in your book. Every moment was laid out before a single day had passed" (Ps. 139:16).

You Are God's Gifted Creation

In his grace, God has given us different gifts for doing certain things well (Rom. 12:6).

God has given me the gifts I need to fulfill my calling as wife, mother, friend, etc., in the manner that pleases Him. You have been given the perfect gifts for you — gifts that magnify the Lord through your life and ministry. No one else in the body of Christ can do what God has called and gifted you to do. You are God's gifted creation, not because of who your husband is, but because God has gifted you with spiritual gifts to be used for His glory. If suddenly you were no longer a minister's wife, you would still have the opportunity to fulfill your purpose based on the spiritual gifts He gave to you. As the verse in Romans goes on to instruct, "You have the gifts, now use them."

If you haven't identified your spiritual gifts, I would encourage you to take a spiritual gifts inventory test and discover them. A website that you can go to and take a test is www.uniquelyyou. com. Once you realize what your gifts are, you will understand why you are more fulfilled when you operate within those gifts. It also adds to great happiness to operate within your God-given giftedness, and, of course, it's a huge plus in ministry life!

Knowing the spiritual gifts that God has blessed you with is very important. Not only that, knowing your spiritual gifts will help you to understand the way you will respond in situations.

For example, one of my spiritual gifts is mercy. This is evident in the ministries I have been involved in throughout the years — for example, cancer support groups, jail ministry, etc. It is because of my gift of mercy that God draws my heart to ministries that help people in difficult and heartbreaking circumstances. As well, my gift of mercy kicks in at times when a strong prophetic voice needs to be heard. Hence, my comment in a later chapter to "let the men be the men." This is so clear to me, God's uniqueness in creating us, and then placing us with our particular spouse. My spiritual gifts and Ronnie's spiritual gifts are at opposite ends. In essence, our spiritual gifts balance and complement one another. Do you think that is by coincidence?

GOD CALLED YOU, TOO

I believe that as ministers' wives we should all take time to reflect on the amazing call of God on our husbands' lives. What I would like for you to realize, as I have, is that we are called into the ministry, too, when we marry a minister.

My precious daughter-in-law Meredith felt that God had called her to missions. She has told me that she fully expected to be living somewhere in Africa in a hut. When Meredith contemplated being my son Nick's wife, she struggled with whether she was abandoning her call from God. As she worked through this issue, Meredith came to realize that she was *not* abandoning her call. Meredith came to the spiritual conclusion that "missions" was a good thing — something she was passionate about and still is — but her call was definitely to be Nick's wife and to be open to wherever God might lead them. Nick very wisely pointed out to her that, as his wife (he feels called to be a pastor), she would be answering her call to missions, though she might not serve in a foreign country or live in a hut.

I never felt called into the ministry as Meredith did, but I did feel called to be Ronnie's wife. Therefore, regardless of whether you felt a distinct call to ministry, or a call to marry your husband, you were indirectly called to the ministry. That doesn't make your calling less than your husband's, nor does it make your calling as a Christian less important. In fact, it shows God's perfect plan in the mate He chose for you and the purpose of your life. Gary Thomas makes the following point in his book *Sacred Influence*: "There is unique glory in both sexes — men and women aren't the same, but they are equal in God's eyes. God gives you the opportunity to define yourself, not in defiance to your husband, but in a way that complements your marriage and blesses your husband."[1]

There is another very powerful quote in that book that I want you to remember: "God, not your marital status or the condition of your marriage, defines your life."

The author makes the above statement plus adds that "as a woman, you need to understand the glory of being a woman made in God's image; experience the strength you have as the recipient of His Holy Spirit; and find refuge in the worth and purpose you have as His daughter." None of these things are determined by the position of your husband in ministry. When you are secure in who you are in Christ and His plan for you personally, you can rest in His will for you and His special calling for you as a minister's wife. Remember, the most important thing is to know who you are in Christ.

Knowing who you are in Christ will sustain you when the difficult times in ministry come, and I can guarantee they will.

Knowing who you are in Christ solidifies your own personal calling to ministry, whether you feel called specifically to ministry or to your husband.

Knowing who you are in Christ liberates you to walk and exercise your giftedness.

Knowing who you are in Christ assures you of your uniqueness as His creation.

Accept the identity that has been given to you in God's creation and Word. You are a woman of influence whether you regard yourself as that or not. God has placed you with your husband in this position at this time to be an "influencer." It has nothing to do with age or sex, but with yielding ourselves wholly and completely to God to be used in whatever venues, circumstances, or opportunities God brings our way.

I don't know about you, but knowing who I am in Christ makes sense of everything in ministry. From who I am (His unique creation), to what I do (His calling on my life), to how I do it (the spiritual gifts He has blessed me with) . . . and the very special blessing of *who* I get to do ministry life with — my husband.

INTERACTIVE TESTIMONY

It is somewhat unusual that we have had the blessing of serving with a couple on our staff more than once. Shawn and Tracey Smith began their married life with us, left to go and serve in some other church ministries, and in time, the Lord brought them back to be on our staff team once again! Shawn serves as our Springdale campus and multi-site pastor. Because of this unique situation, I have seen this wife, Tracey, grow as a "staff wife" in incredible ways, from being a newlywed — fresh in ministry — to a seasoned and godly woman who challenges the socks off of me! I will never forget the first staff retreat that Tracey attended. I was flippantly spouting off the term "staff wife this, and staff wife that" when she raised her hand and asked me this question, "Miss Jeana, exactly what *is* a staff wife?" It made me stop and think about the terminology used — taking for granted that everyone understood what it meant to be a "staff wife." I realized there was some lack of understanding of the expectations that came with the role of this very young and very inexperienced "staff wife." I'll never forget that. Read these words from Tracey, as I asked her the following questions.

Jeana: Since that day that you raised your hand in sheer naivety and innocence and asked that question, "Just what is a staff wife?" how has your comprehension and understanding of what it means to be a "staff wife" changed from those early days to now — having served now for 19 years in ministry by your husband's side?

Tracey: My comprehension and understanding of what a staff wife is has changed dramatically since I asked that question almost 19 years ago. My focus and understanding at the age of 23 was completely based on what a staff wife "does." My perspective was strictly performance driven. "Women watch women." As a young wife with little church experience, I was watching and listening very carefully to every staff wife I knew. Every wife I knew dressed, talked, and acted differently. They were all involved in different things. Yet they all seemed to have a singular understanding and confidence in wearing the title of "staff wife." I constantly compared myself to others. I had no idea how to make a napkin ring, speak to a group of ladies, lead a Bible study, put together a budget, shop for bargains, look like a million dollars, host a party or shower for 100 or more — the list was endless and so were my tears.

I asked that question in desperation. You answered my question that day by sharing many of the things you wrote in this chapter. You told me I was unique, chosen, gifted, and called by God. You didn't use those exact words at the time but the message was the same. It is not about what I did but about who I was. I had never really looked at myself before from this perspective. The confidence I saw in the women around me came from their understanding of this. I had memorized 2 Corinthians 3:4–6 for a Bible study in college. The chapter and verses became a standard for my identity first in Christ and then as a staff wife. The verse states: "Such confidence as this is ours through Christ before God. Not that we are competent in ourselves to claim anything for ourselves, but our competence comes from God. He has made us competent as ministers of a new covenant — not of the letter but of the Spirit; for the letter kills, but the spirit gives life." Verse 17 says, "And where the Spirit of the Lord is, there is freedom" (NIV). God wanted me to see this truth and to base my identity in His Word. My choice to do this completely changed my understanding of "who a staff wife is."

Jeana: Has your identity as a staff wife been a positive thing?

Tracey: My identity as a staff wife has been a positive thing. We have served in several churches in different places. In 19 years there have been many expectations, opinions, and opportunities presented to me by a variety of people and circumstances. It did not take me long to realize that all of these often change and at times even contradict each other. It is because I wrestled with the question of "who a staff wife was" that I can say that though not everything experienced has been positive, my identity has not changed. God has used every experience for His glory and His good. This, thankfully, is always a positive thing.

Jeana: How do you separate your identity in Christ from your identity as a staff wife?

Tracey: I keep the two identities separate by looking to God's Word. God is so good to give us many verses about who we are in Christ. I have read, studied, and memorized many of these. I have looked to His Word to examine women of the Bible to see how they responded, served, and struggled. It took me awhile to learn that if I tried to look anywhere else other than the Lord for my identity that I would be confused and frustrated.

My identity as a staff wife is built on this understanding. Who I am in Christ will be intertwined with who I am as a staff wife, friend, mother, daughter, or any role I am given. My identity in these roles constantly changes, while who I am in Christ remains steadfast. It allows me great freedom to admit failures, say no, and try new things while all along standing on this strong foundation. The circumstance and seasons I am asked to serve in through these roles also change. Some are difficult and others are great fun! I pray often about all of these.

Jeana: What changes have taken place as you have grown and matured in your Christian walk as well as a staff wife?

Tracey: My perspective and understanding have changed greatly as I have matured in my walk with Christ and as I have continued in my role as a staff wife. It has affected every area listed below.

I still watch women, but for an entirely different reason. My primary purpose is no longer to compare myself or rate my performance. It is to encourage and affirm others so that they can be confidant in who they are in Him. I confess that I do not always succeed in this. It is my nature to compare, etc. I am thankful to be His work in progress.

I have learned to filter all things through His Word. This has helped in what I would deem life's greatest storms and in the countless little things of daily life and ministry.

I have learned to filter all things through my husband, our marriage, and our season of life. I am a wife. I simply can't just consider myself. This will at times define what I can and can't do.

I have grown in my talents and gifts. I can even do most all of the things listed above and even a few more.

Last, and I think most importantly, I have learned to be grateful for the title of "staff" in front of wife. There is no greater joy than to be married to a minister. My husband is called to serve a sovereign God. He is charged to reach the world for Christ and to impact the present for eternity. He has the opportunity to touch others' lives for Christ. I am called serve him and with him. What a privilege! There are so many people I have had the opportunity to serve because of this role. There are so many lessons I have learned because of places we have served, but there is only one man I have had the opportunity to be married to for 19 years. May God continue to grow and mature me for this task as a minister's wife.

Endnotes
1. Gary Thomas, *Sacred Influence* (Grand Rapids, MI: Zondervan, 2006), p. 21.

3

IT AIN'T THAT HARD

WHAT I AM ABOUT TO SAY MIGHT seem a contradiction to the chapter title. Ministry is more complicated today than ever before. Even as recently as five years ago, the way we do "church" has changed drastically. People's commitment to church has changed. The methods we use to reach people have changed. No longer is "church" the main thing — it's just "one more thing," sad to say.

But there are some basics in ministry life that I believe are timeless. These basics of ministry life are what will keep you on the right path. We can't make it harder than it is, because really and truly, "It ain't that hard!" I am fully aware that "ain't" is not grammatically correct — but it so aptly explains how I feel about the content of this chapter and is a phrase coined by a friend and myself as we were discussing ministry life!

I want to share some things with you that I believe are basics to ministry life. I'm not saying these will make or break your success in ministry, but I do believe all are helpful and biblical and will only serve to help you survive and thrive in the life that God has called you into.

Walk with Christ

You must have a personal walk with Christ. I've already discussed this in great depth in the first chapter, so I won't go into more detail on that point, but will just re-emphasize the importance of that aspect in personal and ministry life. Our walk with Christ will determine our attitude toward conflict, problems, and even joyful times. Good times and bad times are all "Father filtered," even when we don't understand or can't make sense of it. Your walk with Christ will not guard you from problems, but will determine your attitudes toward them and should definitely influence your actions. This applies to every area of your life. From church issues, to family issues, to whatever, Christ is your salvation, not just eternally, but daily.

This Scripture really covers it all if we take it to heart: "Love the LORD your God with all your heart and with all your soul and with all your strength" (Deut. 6:5; NIV).

Presence

Our church families need to see our "presence." Consistent presence speaks volumes to our people. Whether you are a "speaker/teacher type" or a "behind-the-scenes" kind of wife, your "presence" sends a message to others. Your presence at church functions sends a message to others. It says, "This is important to me." If we really believe in what we do, we must recognize "presence" as important. If "presence" is not important, then why do we have high attendance days? Or why do our husbands become discouraged on bad weather Sundays or summer slumps? It's because presence does matter.

Most importantly, it is essential for our own personal walk with Christ. Consistent "presence" says to others, "This is important to me because I *need* to be with God's people, be under His Word, worship, and to grow together." In most of our churches, there are many ministry options that are offered. That plus the weekly corporate worship experiences offer many opportunities for "presence." Like it or not, people are watching us and watching our families. I don't think people in our congregations expect perfection, but they do expect us to "be there." They are looking at us to see how we make this life work — what *source* we draw from! This isn't something we only do for others, it is Christ's command for us. The church of today is much more forgiving, accepting, and has fewer expectations for ministers' families. Believe me, I know — it's the only life I've ever lived. But in all these years of ministry, one of the things that has never changed is the expectation of "presence." "Presence" on our part is living out with our life what we say we believe in and what we expect from our members. Just be there — "it ain't that hard!"

Love One Another

Treat others the way you want to be treated. This is a simple command that most of us know, but oh so powerful as we carry out the purpose of the Church. We all learned the Golden Rule as children: "Do unto others as you would have them do unto you." That sounds easy from a child's point of view but is not always easy to carry out in the true sense of meaning. Does treating others the way you want to be treated guarantee you'll always be treated equally as well? Not at all, but it is the right thing to do regardless of how others treat you. The world is screaming to see a picture of authentic love between married couples — that's us — church staff — that's us, too — and love for Christ — and oh, that would be us, too! How much more should we as ministers' wives practice this simple, childlike principle of loving one another whether it be your husband, your fellow staff members and their wives, or someone in your church! They need to see that we as a staff love one another, we love people, and we love Christ's Church. I am sure that most of you have heard that one of the greatest things a man can do for his children is to love their mother. As well, I think one of the healthiest things a church family can see is your staff team loving one another. It is most important that we lead the way in our love for Christ and love for one another in our personal and daily walks. Our congregations are watching us and searching for "how to do life." Practice loving one another as a couple, as a staff, and as the church family. It ain't that hard!

> *Therefore, whatever you want others to do for you, do also the same for them — this is the Law and the Prophets* (Matt. 7:12; HCSB).

Acknowledge Others

In Susie Hawkins' book to ministers' wives (*From One Ministry Wife to Another*) she makes this statement: "Recognition involves respecting the dignity and equal worth of every person and valuing their contributions. . . . Perhaps just being purposeful in noticing others and making the effort to acknowledge them is more significant than we realize."[1] We must never forget the power of giving ourselves away to others. When we simply take the time to acknowledge others — taking the time to speak, to touch, to care for others — we give ourselves away.

It really is "more blessed to give than to receive." You are in ministry because God called you to your husband. Regardless of whether you feel personally called, your husband obviously is; therefore, it is critical that you be willing to give yourself away to others. Don't make that harder than it is, just be willing. There are no prerequisites to do this — just get beyond yourself. God places each of us in different circles of influence, and He does that on purpose — so that we can have the opportunity to touch a lot of people. Don't allow personal insecurities to keep you from this. You would be amazed to know that people in your congregation really *want* to know you, to glean from you, to learn from you, or just have a relationship with you. You don't have to be "something" — just be yourself. One thing my mother, who was a minster's wife for over 50 years, taught me was just to be myself. Great advice. Just be yourself. It ain't that hard. Are there boundaries? Definitely. We will discuss that in greater detail in chapter 9. But giving yourself away with wisdom will always bring blessings on your life. It is a spiritual principle of giving and receiving. Christ is the one who calls us to give to others following His example of the greatest sacrifice on behalf of others. There will never come a time — regardless of how church changes or the way we do it — that acknowledging others, touching people, or giving ourselves away will ever become obsolete.

This is an area that is easy to withdraw from. Sometimes it's just easier to live our lives separately from our church members. At times, that can get "messy," but we also miss out on the blessings of relationships, plus, we are not called to "ourselves" but to "others" and to be active followers of Christ, encouraging one another and being available to reach out to others. Living the "me" life only leads to wanting more time for "me." I challenge you to take on the call of giving yourself away to others — find creative ways to do that. As a ministry wife, you must be more conscious of this as you give yourself away. Use the opportunity when you are at church functions to mingle with many and not just a chosen few. Your visible presence to "others" will speak volumes to your church family. Just acknowledge others — "it ain't that hard."

Love Your Husbands

Last but not least, love your husbands. I will go into greater depth in the next chapter, but there is not a greater example of influence you can have before others in today's world than having a strong, loving, submissive love relationship with your husband. This world is crying out to see this example, and even the *Church* is crying out to see this example. It is a very powerful picture before our world to see a couple in ministry united in love and focus for the Church of God.

You don't have to have it all together and have a perfect marriage. That will never happen. Marriage is a journey and a pilgrimage. Marriage is learning and growing and changing. When you stop — that's when you are in trouble. Usually when you stop working on your marriage, it's because you've stopped caring about your marriage.

Spoil your husbands, not your children! Husbands easily get lost in the priority list when small children are involved. Children will always demand attention, and husbands are forced to or choose to take a back seat to the demands of the children. Although normal for that season of life with young children, be intentional about not neglecting your husband. Be aware of and sensitive to his needs above your children. This may be another one of those areas that makes you say, "That's hard," rather than "It ain't that hard" . . . but you must continually work to give your husband his rightful place in your heart and in your home.

I could sum up this chapter by saying these three things:

> Love God.
> Love the body of Christ.
> Love your husband.

The above things are timeless, regardless of how ministry changes or where you are serving. They will not waver with time regardless of what kind of services you have, where you have them, what time they meet, or who is leading them. But people will always be influenced with our presence because it says it's important to you and it should be important to them. Acknowledging others and making others feel worthy of your recognition, time, and attention will never grow old. It's basic to human life and nature. And God's command to love one another, and especially to show love for our husbands, is vital to ministry — there is no option here. We must be intentional in our love for one another in our marriages, our relationships with our church staff, and our love for Christ.

So even though these are very basic, they are timeless and unchanging. Make an intentional effort to walk with Christ daily, practice presence, acknowledge others, and love one another.

INTERACTIVE TESTIMONY

The phrase "It ain't that hard" was literally coined with my dear friend Susie Hawkins in conversation over ministry life. We are two gals who have loved being pastors' wives, although Susie's husband, Dr. O.S. Hawkins, now serves as the head of Guidestone Financial Resources of the Southern Baptist Convention. O.S. and Susie have two grown daughters married to fine young men, and five precious grandchildren. I mentioned Susie's book earlier in this chapter, and I applaud everything she said in *From One Ministry Wife to Another*. Susie was a pastor's wife for 30 years. We both feel that the positives far outweigh the negatives and decided that sometimes we complicate ministry ourselves, because "it ain't that hard."

Jeana: What are some things that ministers' wives do that makes ministry "hard" when it doesn't have to be? And what would be your remedy for it?

Susie: Ministry brings enough challenges without us creating extra ones! In answer to your question, first I think that we might need to look at the expectations we have for ourselves. Sometimes we, as pastors' wives, feel that we must live up to every church member's expectations, or we must at least be like the pastor's wife who came before us (and, of course, she was just perfect and so wonderful!). Most people are content with you "being yourself" and just want to know that you really care for them. Let go of all that and don't fall into the comparison trap. If we compare ourselves to others, we always end up feeling inferior. And that doesn't help anyone!

I also think that sometimes we feel like we must have "all the answers"—whether it is a biblical question, in a counseling situation, or even regarding decisions that are made regarding church policy or business. There is nothing shameful about saying to someone, "I don't know the exact answer to your question, but I will do my best to find out." Or referring the question to someone else can also be a wise thing to do. We don't have to know everything. It's not that hard to say, "That is a good question and I will do my best to find the answer, or someone who knows the answer for you."

Jeana: What are some practical ways that you made yourself "personal" to your congregations?

Susie: I really believe that church services afford the best opportunity for "spreading cheer and goodwill"! Taking the time to be a few minutes early and speak to people, or visiting with church members after a service doesn't sound like anything particularly spiritual or clever. However, it shows that you care about your people, that you are interested in their lives, and that you actually like them! Also, making a call or sending an email or a note to someone who is hurting can be such an encouragement. At those times I always remind myself that it's a small thing for me to jot a note or an e-mail — it just takes a few minutes. But it may be just the thing the recipient needs to feel comforted or noticed — and that's a big thing! I know how "big" it is, because I know how I feel when I am down and receive unexpected encouragement from someone. These small acts send big messages. Bottom line: it's not that hard to speak to people and at least act as if you care about them!

Jeana: Did you practice "presence" when you were a pastor's wife? How did that speak to your congregations?

Susie: I feel it is very important for staff wives to be present at church services. It's a principle of leadership — if your husband wants your church members to be faithful in church attendance, then his family must lead the way. You can't ask others to do something that you are not willing to do. I also believe that wives need to sense the direction of the church, which is only possible when they listen to their husbands' messages and participate in corporate worship. Don't underestimate the importance of your visibility — it sends the message that "I believe our church service is important! And I don't want to miss it!" It's not that hard to attend church services and pay attention to what is happening. Everyone else does.

Jeana: Why would it be important for the pastor and his wife to present a true picture of love and respect, united in focus for the ministry of the church?

Susie: First of all, every Christian marriage is a picture of Christ and the Church. But second, the couple that serves a church should be a picture of love and unity, as a positive example of those whose lives have been committed to Christ. Like it or not, people watch us. Our mutual respect for one another is also a picture of the shared call of ministry of a husband and wife. As one in Christ, we serve together, complementing each other, using our gifts and opportunities to further the Kingdom.

Jeana: When you were a pastor's wife, what things did you make sure you did to make your husband's ministry easier on him?

Susie: The wife's unique role gives us an idea about how this question can be answered. Concentrate on doing things for him that *only you can do* — planning social outings, family gatherings, sensing when you need to have time together alone, helping him find time to rest and regroup, and meeting his physical and emotional needs. Surely a wife knows best how to pray for her husband, what his dreams and heartaches are, and the decisions that are weighing heavily on his mind. There are always others who can help in the various ministries of the church, but our first priority should be meeting his needs in the way that only a wife can! Now some of this *can* be challenging at times, but it is our joy to love our husbands and serve the Lord with them!

Endnotes

1. Susie Hawkins, *From One Ministry Wife to Another* (Chicago, IL: Moody Publishers, 2009), p. 96.

4

LOVE THE MAN
YOU MARRIED

REMEMBER HOW TENDER YOUR HEART was toward your husband when you were dating or you first got married? There is a reason you married your husband. At some point, you were drawn to your husband. What was that? Was it his looks? Personality? Was it his enthusiasm for life or his humor? His love for Christ? You treasured every minute you could spend with him. You also had the ability to overlook many of his faults because you were so in love with him and wanted to give him your heart totally!

Recognize the difference between saying 'I love you' and 'I'm in love with you.' 'I love you' means I choose to love you. 'I'm in love with you' means I think about you, talk about you, want to be with you." Ministry marriages need both — the deliberate choice and the "I can't help myself." Let your husband know you are "in love" with him.

Give some thought to what attracted you to your husband in the very beginning. As we enter ministry after marriage, sometimes it is easy to forget those things that attracted us to our husbands in the beginning.

I want to challenge you to consider this thinking: Your Husband, Your Treasure. A treasure is something of great value to us, something we cherish, appreciate, and hold in high esteem. Could you say that about your husband? As women, we more naturally treat our treasures with tenderness. Do you treat your husband with tenderness?

Why should we treasure our husbands? Or maybe the more difficult question for ministers' wives might be, Why don't I treasure my husband?

You may not consider your husband your treasure for a myriad of reasons. Maybe you are angry or bitter over past hurts that have not been resolved. Maybe you married a man who was not in ministry at that time, and that was not a part of your lifetime plan. Maybe you feel resentment over unmet needs or unforgiveness in marriage or ministry life. Sad to say, some women — yes, even ministry wives — may not see their husbands as "worthy," much less "treasures." If reading any of the above struck a nerve with you, you may need to take a spiritual inventory personally. Some reading this chapter will need to deal with their attitudes toward their husbands. Some of you need healing for very real hurts in your marriage, and most of the time our effectiveness in leading others is often diminished because of our own personal issues. We become our own sabotage when we do this! Deal with these issues — and if necessary, get wise spiritual counsel.

The bottom line is, we cannot be what we need to be until we truly see our husband, the man we married, as a treasure — a treasure to us, to our families, and most of all to God. Let your attitude toward your husband be such that it will be an honor to God first of all, which is in turn an honor to your husband.

A Scripture that I love to remind our staff wives of is Proverbs 31:11–12: "Her husband can trust her, and she will greatly enrich his life. She brings him good, not harm, all the days of her life."

Could your husband say the above Scripture is true about your life? Exactly *how* can you show your husband — the man you chose to marry — that he is your treasure?

One of the most obvious ways to show your husband he is your treasure is with your *mouth*. What comes out of our mouths can either build up or tear down our marriages.

A wise woman named Barbara O'Chester, wife of Dr. Harold O'Chester, who served as a pastor's wife and influenced my life greatly, taught me this principle, "Never dishonor your husband in public." As I have lived many years as a pastor's wife and observed women who have demeaned their husbands, I have seen the great damage that can be done. When you dishonor your minister husband in public, you risk diminishing the respect due him from others, and you also diminish your own personal respect from them.

Refrain from emasculating your husband publicly or privately. We've seen that visualized before us in many ways. Our world does not applaud a "quiet and submissive wife." This is commonly seen in movies, television shows, and magazines, just to name a few. Unfortunately, we have all known ministers' wives and laywomen who emasculated their husbands over and over, and eventually it will take a toll on a marriage. I feel so strongly on this point that I am embarrassed for a woman who demeans her husband in front of others. Little does she realize the damage she is doing to her marriage. Equally as damaging, a woman who dishonors her husband in private will pay desperately with her personal relationships with her children and husband.

An extremely sad situation was played out before our eyes in the reality show *Jon & Kate Plus 8*. I would not by any means pass judgment on either of these two individuals. Only those two people truly know the details of their life and marriage. I do believe that we can learn much from their situation, and because it was a top news story for many weeks, I took note of Jon's response about his new relationship. In the interview following the divorce, Jon states that his new "love" encourages and respects him. Doesn't that sound like a familiar biblical challenge for wives — to love, honor, and respect her husband? Here we have a man on secular national television telling what he really desires from a woman. Maybe that is a message that would come from all husbands regarding their desired respect from their wives.

James 3:8–11 is probably familiar to you, but let's review the importance of this Scripture in reference to our tongues and the damage it can do: "But no man can tame the tongue. It is a restless evil, full of deadly poison. With it we bless our Lord and Father, and with it we curse men who are made in God's likeness. Out of the same mouth come blessing and cursing. My brothers [sisters], these things should not be this way. Does a spring pour out sweet and bitter water from the same opening?" (HCSB).

James 3:13 gives us some great advice: "Who is wise and understanding among you? He should show his works by good conduct with wisdom's gentleness" (HCSB). Don't we all want to be known as wise and understanding women? Good conduct and gentleness go a long way in accomplishing God's purpose for us as well as helping us be what we need to be to our husbands.

You may be embittered toward your husband. There could be a number of reasons, and you may even feel justified. Sometimes the bitterness has nothing to do with your husband and his ministry but is about the past and your inability to deal with it. Either one can become your "whipping post." We punish our husbands by holding back a part of ourselves, whether it is physically or emotionally, or making ministry life miserable for him.

What's in your heart will eventually come out of your mouth. You may be able to hold it in for a period of time, but eventually it will "spew forth" unless you deal with it. In the heat of the battle — and there can be many in ministry — what's in the heart will come out through the mouth. That is a tool of the enemy, Satan. Sometimes we are even surprised at what comes out of our mouths!

I heard it said one time that your husband's *appearance* is a reflection of you, and your *countenance* is a reflection of your marriage. An angry and bitter woman is easily recognized. And I might add, an angry and bitter staff wife is always obvious to those around her. Guard yourself from becoming that woman.

> As a face is reflected in water, so the heart reflects the real person (Prov. 27:19).

If you really feel that you have a serious problem with anger and resentment, an excellent resource is the book *When Anger Hits Home*[1] by Gary Oliver and H. Norm Wright.

As you consider your own relationship with your husband, ask God to help you control your tongue and to honor him in every way in public rather than live with the regret of a loose tongue that seeks to destroy rather than build up.

Another way we show love for the man we married is through our *time*. This is always a challenge for ministry marriages. Ministry demands, children, extended family responsibilities, friends, and the daily business we all have will compete for the time we have for our husband.

I have found that my husband's schedule supersedes mine on most occasions. Because I love the man I married, I honor our time together, making it a priority and helping him to be successful as he manages his time also. To this day, there is no one I'd rather be with than my husband. Make a conscious effort to spend time with your husband. Be intentional about planning around *his* schedule. Be sensitive and understanding in your planning. Be creative and not demanding. And never compare your husband's schedule with that of another staff member. That will lead you to nowhere.

Do you ever press your husband for time with you when you know he has others pressing him also? Give him room to grow. Marriage is a pilgrimage and ministers don't get to skip over the journey to perfection instantly. Most all of us have had to grow in the area of time management.

Something that Ronnie and I have practiced for a number of years, is spending Fridays together. Although I realize that not everyone can take Fridays off, I would be surprised to find that you and your husband cannot find some block of time every week that you designate for you and your husband to spend time together — alone. I really believe this is critical for a healthy marriage and healthy ministry couple. This will involve you laying aside your plans at times in order to make this time available for your husband. Believe me, it is a wise investment of your time. Make every effort not to cancel out or fill this time with activities that involve others. Just spend time with your husband — he is your priority! My husband works extremely hard in order to be able to take this time off. Not only is it critical to our marriage, it is of great benefit to him personally. I think we would all agree that our husbands need some time off every week to be refreshed and recharged. These men extend much mentally, physically, emotionally, and spiritually when they are being all that God wants them to be. However you can do it — whatever time you can set apart, whether it's a few hours or an entire day — make every effort to spend some time alone with your husband every week. The benefits are huge!

Loving the man we married involves another very important aspect. It's not very popular in today's world of thinking, but it is the aspect of service. In a world of feminist views and busy schedules that has even invaded the Church, service to husbands has all but gotten lost. Loving the man we married involves *serving* that man. You may be saying, "But hey, that's not my spiritual gift." Service to our husbands is something we do because we love them. It is a God-given opportunity to meet needs regardless of what your spiritual gifts are. Free your husband up to accomplish the ministry God has called him to. Be his greatest encourager, not discourager.

God chose you to meet his needs, not someone else. You have been called to be his wife, not someone else. A word of warning to wise women — there are women in your congregation who would be happy to serve your husband and meet his needs. Make sure those needs are met by you, not another woman.

How would you rate your "service" barometer to your husband: low, medium, high? Love the man you married by serving him.

Being in ministry can provide unique challenges in the way of friendships for your husband. Friendships do not always come easily for ministry men. *Make sure your husband knows that he is your best friend.* This takes precedence over children, other family members, friends, and church members. You love the man you married by being his friend. Make your husband your lifetime study. I have already mentioned an excellent book on marriage that I highly recommend, *Sacred Influence*[2] by Gary Thomas. There is an excellent chapter about knowing your husband and studying him. That study should be unique to your husband alone. Never compare your husband with another man — that's another step that leads to nowhere. Do you really know what makes your husband happy?

I have friends whose husbands are CEOs of large companies, college coaches, doctors, and executives. Each of these men has very specific jobs and responsibilities and requirements. This is their job. After spending time over these years with women whose husbands are in a variety of vocations, I've realized each vocation has its own challenges. Your husband's vocation happens to be ministry. Since being called to ministry is a high calling from God, it involves excellence in day-to-day performance. Do you think the executive or college coach's wife *loves* everything about her husband's job? Every job — ministry included — will always have parts that are more desirable than others. That is life. What gives you the right to whine over certain job responsibilities involving your husband?

If your husband is the senior pastor of the church, no one will bear the responsibility of the church any more than your husband will. You role is to take away as much "stuff" from him as you can and make your home a "haven" for him to come home to. Whatever ministry your husband serves in, it should be your goal to relieve him of as much stress as you possibly can.

We've talked about some really practical ways to love the man we married, but I feel it is most important that we consider the high calling of ministry on your husband's life.

Ask yourself these questions:

> Am I in "awe" of the high calling of ministry on my husband's life?
>
> Am I in "awe" of what God does through my husband's ministry?
>
> Do you ever consider the "awe" that God allows you to be a part of supernatural ministry because you are married to your husband?

Are you in "awe" of God's working in your church? It's not a building but the presence of God that is awesome, and to think that God would call us to serve Him in ministry is a high calling. Psalms 68:35 says, "O God, You are more awesome than Your holy places" (NKJV).

One of my favorite passages in the Old Testament is after the ark of the covenant had been brought into the temple. First Kings 8:10–11 says, "And it came to pass, when the priests came out of the holy place, that the cloud filled the house of the LORD, so that the priests could not continue ministering because of the cloud; for the glory of the LORD filled the house of the LORD" (NKJV).

My personal prayer is that I never get over the "awe" of God's call on my husband's life, His work in my life, and His work in our church. May we remain in "awe" of God's temple, His work among us, and the call of God on our husbands' lives.

We recently had a guest pastor come and preach at our Sunday services. His wife came with him, and we had the privilege to be able to spend time with them beyond the services. They shared their love for their congregation and place of service — how their children were learning what being "at church" really meant and other positive statements. The wife enthusiastically shared what areas of ministry she was involved in and how much their church meant to their lives. In the time that we were able to spend with them, I felt a kindred spirit and love for them quickly.

That night, in the service after he finished preaching, during the invitation this pastor and wife knelt on their knees to pray. After a few minutes, they stood and began to join in worship — holding hands and lifting them upward. I was deeply moved by the picture I saw — a pastor and wife loving God, loving His Church, and loving one another. Ladies, love the man you married.

INTERACTIVE TESTIMONY

I have quoted Barbara O'Chester in this chapter already. Barbara, wife of Dr. Harold O'Chester, who is the pastor emeritus of the Great Hills Baptist Church in Austin, Texas, had a huge impact on my life as a young minister's wife. Barbara led a full-fledged retreat ministry for women for a number of years. In reflecting on her years in ministry and the message that reflects her life most, I would say that more than anything, Barbara O'Chester taught us how to love our man — in every sense of the word. Here are some of Barbara's thoughts on how to "love the man you married."

Jeana: As a pastor's wife who served by her husband's side in ministry for a number of years, can you tell us what is one of the greatest ways we show that our husband is our "treasure"?

Barbara: The way we look at our husband while he is preaching or just in conversation shows he is our treasure. You can embrace him with your eyes without touching him physically. Even if we have heard the message before, we should be engaged, taking notes, and not looking around seeing how others are receiving the message. Our eyes should be on him as if every word is important to us. I always sat on the second row of the auditorium so if he needed anything, he knew where I was. Be involved in the ministry of your husband and faithful in attendance. This shows that his task matters to you and that you are unified in the purpose of serving God.

Jeana: What words of caution would you give to wives about dishonoring their husbands either in public or private?

Barbara: In private: When we were children we learned three words: stop, look, and listen. These words serve us well in marriage. When your husband comes home, stop what you're doing, look at him, and listen to what he has to say — 58 percent of communication is facial expression, 42 percent is body language and voice inflection. We have to learn to listen with our ears, our eyes, and our hearts. Don't be too quick to give advice — sometimes he just needs a "sounding board." If he wants advice he'll ask for it.

In public: We can show our respect by the way we talk about him to others. Anything we say that puts him down even in jest can be taken as disrespectful. Any time we begin a sentence with "my poor husband" or end a sentence with "bless his heart" is a put-down.

Brag on him to others in front of him. It doesn't matter how many people think he's wonderful, he's most concerned with what you think about him.

Jeana: After serving many years in ministry, what does the "high calling of being a minister's wife" mean to you personally?

Barbara: My husband has always said, "A pastor would have to step down to be the president of the United States." I agree. The Lord showed me many years ago that of the billions of people in the world, He chose a minute number to serve Him in a full-time vocational capacity. I am humbled to have been a pastor's wife. We are privileged to serve. Ask the Lord to give you a servant's heart. Guard against an attitude of entitlement.In the ministry we hold many lives in our hands. What a privilege that God would entrust us to love and serve His people. Has it always been easy? Definitely not! Has God always been faithful? Definitely yes.

Endnotes

1. Gary Oliver and H. Norm Wright, *When Anger Hits Home* (Chicago, IL: Moody Press, 1992).
2. Gary Thomas, *Sacred Influence* (Grand Rapids, MI: Zondervan, 2006).

5

BALANCE IS THE KEY

I CAN'T DO IT ALL! I'M OVERWHELMED! Why are we always at church? How do I balance life and ministry? How can I get my husband to spend more time at home instead of the church?

I believe many ministry problems are created by a lack of balance in many areas of life. Balancing time, family, and church will always be a tension in ministry life. I am married to the greatest organizer and the most disciplined person I've ever met. My husband sees order to everything! Not only that, he's a master at time management. I, on the other hand, struggle in those areas! Life in general, along with marriage, children, and ministry responsibilities, has forced me to grow in those areas not just to survive, but to thrive. There is a huge difference between "surviving" and "thriving" in ministry, and balance is key. I want to share just a few of the areas that I believe are most critical in the area of balance.

BALANCE IN FAMILY TIME

I think one of the most critical areas we struggle to balance is the area of time management. As I already stated, my husband is a master at time management, but few people are as gifted as he is in that area. This has been of great advantage for our family as we serve in ministry. Most are more like me — struggling to survive and make it all come "together." I have made great strides throughout these years of marriage and ministry, and because of that, I believe we have escaped much conflict with our family and within church life.

At times we blame the church for a lack of family time and mismanaged schedules. I really believe that *we* are to blame many times because we are poor time managers. As ministers' wives, we can either help or hurt the situation. If your husband is a good time manager, bless him greatly! If he's not, be his best advocate and help him to grow in this area. We're all on a journey, and I am grateful that grace has been extended toward me in this area because it affects *everything*. God desires for us to live lives of order not disorder (1 Cor. 14:33). God is trying to do us a huge favor here if we will just heed His Word on this.

"Let all things be done decently and in order" (1 Cor. 14:40; NKJV). To me, that applies to all of life. Having order in your life simply makes everything better. Whether it's at home or church or other activities, order makes everything better. There are plenty of tools and resources to expose yourself to; make yourself aware of the options and choose what works for you. Each individual and each family must decide what works best for them. There are obviously different levels that each family will achieve when it comes to order, but one thing is for sure: we all know when we have it and we all know when we don't! When we don't develop a sense of order, life is full of chaos.

You must grow in this area if it is a weakness in your life. "I'm just not organized" won't cut it in ministry life. Although we are not talking perfection in any way, you must come to the point that you have some sense of order in your family life. If not, there will be constant turmoil and conflict in your home that will carry into ministry and affect your husband greatly. Don't let that be a stumbling block to the effectiveness you and your husband have in ministry together simply because you just refuse to "get it together." You are going to be the key to this in many ways. Whether you like it or not, you will be, in all probability, the keeper of the "calendar" for your family — which can be very complicated when combined with a busy husband's schedule. If you do not get ahold of the schedule on your end, it is highly likely that you will suffer lack of family time, which is critical for all ministry families. I am convinced that quality, meaningful time can be managed, but it's going to take a huge part of you working that out and being flexible with your husband's schedule at the same time. In other words, plan, plan, plan! God does not intend for us to sacrifice our families on the altar of ministry. But each ministry family must make decisions that will enable quality time to be experienced and enjoyed. And most of the time, it just takes effort — real effort — to balance time.

Lack of order in our lives loves to show up on Sundays! Ever been in a heated conversation with your husband before church about not having his shirt ironed? Or his suit picked up from the cleaners? Or some other detail you forgot or failed to take care of? Satan can use the most trivial things to ignite an argument between couples. Then who ends up going to church mad and hurt on the inside, but pasting on the fake smile before those in our congregations to make them think that everything is just great! Ladies, take care of business at home — live a life of order! You may think this is a little silly, but many years ago, Ronnie and I determined that we would make every attempt in our marriage to stay away from anything that might engage us in conflict with one another on Saturday and Sunday. It is our belief and conviction that for Ronnie to be anointed when he stands up to proclaim God's Word, we need to be in total unity.

Balance with Extended Family

Behind every ministry family is an extended family. These extended families can be healthy or unhealthy. There can be illness, financial problems, aging parents, relational problems, and a myriad of other family situations. These circumstances affect all of our lives and can sometimes create additional challenges above what we already deal with in church life. I am not a counselor, but there are plenty who can advise in this area for very difficult family situations. The caution I would give is not to let those extended family situations control your obligations to your current ministry responsibilities. Few extended families really understand "the call to ministry," and therefore they are not always sympathetic with the lives we live as ministers and wives. I am fortunate to have come from a ministry family; my father was a pastor for over 50 years, so my parents understood our ministry life. As well, Ronnie's family, although not in ministry, blessed and released us to carry out God's call on our lives.

I am not suggesting that you forsake extended family. I am suggesting that you recognize your greater obligation is to your ministry call, whether understood or not. I also believe that with diligence, patience, love, and understanding, the two can walk together in great accordance and harmony most of the time. A ministry wife who constantly has to run home to mama and daddy and neglects her husband is forgetting that she is to "leave and cleave" not only for the sake of the ministry, but even more importantly for her marriage.

BALANCE IN CHURCH LIFE

Although not totally under your control, you can have great influence in the area of church life. You can control your involvement in church activities. I am talking about ministry activity beyond normal Sunday worship times and whenever else your particular ministry corporately meets. Those are non-negotiable. How can we expect our people to meet together in corporate worship and the minister's wife not be there? I am not only referring to the senior pastor's wife, but wives of the support staff as well. Attendance is important. Your presence in corporate worship says to others, "This is important to me." If we really believe in what we are doing, then our presence is important and necessary. Only in recent years have we had to ask prospective staff wives if they regularly attend church. What a shame.

But beyond our obligation to corporate times, most have the opportunity to choose those extended times of involvement. All of us have gifts that are to be used, whether we are ministers' wives or not, for the Kingdom. The great thing about church life today is that most churches do allow and encourage wives to be involved in those ministries they feel called to and not just fill a position. It is the difference between serving out of "passion" and serving out of "position." Speaking from personal experience, I have done it both ways. I have served out of obligation and I have served out of the passion for specific ministries I felt God called me to. Guess which ones were more effective for the Kingdom of God? Guess which ones were most fulfilling to me and even seemed to work to the time advantage of my busy schedule? You are correct — the ones God called me to! And learning to discern the difference is invaluable to balancing your time at church. It is crucial for you to serve where God wants you to serve. Factor in and recognize the demands on your husband's time, and realize that at times, you may have to "pick up the slack" at home because your husband can't always be there. Your husband's position and obligations supersede your obligations. I realize that's not a very popular thing to say in today's world of feminist views that have even invaded the Church, but the bottom line is this — your husband's schedule takes priority over yours.

My husband made a huge commitment to our family many years ago. At that time we were serving in a very committee-structured church, that dominated much of his time. Our children were very young. I was extremely resentful of his time away — feeling abandoned and lonely much of the time. My response in the beginning was not what it should have been. In fact, I was guilty at times of ruining what little time we had when he finally came home, because I was so resentful. God did a work in my heart and I stopped the nagging and complaining. I simply stopped. God dealt with my mouth and my heart. Some months later, my husband made a fresh commitment to our family. God had worked in his heart also, and he made the commitment that he would never sacrifice his family on the altar of "church." Ronnie has held true to that commitment, never sacrificing our family and remaining faithful and diligent in his call to ministry.

Balance in Availability to Others

I do not believe that God expects us to be "on call" 24/7. Maybe in years past that was the thinking, but not in the church world today. If that is the case in your church world, pray and ask God to give your congregation a more realistic view of the minister's responsibility. There are some things you can do to protect yourself. I also believe that God does not intend for us to take on every ministry project and person, but to share that responsibility with others. There is no way that you can be available to others constantly and meet the needs of your own husband and family. I am a firm believer that we must remember God called our husband to be the minister and we are to walk by his side. When God does call us to minister to individual persons in our churches, there is even a limit to what we can do. God did not intend for you to resolve every conflict and meet every need that comes your way. Yes, there are times and individuals where God will specifically use you to guide them in their walk, but make sure that you do not take on the entire church world and its problems.

Balance in Taking Time Off

Balance must also come in ministry life in the form of "drawing aside" or a period of "rest." There are times when we must pull away, for a brief time, to renew ourselves. Even Jesus drew aside at times. I strongly encourage you and your husband to make sure to take time off. Everybody needs time away, and that is another part of planning ahead so time is available to do that. Otherwise, your husband will tell you he has too much to do and cannot afford to take the time off. Ronnie has always made sure that we had family vacations, apart from the time spent with extended family. I realize that this will take great planning on your part, but it's a must. Make sure you make this happen — it's an integral part of the balancing act!

INTERACTIVE TESTIMONY

Carol Young is the wife of Jeff Young. Jeff serves on the staff of Prestonwood Baptist Church in Plano, Texas, as the minister of spiritual development. When Jeff and Carol served on our staff, I recognized Carol's ability to juggle life with three children, each in different age groups — elementary school, junior high, and high school. Add to that a busy husband, involvement in women's ministry, and both sets of parents living in another state. How did she do it? Not that she has all the answers, but I think Carol is a good example of someone who recognized that "balance is the key."

Jeana: In what ways does having order in your home benefit your children in their daily lives and your husband in his ministry?

Carol: For the Young household, life is very busy. My husband's job keeps him extremely busy during the day and often on the weekend. We discovered very early in our marriage that our home ran more smoothly if I handled the day-to-day details of our home. This doesn't mean we don't come together and discuss big issues; however, with his blessing I handle school, household, and most financial decisions that come up on a daily basis. As I do this, he is able to come home and relax, enjoy our children, and focus on his ministry. The last thing he wants to do when he comes home is make decisions or handle our finances. My goal is to make our home a haven for him — a place he wants to come home to. God's Word tells us in I Corinthians 14:33 that "God is not a God of disorder but of peace" (NIV). Our home is just more at peace when there is order. This often meant that we had a five p.m. cleanup time before daddy got home. We tried to make his entry back home as peaceful as possible.

For our children, this has meant that certain actions are required by them each day. When they started kindergarten they were expected to make their beds and straighten their rooms each morning before school. I've helped them to organize their rooms so that everything has a place so that after they play it goes back where it belongs. Because this is done daily and not weekly, our house is rarely a total wreck. They tend to keep things neater when they know what's expected. They each have chores that they are responsible for each week. This is a family and everyone helps and does their part — I am not their maid! I hope I am teaching my children to be organized and run an orderly home. My daughter just moved into an apartment this year at college — I am just beginning to see fruit from my labors. When you begin living in chaos and clutter you start to appreciate order and realize how it leads to a peaceful household.

Jeana: What is the greatest struggle you face in trying to keep "balance" in all areas of life?

Carol: Our greatest struggle between ministry and home life is our activities. Church attendance and major church activities have not been negotiable in our family. We never have to decide if we are going to church on Sundays — it has already been decided. This is our biggest priority. At times, this means we don't attend late

Saturday evening activities. We didn't plan many sleepovers on Saturday nights or sign up for activities that occurred regularly on Sundays. This was fairly easy to manage when our children were younger but has grown into quite a struggle as they get older. More and more activities and sport games are occurring on Sundays. We have tried to maintain our priority while not being completely closed-minded. We talk with coaches before joining teams to make sure they respect Sundays and are like-minded. We utilize Saturday services and other times to worship so that our children are learning that "worship" is important.

I have not expected my children to be in every activity that our church has to offer. Two of my children are social creatures and love being a part of everything. This is not always beneficial for them. One of my children is a "home body" who needs down time to function and feel healthy. As the parent, I feel it's my job to help my children make godly decisions about the activities we will be involved in. Some activities are non-negotiable — worship, youth discipleship, and Sunday school. We usually pick one sport activity, music lesson, etc. I think many kids are totally stressed out by the multitude of activities (sometimes good activities) they are involved in. There are seasons when we do a good job of managing our activities, and there are times when we have not managed this well. As stated — this is always a struggle. Good activities are constantly vying for our time. It is important for us to ask God about our schedules before we say yes to anything else. We are constantly evaluating our family life — what is going good and what is not! What we can eliminate in order to make room for something else.

Family time is another non-negotiable. When the children were young, this was Saturday night. We made this a fun time and something they looked forward to. As our children have grown, a specific night each week is impossible. We still share a family meal two to four times a week. We share about our days, school activities, struggles, etc. We also regularly plan family activities. We try to make these fun times that they will enjoy being a part of. Our family is very important to us, and we constantly evaluate our schedule to make sure it allows time for our family to be together.

Jeana: What advice would you share with other ministry wives that has been of great help to you to maintain balance with ministry and family life?

Carol: Someone shared a great tip with me many years ago as I was struggling to keep my household "in order," which was, "It's okay to say *no* to good things." I spent many early years saying yes to everyone's request and was completely frazzled at home. I have tried to recognize the areas God has gifted me in, and serve in these areas. I make sure I take the requests to God in prayer and seek His wisdom about my schedule.

Another tip we received from a mentor couple early in our marriage was to continue to date each other or plan times to be together. When our children were young that meant saving up for babysitters. We have never had family close by, so we had to budget for this and it was a priority for us. We made sure our children knew that our relationship was important and we wanted to spend time together. When they went to preschool or school, we started having weekly dates on my husband's day off. Friday is usually my husband's day off, so I hold that day as almost sacred. I don't plan appointments or lunch dates with friends on Fridays. This is my day to be with Jeff. Some Fridays we may have time only for lunch, or some days we may spend the whole day just hanging out, doing errands, driving in the country, or shopping. Of course there are times when things come up that have to be done on Friday; however, this is the exception instead of the norm. This has given us time to communicate as a couple, to evaluate our family, and to make our relationship a priority.

6

LET THE MEN
BE THE MEN

I GREW UP IN A PASTOR'S HOME. I said I would never marry a pastor, but that is the only life I have ever known. Growing up in a pastor's home undoubtedly molded much of my thinking as I became "the pastor's wife." Much of what I learned in a minister's home has been resourceful and invaluable. I learned from my father to love the Church and God's Word. My mother was a wonderful example of a quiet and gentle spirit and served with a true servant's heart.

Regardless of what I said in innocence or immaturity, I would not want to do or be anything else to this day. My husband and I have been in ministry — he as a senior pastor — since the day we got married. In fact, he became a full-time pastor four months before we married, almost 33 years ago at the time of this writing. I love my job as pastor's wife and desire for other staff wives to enjoy this journey as much as I have!

One of the greatest lessons and realizations I learned early on as a pastor's wife was that I was *not* called to be the pastor.

God did not intend for us to bear the burdens of the Church. He has called our husbands to do that. He has called us to walk by their sides and be supportive of their calling.

"Let the men be the men" is a phrase I coined years ago as I challenged our staff wives on how to cope with ministry issues. This is an area where many staff wives get themselves in a great deal of conflict and invite trouble into their laps. For you to try to solve staff issues that your husband should be dealing with is a rebuke to you and your husband. That is not the message you want to send to your staff or congregation.

Of particular importance to the senior pastor's wife is that God called your husband to be the pastor, not you — you are to be his helpmeet. When you step in and try to act as "pastor" you lessen his authority, effectiveness, and respect from others. To put it very clearly, you make your husband look like a weak leader.

Also for the senior pastor's wife, let your role be to love and minister to those wives on your staff team. When you take on a role that is not intended to be yours, you reduce the amount of influence you have with them. "Let the men be the men" and handle the conflict, and use your energy to love, influence, mentor, and challenge those precious wives on your staff.

I have never wanted to be the "staff wife Gestapo." I would much rather be considered their friend or spiritual adviser! Because dealing with staff will occasionally involve conflict, Ronnie and I have always practiced that if there is a problem with a staff wife, it should be handled by the appropriate men on staff, either the senior pastor or the designated staff member who deals with those situations.

Almost always, if there is a problem with the wife, there is a problem with the husband. Getting to the root of the problem is not always easy or obvious, but after serving many years as a pastor's wife, there is usually an underlying problem that causes a wife to act in a way that is either inappropriate or unacceptable. There are many reasons that we all act like we do, but today's world and the various backgrounds that people come from are profound influences on ministers and their wives.

We cannot hang on to a victim mentality or excuse immaturity, but many ministers' wives have not come from stable Christian backgrounds, may have not been exposed to church life at all, or may have been saved at a later age. After having served for so many years as a senior pastor's wife, I realize that every staff member we hire comes with baggage and background. Sometimes this is good and sometimes it can be challenging in the ministry. Realizing that each one comes from an individualized background, family, experience, etc., has helped me to understand some of the struggles some wives have.

I believe the key here is the same as with any other Christian, regardless of the background we come from. If we have been saved, we are "new creatures" — old things are passed away and all things become new. It is up to us as Christian believers to grow in the grace that Christ has so wonderfully given us, to mature and become all that God would have us to be. There is great accountability and expectation from our congregations that we do that. I do not believe that our congregations expect perfection from the staff team, but I do believe they deserve our utmost attempt to follow Christ, to grow in our walk with Him, and to serve Him with our "whole hearts."

Men handle conflict and challenges differently than women. They resolve issues more easily and with less feeling and emotion than women do. That's why we should let the men be the men. Men have the ability to disagree completely and go out and play golf together the next day. Women tend to hang on to hurts and nurse them for a while before we are able to move on. Again, another reason to let the men be the men.

Many problems can be created by a wife who wants to lead, be involved in situations that do not include her, or to control situations that are of concern to her. In a sense, she wants to be "the pastor." I am not saying that literally but am referring to the way she conducts herself. This can be the senior pastor's wife, as well as another support staff member's wife. For whatever reason, women seem to think sometimes that they have a better way of leading and doing things. This is not to say that women have no place in advising their husbands in ministry. Our husbands are wise men to listen to sound, spiritual advice given to them by their wives.

I am referring more to strong women who refuse to understand their important place to walk by their husband's side, not to lead the church or continually stir up trouble. The caution here is to not emasculate your husband's leadership — whether he serves as senior pastor or a support staff team member — by your actions or words.

When you attempt to lead or overstep your boundaries as a wife, you put a strain on your relationship with the other wives. Plus, it may fuel their fire to attempt to do the same in their husband's ministry or marriage.

I firmly believe that if we will "let the men be the men," God will use them to lead in powerful ways. God created men to be leaders under pressure. God created men to be less emotional and more rational. God created men to be less reactionary in difficult decisions. I also believe that God, because He called our husbands into His ministry, will direct them in wise decision making. A Scripture I have claimed for my husband many times when he has faced difficult decisions is this one: "But His secret counsel is with the upright" (Prov. 3:32; NKJV).

At times, all our husbands will face very difficult circumstances. There are certainly times when I am so thankful that I am not the one in charge — the one who has to make the tough decisions. God has gifted our husbands as men who can be courageous in the face of those difficult times.

Another favorite Scripture I turn to regarding difficulties I know my husband must handle is, "The wicked run away when no one is chasing them, *but the godly are as bold as lions*" (Prov. 28:1; emphasis added). What a great prayer to pray for your husband — that he would be as bold as a lion! God knows we need courageous men leading our churches in today's world!

Although rare, there have been occasions when my husband, after having received counsel from others and knowing there is no alternative, and having given much prayer to each situation, realizes that a termination must occur. That is never fun for anyone. Your husband cannot make difficult decisions about staff based on friendships or involvement with a wife on the team or in the church but based on what is best for the church. Men normally have the greater ability to be more objective in difficult situations.

These times are especially difficult. I, of course, always consider the wife's feelings and how the layoff will affect the children and so on. Our husbands must make the decisions based on *what is best for the entire church*. Women tend to make decisions of the "heart." Another reason we need to let the men be the men.

Also, I believe God has a huge, important role for the women who walk beside their husbands in ministry. When we get those roles mixed up and confused, there are guaranteed problems. What a great responsibility to pray for our husbands as they serve in those important roles as leaders in ministry. What a great call for us, as their wives, to offer godly support — and even occasional advice. What a tremendous call on our lives as well to be the instrument that God called us to be — walking beside these great anointed men of God.

I encourage every minister's wife, whether your husband is the senior pastor or a support team member, to search your heart, your thoughts, and your actions. Do your actions give the impression that you would really like to be the pastor? That you always think you have a better plan? Do you feel like the man in your life — or the men on your staff team — are not making the right decisions and need your advice? Do you criticize their leadership behind their backs? Do you undermine decisions to others? Do you cause your husband to doubt his own leadership? Do you enjoy knowing everything about everything whether it involves you or not? Do you make the effort to calm a storm or create one on your staff? These are important questions to make you search your own heart and answer.

I promise you this, if you will concentrate that energy on loving and supporting your man and letting "the men be the men," it will be much more enjoyable to serve as a minister's wife by loving and encouraging those wives you serve with. Let this be your goal . . . and "let the men be the men."

INTERACTIVE TESTIMONY

Jennifer Landrith is a pastor's wife. Her husband, David, serves as senior pastor of the Long Hollow Baptist Church in Hendersonville, Tennessee. They have three children. Jennifer is the author of *In Our Shoes*, which is a Bible study for ministers' wives that I would encourage all of you to use with your staff.

Jeana: What does "let the men be the men" mean to you as a senior pastor's wife, and how would you advise other wives on your staff to heed this advice?

Jennifer: When I first heard the phrase "let the men be the men" I thought, *I have never heard that put in that form.* This statement is so true and yet so simple. It impacted me because I thought so many times that when we as wives get involved we bring emotions into the picture and we stay injured or hurt over things when our husbands have long moved on and forgotten the situation.

I do advise our other staff wives to heed this advice because I think it will help them and their husbands in their ministry. This just makes sense. Staff wives will avoid some pitfalls along the way if they can learn this lesson early.

Jeana: What kinds of problems have you seen develop when staff wives try to take on problems that are not theirs to solve?

Jennifer: Wow, I have seen staff wives who have tried to talk to committees about their husband's salary, wives who have gotten on to another staff person if they didn't attend their husband's event, and wives who have taken up their husband's offense when he needed to handle the situation himself. When the wife gets involved it can be uncomfortable for all of those who are involved. When she feels ownership or control over a certain area then she has forgotten the bigger picture of the church and her role in it. Interfering in something that you are not involved in only further escalates any problem and allows for more hard feelings between staff or members in the church. This brings further stress on her husband instead of less.

Jeana: When you consider your role as the senior pastor's wife, how does that affect your response to difficult circumstances knowing that you are being "watched" not only by the other staff wives but also by church members?

Jennifer: I try not to think about the "immediate eyes" upon me in a certain situation but try to think of how my attitude or answers can please the Lord. He is the one that I want to honor, so I want to respond as He would have me to. I want to share from my heart and be real but I must also be smart. Real doesn't mean you reveal things you shouldn't. You don't have to address everything, and sometimes you just need to redirect things. For instance, if someone wants me to pass on a message to my husband, then I may reply it would be better for this person to call his assistant because I might forget. Hopefully, as I respond in difficult circumstances, then other staff wives will watch and see me model the right attitude. Also, remember to use humor when you can to possibly lighten any tension. This always helps when it is appropriate. Be willing to give people another chance and try not to take things personally. Everyone has a bad day every now and then, so it is good if you just don't write someone off. On a lighter side, it also doesn't hurt to learn to walk fast when you encounter difficulties and/or difficult people along the way. Find a quick distraction and stay on the move.

Jeana: How might reacting in the opposite manner of "letting the men be the men" cause your husband to doubt himself?

Jennifer: I think a husband must doubt his leadership role if his wife is taking up his offense all the time. He will think he is not capable and probably resign himself to letting her handle it. Instead of the husband growing in this area and gaining the respect of those he works with, he may give up or stop trying. This leads to other people not having respect for him. This could also lead to depression in the husband at some point. You are becoming a stumbling block to his leadership when you don't allow him to handle his own issues at church. You are not allowing him to become the man God intended if you are trying to take over his role. This will make him feel inadequate in leading and doubt his ability to make decisions.

7

IT'S KOOL2BAPK

"HOW CAN WE PRAY FOR YOUR FAMILY?" was a question often asked when our children were little. Our answer was always the same, "Pray that they will grow up loving Jesus and loving His Church." I have rarely felt that I could speak as an authority on raising children in the ministry, not wanting to put our children on display or place more pressure on them. I also had the feeling that the "jury was still out." Our sons are now 29 and 25. Both married godly and lovely girls and have already given us four beautiful grandchildren with another on the way. I guess I can finally say with confidence that those prayers have been answered. I say that with a little reluctance, not because of any behavior that our children have portrayed, but because I know that one of the greatest ways Satan loves to attack is through our children. Our oldest son is a coach and believes one of his greatest opportunities is to influence young men's lives through the game of football, and our youngest son is in full-time ministry. Both love Christ and are highly committed, along with their wives, to the local church. I am grateful for those prayers that were offered up for many years on behalf of our children.

"Preachers' kids" have been looked upon with a certain disdain for a number of years. Why is that? That is obviously a question that could be answered by a number of explanations. Gone are the days, I believe, when ministers' children are set apart with higher unrealistic expectations. There will always be some people who will be watching your children, waiting for them to make mistakes or fall short of their own preconceived expectations. Such is life. I have a feeling other professions might deal with the same sort of issues. Regardless, the best thing we can do as pastoral parents is to make sure we've done our job to the best of our abilities under the power and leadership of the Holy Spirit. Does that guarantee perfect children? You already know the answer to that.

Many ministry parents, under God, raise their children in the nurture and admonition of the Lord. And for whatever reason, some children choose to go a different direction. That is heartbreaking, to say the least. But how many times do we, as children of the King, fall short in our obedience to Him?

One of the most important things in raising children in the ministry is the same for all parents. You are the parent. You are not their best friend. You are the parent. Don't be afraid to say no to your children or to discipline them. There are plenty of Scriptures that admonish us to do this. I personally feel that many children, and not just children of ministers, are left to make their own decisions when they are not capable of making wise and mature choices.

Proverbs 20:11, 30; 22:15; and 29:15, 17 are Scriptures beneficial for raising children.

Don't be afraid to correct your young ones; a spanking won't kill them. A good spanking, in fact, might save them from something worse than death (Prov. 23:13–14; Message).

Because this book is not solely about solving issues with children, I would like to approach this chapter from the standpoint of some things that I believe should be real convictions as we raise our children. What's interesting about this, I believe, is that these principles could apply to all parents, not just ministry parents.

There are many good resources for raising children that can address specific areas of concern, so I will not go into detail in specific areas but in areas that I feel need to be addressed as ministry parents.

I want to mention a few things that Ronnie and I did practice with our children. I'm not saying that our children are the perfect examples, but we practiced some biblical and practical principles that we feel very strongly about. My prayer is that you will search your heart, pray for spiritual discernment as you read this, and allow God to form in your heart those things that are non-negotiable in raising your children.

Your children will know if you really love the church by the things you say at home, when church members are not around. As well, they will see how you value church members by what you say about them outside the church doors. All professions have positives and negatives. Be careful not to pass on a martyr complex of "I'm so mistreated because my dad is in the ministry."

Life is not fair in either the secular world or the ministry world. There are some disadvantages for ministry children, but

I've found the positive outweighs the negative by far. Always point out the positive aspects to your children about the blessings and advantages they have because their dad is a minister. Instilling in them negative attitudes toward church and church people can be costly to their future walk with Christ and commitment to His Church.

If we protect our children from every slight or injustice, or come to their defense all the time, we are doing them a disservice and we make them "handicapped" to function in the real world. Church isn't the only place where injustice can happen. Life is not perfect, and they need to learn that lesson early. Consider that strongly the next time your son or daughter complains about some situation at church or some other circumstance before you go marching up to the church to defend your child's actions or behavior! There are times when we must stand up for our children, but let that be the exception and not the rule.

Don't always rescue your child when he does not get what he wants. Sometimes it may even be within your power as a staff parent to do that! But God may have a different plan — and you may need to step aside and let Him do His work in the life of your child. Don't always defend your child as being right. Sooner or later you will embarrass yourself! Children do embarrass their parents from time to time with behavior that goes against how you trained them. When you defend your child and you know he was wrong in his behavior, you send a message to your child that he is always right, doesn't have to suffer the consequences of those choices brought on by himself, and you teach him to be dishonest in his ways.

You as a parent and as a minister's family are establishing a reputation among your church people. Much of that is under your control and is influenced by your behavior. What do you want that reputation to look like? Don't protect your children and attempt to make their world perfect. There is a general tendency in our world today that promotes an "entitlement mentality." I see it on all levels and ages, inside and outside the church. Be careful not to raise your children with that mentality — if we all got what we deserved, it would only be death and hell.

Here are some questions to think about and ask yourself:

Do others enjoy my children?
Is there constant conflict with other parents and other children?
Am I raising my childen to be able to cope in the world of "others"?

Depending on your answer to these questions, you may want to re-consider how you are raising your children. Hopefully you can answer each of these questions positively. If not, it's never too late to change the way you parent.

Teach your children to honor the Sabbath. Today's world has forgotten to honor the Sabbath. Sadly, Sunday is just another day of the week to the majority of humanity. It's a day to shop, have athletic events, go to movies, and many take part in other options, and if you can squeeze it in, attend church. Even though the world looks at Sunday as just another day of the week, it is still important to teach your children that Sunday is the Lord's Day.

Both of our sons were exceptional athletes. At one time, our oldest son was invited to be a part of a competing team. What an honor to have been asked to be a part of that elite team! The problem was that they traveled many weekends, which meant our son would not have been in worship with our family. As parents, we chose not to allow him to be a part of that team. Now, years later, although that decision seemed difficult at the time, we know without a doubt we made the right decision. By the way, our son continued in his athleticism — breaking several national records in his sports career. I don't think our decision to not let him be a part of that team hurt him, and I believe the spiritual benefits paid off immensely. Teach your children the importance of honoring the Sabbath.

Church attendance was never optional in our home. Even when our sons got into high school and could drive on their own, it was not a choice to be made on their part. Children can become quite creative in coming up with excuses of why they shouldn't have to go to church or church activities: boring teachers, their friends didn't have to go, they're too tired — just to name a few! We also required our children to be involved in extracurricular activities along with corporate worship times. Some of the most influential, spiritual, life-changing moments can come at summer camp, lock-ins, Disciple Now weekends, and Bible studies. I realize the names we give these may have changed in today's world, but the end result is the same regardless of what contemporary name we give them. Having your children at those events and experiences may be the times when God calls them to make very important life decisions. You are placing them in a position to hear from God in the early and formative years of their lives. It's not just filling their lives with churchy activity — it's placing them in positions and opportunities where God can speak to their hearts. That's why you do it!

Apply spiritual truths and principles every chance you get. Our words and actions have the power to influence our children in a positive or negative way. After being a parent for 29 years and observing other parents for even longer, I have made a profound observation: children become like their parents.

Critical parents raise critical children.

Selfish parents raise selfish children.

Cynical parents raise cynical children.

Rebellious parents raise rebellious children.

Parents with integrity raise children with integrity.

Parents who love the Church raise children who love the Church.

Are there exceptions to this observation? Of course there are. Your children will make mistakes, regardless of what your vocation is or how hard you try to be the perfect parent. Being in ministry doesn't guarantee anything. Our children will make wrong choices at times, even when we as parents have done the best we knew how to do. But I do believe there is validity in my observation when I see parents who are permissive, indulgent, not teaching respect for authority, or failing to teach their children in spiritual matters.

One of the greatest things that you can do for your children is to love one another. Children who see their parents loving one another feel more secure. Children who see their parents loving one another see God's love in action before their eyes. What better example could you show your children?

INTERACTIVE TESTIMONY

Janice Thomas has been a friend for many years. She was a neighboring pastor's wife when we served at Nederland, Texas.

Her husband is Dr. Claude Thomas, a pastor for many years. At that time, my children were very young, but I observed her "mothering" and "ministry" skills in raising her four boys. Those four boys have grown up and married, and Janice now has 13 grandchildren! I have watched all of them turn out to be godly men, three of whom are in full-time ministry, and the other serves the Lord through his law practice. My question to Janice was — how did you do it? Her answer was always the same — "on my knees." Janice has been one of those wonderful role models in my life as a minister's wife and a ministry parent. I knew that I wanted to include some of her wisdom on this topic of raising children in the ministry. I asked her to respond to some questions about raising her sons in a home where their father was pastor of a local church.

Jeana: Do you believe being in ministry was a positive or negative experience?

Janice: Our four sons were given to us by God as precious gifts to value, cherish, train, protect, and rear in our ministry home. Their father was a pastor and we had the expectations, demands, heartaches, joys, and blessings that all ministers' families experience. Our first responsibility was to our family. We were committed to care for, nurture, and cultivate the soil of our four sons' lives to help them develop into the men God has called them to be.

I believe the ministry has been a positive influence on our sons' lives. However, they did experience some of the negatives of ministry life. They felt the "glass house syndrome" and disappointments of people that come with being a ministry family. But with each situation, we found that it was most important how we as parents handled the ministry stresses, expectations, heartaches, and joys. It is our belief that we as parents in ministry must model for our children the life that Christ modeled for us. What we did to fulfill our responsibilities to the local church ministry was important, but we knew it was imperative to show day by day what Jesus taught in the Bible by living the teachings of Scripture each day. While we acknowledged our own "failings," we sought to live out an authentic relationship with Christ in our lives and homes, seeking to follow Jesus with all our hearts and walk in His teachings with the needs of our children in mind.

And there were the positive opportunities that came their way due to being raised in a ministry home. They were privileged to meet and know some of the greatest people on the planet. The people we meet early in life affect the way we live life. It has been true for our sons. They were also constantly exposed to the Scripture and its impact on life. We wanted them to experience Christ at the point of His Word. And we wanted them to have the opportunity to see how the teachings taught through the ministry of the church impacted the life of the pastor's family every day, especially a growing relationship with Jesus.

Jeana: What are some of the important aspects of ministry that you made sure your children "got"?

Janice: The first truth we wanted each of our sons to "get" was and is that God unrelentingly and unconditionally loves them and so do we. Through ministry we sought to reinforce that reality and that nothing could diminish that love.

The second truth we wanted them to get was that we were always there for them. We want to talk to them, we want them to talk to us . . . we want to hear their heart and we want them to hear ours. We are a family living life together.

The third truth that we wanted them to know is we live in a "fallen world." Perfection does not reign in our world and neither does it in our family and certainly not in the ministry world. Our journey in life has many joys and sorrows. People will disappoint you. Life is not always fair — but God is always good! He has plans for our lives that give us a future and a hope (Jer. 29:11). Success in the journey of life is found in submitting to His plan for our lives. We knew if they would grasp these realities and live them out they would be walking in God's power for life.

The fourth truth is that God is our source. Jesus died for each of them and is the source for their day-to-day living. The truth of the Scriptures was always talked about in our home. I used unconventional methods to get the Word of God into their hearts and minds, such as taping selected Scripture verses on the inside of the cupboard next to the peanut butter jar as a constant reminder.

The fifth truth is that we are not created to live in isolation but in community. The community of faith, the Church, is God's design for us. And fulfilling that design builds every other area of life.

Jeana: As your children are grown, what important lessons do you think they will hold on to forever?

Janice: I believe and pray that they will grasp continually that God loves them unconditionally. I believe and pray that they will be truly "rooted" and established in love so that they have the power to grasp how long and high and deep is the love of Christ and know that this love surpasses knowledge — so that they may be filled with the fullness of God (Eph. 3:17–19).

I believe and pray that they accept the fact that we live in a fallen world with fallen people. Perfection does not reign in this world or the ministry, and God does not require them to perform for the approval or acceptance of Him or others. They just need to seek God's sovereign activity and His righteousness (Matt. 6:33), which means that Jesus is the voice that will steer them through every situation. Jesus is the peace that will set their troubled hearts to rest. Jesus is the power that will hold them up in a storm. Jesus will be closer than any friend could ever be.

I believe and pray they embrace that life is an amazing journey to be celebrated. This journey of life is for the purpose of being a reflection of Jesus here on earth.

Jeana: What is the best thing about raising children in a minister's home?

Janice: I am uncertain that I can identify the "best thing," but I do believe there are some great things about being raised in a minister's home. The minister's home can be a place where the very life and teachings of Jesus are lived out. It is to be a place where love abounds and lots of grace is expressed. It is an opportunity to experience up close and personal how to: (1) integrate every aspect of your faith in lives lived, (2) demonstrate the value of church as a community of faith loved by Jesus with a definite mission in the earth rather than a place of employment and institutional identity, and (3) the relationship with Jesus lived in a real and vulnerable way. Conflicts and problems do arise in ministry, but the ministry home is a safe place to work through these conflicts as the textbook of the Bible is taught and lived. It is my heart's prayer that these teachings were modeled in our ministry home just as Jesus modeled them for us.

8

LET IT GO: DEALING WITH CRITICISM, CONFLICT, AND UNFORGIVENESS

DEALING WITH CRITICISM GOD'S WAY

WHAT IS CRITICISM? Criticism, according to Webster's dictionary, means "to find fault." Anybody relate to that? Have you ever had to deal with the criticism pointed at your husband, children, or the way your husband does ministry? Maybe even *you* are the one who is being criticized.

One thing you can count on dealing with in ministry is criticism. Everyone deals with criticism — we might even agree that "criticism is no respecter of persons." It comes to the young and the old, the rich and the poor, and all in between. Criticism comes in ministry life no matter how young or old you are, what your personality type is, or how short or long you've served somewhere. Count on it, you will be criticized.

Everyone has had — or still has — critical people in their life outside of ministry life. It can come from within our families — a husband, our parents, our in-laws, even our children, possibly a co-worker, maybe even a close friend. Sometimes the criticism that comes from within is much harder to deal with than criticism that comes from the outside.

How Does Criticism Affect Us?

Criticism . . .

> paralyzes us,
> makes us feel defeated,
> stifles us,
> makes us feel "less than,"
> makes us feel insecure, and
> hurts us.

Criticism makes us angry, defensive, and want to fight back. Criticism in ministry can be very discouraging to you and your husband if you allow it to. In our flesh, we calculate the sacrifice we consider ourselves to make for the "cause of Christ" only to be met with the criticism of others, and it can cause us to crumble quickly. We then immediately move into the "martyr role" or take on the "how dare they criticize us" mode — or any other "poor me" syndrome that we can muster up! No one enjoys being criticized.

At times like this, a very good Scripture to remember before we spout off our displeasure is Proverbs 13:3: "He who guards his mouth preserves his life" (NKJV).

Are There Lessons to Be Learned from Criticism?

There is always something to be learned from the adversity in our lives. God can use criticism to make us better and to bring about His bigger purpose in our lives. A verse that has proven to be true over and over again in my life says: "Blows that hurt cleanse away evil" (Prov. 20:30; NKJV).

Most of the time, our initial response is to blame others, but when is the last time you did some soul searching to see if you warrant your own criticism?

Consider these questions:

> Is there a legitimate reason for criticism?
> Is there any truth to what others are saying?
> Is there something in my life that warrants criticism?
> Does my behavior ask for it?
> Am I a critical person? Sometimes we are guilty of what others accuse us of. We *are* the critical person.

Just as we can be wounded by the words of others, we can hurt others. We have the power to breathe death or life into others by what we say with our tongues. Proverbs 18:21 says, "Death and life are in the power of the tongue" (NKJV).

If we do something that we know is wrong or questionable and we are criticized for it, why should we be surprised?

The Bible also cautions us to be aware of the influence others can have on our lives. Proverbs 22:24–25 tells us, "Don't make friends with an angry man, and don't be a companion of a hot-tempered man, or you will learn his ways" (HCSB).

If you are critical of others, more than likely you will be criticized. It's the "law of criticism." What goes around comes around.

Sometimes it is to our advantage to *listen* to criticism just as the Scripture says. Proverbs 13:18 says, "He who regards a rebuke will be honored" (NKJV).

How Should We Respond to Criticism?

"A soft answer turns away wrath" (Prov. 15:1; NKJV) would be a good place to start in how we respond to criticism. We would be wise women to let that become our initial response, although that is usually totally against our flesh. Our flesh seeks to defend and explain our point of view or course of action. In other words, most of the time we "come out swinging"!

There are two kinds of criticism.

A. *Deserved:* many times we get what we asked for. Throughout these years of ministry, I have seen this happen more than once, and church staff members can really ask for their own criticism with dumb decisions and actions. I know no other way to say it but that. And then we wonder why we are being criticized!

God's way to respond to criticism is with humility and repentance, especially when we have done something to warrant that criticism. God's ways will lead us to ask for forgiveness and take steps to correct our mistakes. If you continue to stiffen your neck and refuse to examine or change your ways, you will only hurt yourself, your marriage, your relationships with those around you, and, ultimately, the ministry you are called to.

If you regard a rebuke, as the Scripture previously stated, it says you will be honored. Regarding a rebuke will take some serious heart examination, extreme humility, and consideration of the actions that may have brought on the criticism. Somehow, we must constantly remember this principle and not react defensively.

My husband has been a great example in this area. He has received more than his share of criticism throughout many years of ministry. He practices the policy to always listen and learn from your critics. Sometimes they are right, sometimes they are wrong. But giving a listening ear and open heart to your critics may serve as a great growing experience in your spiritual life. God uses all things in our lives, sometimes even criticism, to draw us closer to Himself.

B. *Undeserved:* what we believe to be unjust criticism

It is important to ask God to give you wisdom and discernment and to make every attempt to check your heart to make sure the criticism is not justified. Remember that the "LORD is a tester of hearts" (Prov. 17:3; HCSB).

Even if you are being criticized unjustly:

1. Examine and humble your heart before the Lord. Romans 12:17–18 is a great Scripture for us to remember in those difficult times of unjust criticism: "Do not repay anyone evil for evil. Try to do what is honorable in everyone's eyes. If possible, on your part, live at peace with everyone" (HCSB).

2. Don't retaliate. Retaliation is our normal, natural response, but we must grow and mature beyond that fleshly act to strike back when we are criticized. Rarely, if ever, does retaliation lead to anything good.

3. Pray and ask God to give you grace on your lips (Prov. 22:11). "Whoever guards his mouth and tongue keeps his soul from troubles" (Prov. 21:23; NKJV).

4. Leave it with God and let it go.

Is it ever right for a Christian to refute criticism? I believe it can be on rare occasions. There is a time for righteous indignation, but it should be only an exception and not a frequent experience in your life. I am hesitant to even mention it, but because of my own personal experience in that area one time, I have chosen to include this story.

There was once an occasion when I listened and listened and listened to the false accusations against my husband. A couple had come in to share with Ronnie their "concerns" about his leadership in our church. The wife accused him of not caring about people (little did she know that the very night before we had been up with a family until two a.m.). She added that all he did was stay in his office, that he was out of touch with the real world and he expected too much from people in our church, and on and on and on. My husband sat there and never defended himself. Finally I couldn't stand it any longer. I "rebuked" her and told her that she knew what she was saying was not true! Believe it or not, she stopped cold in her accusations and said, "You're right." This is the only time in our ministry life that I *ever* remember doing it, but it was so obvious that I could not ignore her accusations and I knew that my husband was not going to defend himself on that particular occasion. The meeting ended cordially with the general feeling that we all "agreed to disagree" on the concerns laid before us. The relationship was never the same, but I can honestly say that I felt I did the right thing on that rare day.

Guard against taking up an offense for someone else. This is extremely hard to do when someone is attacking someone you love — whether it's your husband, your children, or someone else you care about. When you take up an offense for someone else, you are carrying a burden that is not yours to carry. Plus, you may ignite or fuel hard feelings for that person toward the offender.

Better to leave it alone — let it go and let God work it out in His timing and His plan.

You make your husband look like a weak man if you run to defend him every time he is criticized. It is a *rare* occasion that I defend my husband — even though he has been criticized often. I have learned to let the Lord fight our battles for us, and sometimes — just a very few times — he has let me speak truth on his behalf.

I learned a hard lesson years ago as a young pastor's wife. After seeing my husband humiliated publicly in a business meeting, I made my way to a church member and his wife and promptly informed them that they were being swayed in the wrong way against my husband — only to see the man who had done the "swaying" observing me.

The Lord kept me up all night under great conviction over my actions, and I knew that I had to call this man and apologize for my behavior.

He was the last person in the church that I would want to call for anything — much less to apologize. He loved to intimidate people and was just not a very friendly or kind person. Having to call him that morning — under the conviction of the Holy Spirit — cured me and, I'm sure, saved me from heartache in the future that I would have brought on myself due to a lack of composure and trying to refute criticism toward my husband.

Remember that Scripture, "Blows that hurt cleanse away evil"? (Prov. 20:30; NKJV). Even though others' actions may have been wrong toward my husband, my action was equally wrong, and learning that lesson has kept me from falling into that pattern of trying to defend the accusations against my husband.

My husband is not afraid to take a stand and be bold; therefore, if I am constantly trying to defend his stance on issues, that task would be never-ending! That's not the way we need to spend our energy. Don't be guilty of bringing on your own criticism and living from one crisis to another. That drama never ends and leads to nowhere.

We need bold and courageous men in our world today! Pray for your husband to be a bold man — a man full of courage to face criticism and speak truth. Don't ever be guilty of holding your husband back for doing what is right.

It is inevitable that your children will also endure some criticism along the way. Let me be clear to say in advance, it's not just ministry children who receive criticism. Remember, criticism is a way of life for *all* of us, regardless of who your mom and dad are or what they do for a living. Don't presume that your children are being criticized and persecuted unjustly for your sake! You do your children a disservice if you run to their rescue and attempt to deliver them from all criticism.

Again, "blows that hurt cleanse away evil." The Lord may use this truth in your children's lives to make them grow in their personal walk with the Lord. Real life involves criticism. Don't handicap your children in coping with the real world by always rescuing them and assuming everyone else is just being critical of them.

It's always best to evaluate the full situation and possibly prevent embarrassment to yourself when you find out the truth may differ from what you've been told. Regardless, God can use all things — good and bad — in our children's lives to mature them and prepare them for life.

Show your children how to respond to criticism — just or unjust — by *your* behavior toward those who criticize. Be a godly example to your children in this area. *Anyone* can act like the world and respond like the world, but it takes someone full of Jesus to respond as Jesus would have us.

HOW DID JESUS DEAL WITH CRITICISM?

Jesus lived with criticism. Two examples come to mind. Jesus was criticized by those He knew in His own hometown. Read the following account from the Book of Matthew.

> He returned to Nazareth, his hometown. When he taught there in the synagogue, everyone was amazed and said, "Where does he get this wisdom and the power to do miracles?" Then they scoffed, "He's just the carpenter's son, and we know Mary, his mother, and his brothers — James, Joseph, Simon, and Judas. All his sisters live right here among us. Where did he learn these things?" And they were deeply offended and refused to believe in him. Then Jesus told them, "A prophet is honored everywhere except in his own hometown and among his own family" (Matt. 13:54–57).

Mary and Martha, two of Jesus' closest friends, expressed their disappointment openly to Him at Lazarus's death: "Lord, if only you had been here, my brother would not have died" (John 11:32).

Jesus was criticized by some of the members of his own family. "For even his brothers didn't believe in him" (John 7:5). Think of how that must have made Jesus feel! They did not fully understand

His calling and that He truly was the Son of God. Not that we should compare ourselves to Jesus, but at times we are criticized by others due to a lack of full understanding of our work and calling.

Just think about this — Jesus' disciples — His closest circle of friends and followers — were also critical of Him.

In Matthew 16:21–23 it says: "From then on Jesus began to point out to His disciples that He must go to Jerusalem and suffer many things from the elders, chief priests, and scribes, be killed, and be raised the third day. Then Peter took Him aside and began to rebuke Him, 'Oh no, Lord! This will never happen to You!' But He turned and told Peter, 'Get behind Me, Satan! You are an offense to Me because you're not thinking about God's concerns, but man's" (HCSB). (Is this a word for us or what!?)

Those in authority also criticized Jesus, the Sadducees and Pharisees, other religious leaders such as the priests and elders, and the soldiers, just to name a few.

There are so many instances where Jesus was criticized for doing great things — like healing people. How could that possibly have been a reason for criticism?

Jesus was criticized on all sides — from those who were closest inside His circle to those who really didn't know Him or understand what He was all about. They criticized Him upon assumption of what others had said about Him or just what they thought was traditionally correct.

Have you ever been criticized unjustly when the person criticizing didn't see and understand the "whole picture"?

What examples did Jesus leave with us in dealing with criticism? The Gospels are full of examples of how Jesus dealt with criticism in a number of ways:

He was silent at times (before the Sanhedrin).

He refuted it at times (in the synagogue when He taught).

He took it to the Father (in the Garden of Gethsemane before He was ultimately betrayed).

In John 13:1–4 we read this account:

Before the Passover Festival, Jesus knew that His hour had come to depart from this world to the Father. Having loved His own who were in the world, He loved them to the end. Now by the time of supper, the Devil had already put it into the heart of Judas, Simon Iscariot's son, to betray Him. *Jesus knew that the Father had given everything into His hands, that He had come from God, and that He was going back to God.* So He got up from supper, laid aside His robe, took a towel, and tied it around Himself (emphasis added; HCSB).

You see, Jesus knew:

1. where He came from (the Father had sent Him);
2. why He came to earth (He knew His purpose);
3. where He was going (He knew He was going back to the Father after His work on earth was finished).

So when the criticism came, even in the most severe form, knowing that He was facing crucifixion, He was totally *secure* in His actions, purpose, and calling. When you are *just* in your actions and you are criticized for it, sometimes you just have to:

1. know where you come from (spiritually speaking);
2. know why you're doing what you're doing;

3. know where you're going;
4. leave the results to God and Let It Go.

Several years ago my husband went through a severe attack from the media. As we walked through that difficult time, we had to ask ourselves these questions. What we learned from those questions was this:

> The criticism was unfounded and unjust.
> The criticism came from the *world's* point of view.

It was a "cause" worth fighting for — not understood by everyone — a spiritual cause worth being criticized for. This was something bigger than all of us; this was God's plan for many reasons. It became an opportunity for the Body of Christ to stand up for our freedom in this country and the courage to stand.

The criticism that came from "within" hurt much more deeply than the articles in the paper. Even though the overwhelming majority of our church members supported my husband, there were some within our congregation who did not. The accusations and criticism that wound us most deeply are often those that come from within. Those wounds are the ones that bring us to our knees and make us want to crumble.

Your response to criticism, conflict, or crises is a testimony to others. "Others" may be your children, other family members, friends, or co-workers.

A Scripture passage that helped me through that time of persecution and criticism and will help you is 1 Peter 3:12–17: "The eyes of the Lord are on the righteous, and His ears are open to their request. But the face of the Lord is against those who do evil. And who will harm you if you are passionate for what is good? But even if you should suffer for righteousness, you are blessed. Do not fear what they fear or be disturbed, but set apart the Messiah as Lord in your hearts, and always be ready to give a defense to anyone who asks you for a reason for the hope that is in you. However, do this with gentleness and respect, keeping your conscience clear, so that when you are accused, those who denounce your Christian life will be put to shame. For it is better to suffer for doing good, if that should be God's will, than for doing evil" (HCSB).

After my husband had been the lead story on the local evening news, front page newspaper articles, and many letters to the editor for a period of weeks, I found myself very uncomfortable going out in public during that time. Sometimes we let our "vain imaginations" get the best of us, and the enemy, Satan, causes us to lose perspective.

During that time, my husband and I attended an athletic event at a local high school. It's normal for us to receive stares — not out of negative circumstances, but his visibility on television causes people to take a second look when they see him in public. Being a little self-conscious that night, I noticed a lady staring intently at my husband as we approached the ticket gate. She was dressed in noticeably tight clothes and puffing away on a cigarette. She began to approach us and I braced myself for a tongue lashing right there in public! As she got closer, she said, "Aren't you that Ronnie Floyd?" "Yes, ma'am" my husband replied kindly. The next words out of her mouth completely amazed me. "I wish the media would just leave you alone. You just keep preaching the Word." Then she turned around and walked off! Needless to say, I was speechless and extremely relieved! That was probably God's way of telling me to ease up and quit worrying! So don't let the enemy cause you to cower and be intimidated when your husband takes a strong stand on an issue in your church or your community.

As I bring this most important chapter to a close, I want you to consider these things:

Is the criticism in my life justified or unjustified?
What can I learn from the criticism?
Am I a critical person?
Do I let critical people influence me?
How will I respond to the criticism in my life?

Can you answer these questions as well from a godly viewpoint without any hesitancy?

Where did I come from?
What is my purpose here on earth?
Where am I going?
Have I left this situation with God?
Have I "let it go"?

Only if you know Jesus Christ as your personal Savior can you answer these questions. It is by God's sovereign will that you were born. You are not reading this book by accident. Jesus Christ came to earth to bring salvation to anyone who is willing to repent of the sin in his life and ask Him to come into his heart so that he might spend eternity with Him in heaven. He wants to give you victory every day of your life — even victory over criticism.

Until we make some choices in the way we will handle criticism, there is a great temptation not to forgive those who have offended us.

We have no greater example of forgiveness than Jesus and His life and death on the Cross. We will never experience the circumstances or criticism in our lives to equal or surpass what Christ's sacrifice of forgiveness was on the Cross for our sins. The bottom line is, we have no choice to not forgive — because we have been forgiven much.

After 33-plus years in ministry, I have learned that having a spirit of forgiveness is not optional. This is definitely not an area that I would say "it ain't that hard" because it's been a real challenge in my own life, but I want to say again that forgiveness is not optional. I deal with hurt *inwardly*, not *outwardly*. I don't strike out — I cut you out. It's not with outward actions but is a matter of the heart. This is not something I am proud of, and I must guard against this in my personal walk with Christ.

Having said that, I know that unless I forgive others I will not receive personal forgiveness from the Father. I also strive to remember the fact that I, once again, have been forgiven *much*.

Here's my reminder — let this apply to your life also: "If you forgive those who sin against you, your heavenly Father will forgive you. But if you refuse to forgive others, your Father will not forgive your sins" (Matt. 6:14–15). We must recognize and remember that God is the judge. We are not.

These Scriptures are the perfect reminders of who should do the judging. "Do not judge others, and you will not be judged. Do not condemn others, or it will all come back against you. Forgive others, and you will be forgiven" (Luke 6:37).

"Do not judge others, and you will not be judged. For you will be treated as you treat others. The standard you use in judging is the standard by which you will be judged" (Matt. 7:1–2).

Not to be misleading or contradictory, but the Bible also tells us to "be shrewd as snakes and harmless as doves" (Matt. 10:16). I believe God gives us discernment with those who hurt and offend us. Forgive? Always. Not optional for a Christian or a minister's wife. But you can also ask God to give you wisdom and discernment for future dealings with those are bent toward hurting you or your husband.

Through these many years serving in ministry alongside my husband, I have learned a lot about the area of forgiveness — many times dragging my feet, with my heart to follow eventually, but knowing God's personal forgiveness for my sin rendered me helpless to do otherwise. The following are some things I've learned:

1. Always leave the door open when others hurt you. Time has a way of bringing things around, and God can work in amazing ways when we don't close our hearts to those who hurt us. My husband has modeled this to me over and over again throughout many years of ministry in one place. While there are many positives to long tenure, it also carries unique challenges. We have served here long enough to see people leave our fellowship for a variety of reasons and eventually come back. Sometimes they come back with repentant hearts, other times they simply come back. Regardless, time does have a way of healing past hurts when we choose to forgive and "let it go."

2. Unforgiveness hurts my personal relationship with Christ more than the person who hurt me. Unforgiveness puts *me* in bondage, not the other person or persons. Why would

we want to allow that in our lives? Satan uses unforgiveness to hinder our relationship with Christ, making us more vulnerable to his attack on our lives. Remember this: God is the judge. I am not. You may need to repeat that in your mind several hundred times a day when you've been really hurt by someone.

3. Forgiveness softens your heart toward those who hurt you. A spiritual goal for all of us should be to have tender hearts — regardless of what happens. I heard it said once that ministers' wives should develop "the hide of a crocodile and a heart of butter." That statement holds much truth.

4. Unforgiveness robs us of precious energy. If you're like me, you don't have any to waste. There is too much to do — too much good to do and focus on — to waste our precious mental, emotional, and spiritual energy being bitter and angry.

My husband has modeled forgiveness before me numerous times in ministry. I have seen him viciously attacked publically and privately and seen him open his heart and arms and graciously forgive. He even forgives those who have not asked for forgiveness, leaving God as the judge. What an example.

We can all think of someone we know who has chosen to not forgive — or refused to "let it go." Is there anything attractive or appealing about that? I think not. If we really consider the whole issue of criticism, conflict, and crisis, under God, we must "let it go." When considering whether "to forgive or not to forgive," we really have no choice at all. As I said previously, we must choose to forgive because each of us has been "forgiven much." Thank You, Jesus.

INTERACTIVE TESTIMONY

Meredith Floyd is one of my two precious daughters-in-law. She is married to our younger son, Nick. Nick and Meredith met at Liberty University, fell in love, married, and have given us two beautiful grandchildren — Reese Caroline and Beckham Grant. Meredith has a love and passion for following God's will for her life unlike any I have seen in very many young women her age. She received her degree from Liberty University in biblical studies, concentration in women's ministry. She was honored with the very first Women's Ministry Award in 2005. Meredith is a gifted teacher and loves to teach the Word to women. Although she is young, God has already used circumstances in her life to help her live out some of the biblical principles I have talked about in this chapter.

Jeana: How has God used the area of forgiveness to cause you to grow in your walk with Christ?

Meredith: The Scripture God has really used in my life regarding forgiveness is Ephesians 4:32. "Be kind to one another, tenderhearted, forgiving each other, just as God in Christ also has forgiven you" (NASB). That gets me every time! I have not come across a situation yet that, when put through the Ephesians 4:32 test, comes out the other side exempt. No matter what the specific situation is, God's answer to me is the same: "Meredith, I hear you . . . but I want you to forgive that person as I have forgiven you . . . how have I forgiven you?" He forgives me immediately, completely, and repeatedly. I have often found myself unwilling to forgive others, but then in the next breath asking God for forgiveness for a sin I have committed. In that moment, I so appreciate how the Lord forgives me immediately as I recall 1 John 1:9: "If we confess our sins, He is faithful and righteous to forgive us our sins and to cleanse us from all unrighteousness" (NASB). There I am receiving such an available forgiveness but unwilling to give the same to another. It is in that moment that the Spirit whispers Ephesians 4:32 to me. I have no choice but to obey. I have learned that I must choose to forgive, even though I might not "feel" like forgiving. It is in this obedience that I find freedom. He is faithful!

Jeana: What does it mean to you personally to "let it go"? What steps did God use in your life to bring you to the point where you were willing to "let it go"?

Meredith: Just "let it go" is what women say to other women all the time, but it is not so easy to do! Ha. Before I can get to the point of just "letting it go" I have found one particularly helpful verse. Hebrews 12:14–15 says, "Make every effort to live in peace with all men and to be holy; without holiness no one will see the Lord. See to it that no one misses the grace of God and that no bitter root grows up to cause trouble and defile many" (NIV). To me, "let it go" means do my part to "make peace" as best I can, and then I must lay it down at the feet of Jesus. I have to entrust the "offence" and the cartful of emotions that comes with that hurt to the Lord! He can handle it.

In hurtful situations, I am only responsible to the Lord for my own actions. We cannot control other people, as much as we might think we know just what they need to do! The other person involved will be accountable to God for his or her own actions. It is up to him or her to work through the issue with the Lord. We are all sinners, and it is only by the grace of God we are not doing exactly to them what they have done to us. Whether or not they ever apologize for their part or ask for forgiveness is irrelevant. My response must be the same. First, I must try to do my part to "be at peace" with all men. I must make restoration on my end if needed. Second, let it go! Lay it at the feet of Jesus. I have to choose to forgive that person based on the command of Jesus (Eph. 4:32). God's Word always works! His way is always best! He created us and knows best how to help us walk through our wounds. I must trust Him. Third, I can begin praying for that person. Praying for the person who has hurt me can do several things. It brings me into obedience to the Word (Rom. 12), it blesses them (Rom. 12), and it helps relax my anxious heart by turning my focus and emotions toward Jesus. Praying for people during these circumstances has been so powerful and freeing in my life. Try it!

Jeana: Although you are young in ministry, how do you plan to deal with criticism or conflict? What source will you run to? How do you feel God has already used circumstances in your life to prepare you for those times?

Meredith: I participated in a Bible study while we were serving on staff at Prestonwood Baptist Church in Dallas, Texas. It was called *self-confrontation.* (I recommend it!) In it, there is a chapter dealing with anger, bitterness, and unforgiveness. It was a very powerful tool in helping us learn how to practically, step by step, deal with the issue of unforgiveness. I just happened to be dealing with that issue right when we came to that specific chapter. Don't you just love how God does that? (No and yes!) Although sometimes awkward and challenging, when I follow through in obedience during these times, I am always glad I did. He is so trustworthy and always has our best interests in mind! By learning what the Word of God had to say about the subject, I was able to practically apply it over the next few weeks.

Although this situation did not happen within our ministry, but outside of it, it did teach me many lessons that I needed to learn about how to deal with conflict, unforgiveness, anger, and bitterness. I knew that a life devoted to full-time ministry would require me to "toughen up"! I was going to have to learn how not to be such a people pleaser and how to deal with all of the emotion that comes from being offended, criticized, or hurt by someone. Little did I know, God had just the recipe to allow me to have some real life practice. Ouch!

To finish the story, I knew God wanted me to follow through with my "Bible study homework" that week, the tall order of confronting the person and asking forgiveness for my part. God gave me the courage. I remember walking toward this person, all the while thinking, *I can't believe I'm doing this. . . . I am so scared . . . my body is moving in that direction . . . there is no turning back.* I went to this person, apologized for my part (I don't think this person ever knew anything was bothering me) for how I had allowed it to affect me and hoped they could forgive me. This person was so gracious! I could feel the anxiety and weight lifting off of me. I had almost let my pride and fear keep me from God's healing in this specific situation. Even though this person never apologized or talked about what I believed "they had done wrong," it didn't matter. I had obeyed what I felt God called me to do in this specific situation and did my part to "be at peace with all men." To this day, the anxiety I had felt for over a year anytime this person was around or was even mentioned is gone! Praise the Lord! It is now replaced with a new memory — a memory of a God-sized moment in my life where God came through for me and gave me the courage to do what He was asking me to do. He healed my anxious heart and humbled me greatly in the process.

I am *not* suggesting that you must confront every person you have harbored unforgiveness toward. This is just what the Lord was asking of me in this specific case. I needed extra work! My experience with unforgiveness lasted over a year, and God really used this entire situation to teach me just what can take root in our hearts after being hurt. Truly, unforgiveness can lead to great bondage and has the potential to spill over into every part of your life. On the other hand, giving the gift of forgiveness brings great freedom! Since that experience, when I notice that I have unforgiveness in my heart, I diligently do whatever it takes between the Lord and me to deal with it as quickly as possible. It is worth working through. Forgive as you have been forgiven. . . .

9

RELATIONSHIPS MATTER

RELATIONSHIPS . . .

Can we have them in ministry life?

Are they important?

How deep can they go?

What's acceptable?

Is anything "off limits"?

Being raised in a pastor's home, I was taught that you cannot have friends in the ministry. Because ministry life and the expectations that go along with it have changed so drastically, I personally believe it *is* possible to have relationships and friendships in ministry. In fact, I will go a step further and say that you *must* have friends and relationships in ministry.

What I have learned after serving in ministry for many years is that all relationships have boundaries. Yes, people will disappoint you, but many will also follow you on the journey of ministry and make it so worthwhile. Are there some cautions to consider? Yes. The sooner you understand the boundaries of relationships, the easier it will be to initiate and maintain those friendships and relationships.

Why do relationships matter? Relationships make ministry fun. Relationships make ministry more rewarding. Relationships take others on the journey with you. Relationships challenge you as you challenge others. Relationships share the joys and the sorrows. Relationships lighten the load at times.

The bottom line is this: relationships in ministry do matter — and they make ministry meaningful. We cannot survive without relationships. Life revolves around relationships with your spouse, extended family, friends, work, and church. That is what life is made of.

Since we cannot actually escape relationships, how do we use them for "good" and not "bad"? How do we know what the boundaries are?

We have much to gain from one another in the Body — from staff relationships to church relationships.

Different relationships meet different needs in our lives — and all have "boundaries." Whether it's your husband or your best friend or your mother or mother-in-law . . . they have boundaries.

I also believe that seasons and phases of life bring about different types of relationships. God knows that we need different kinds of support at different times of our lives.

YOUR PERSONAL RELATIONSHIP WITH CHRIST

We've already discussed in great depth this area of your personal relationship with Christ. You may survive ministry life without a vital relationship with Christ, but you will be miserable trying! I'm not talking about salvation but day-to-day walking with Christ.

At times, in ministry life, nothing can encourage your walk with Christ more than other relational problems. By that I mean that your problems *push* you to Christ. You had better learn to develop your personal relationship with Christ or all other relationships will end up disappointing you at some time or other — including your spouse, family, friends, and church members. Disappointment in others can send you spiraling down the stairs leading to nowhere.

Christ must be who you take your relationship problems and concerns to. Having a vital walk with Christ will give you a different outlook on all relationships. Regardless of what your struggle is in a relationship, having a walk with Christ will give you a spiritual perspective, help you to have reasonable expectations, and enable you to live within acceptable boundaries.

Your Relationship with Your Husband

Please remember that under Christ, your husband is your priority. It's easy when you have small children for that to get knocked down the scale because young children demand so much from their mothers. That is normal and will never change. Much of relationship success is a balancing act for a woman. But it is very important that during those childbearing and childrearing years your relationship with your husband remain a priority under God.

Be loyal to your husband above others on your staff. If you point out and talk about his faults to other staff wives, they will be tempted to look at him through his weaknesses because you have planted those thoughts in their minds. It minimizes his role as a staff leader when you are critical of him. We already recognize humanity in all of us, and all you are doing is giving them ammunition with which to criticize your husband, whether he is the senior pastor or serving in a support staff position. As already stated in a previous chapter, always honor your husband publicly. The dividends are tremendous, but failing to honor him can be devastating to your marriage and ministry.

Our husbands, although strong in nature as men, still need us and are vulnerable without our focus on them. Don't put your husband in a position where he must receive affirmation or attention from others besides you. There will never come a time in your marriage when another relationship should supersede your relationship to your husband. If another relationship is more important to you than the one with your husband, you have already crossed over a boundary that is wrong. Especially wrong is any relationship with the opposite sex that is more important than your relationship with your husband. Also, women can devote more time and energy to female friends or family relationships than their husbands, and this is not God's intended plan for marriage. If you desire to spend more time with your girlfriends or a family member than your husband, you need to ask yourself why. Down the road of life and marriage and ministry, sooner or later this lack of relational value will catch up with you in a negative way. I can honestly say that there is no one I'd rather be with than my husband. He is my favorite person to be with — always.

Relationships with Church Members

Healthy relationships with church members can be a wonderful blessing. Unhealthy relationships can almost mean death to your ministry. Great caution should be exercised as you enter those relationships, knowing they can be a blessing or a curse.

I referred to Barbara O'Chester already, who poured much into my life as a young pastor's wife. Barbara taught me that you can enjoy lots of things and topics, but a wise staff wife will stay away from discussing church-related issues! Talk babies, cooking, hobbies, and any number of things — but leave the discussion of church issues alone. Make and enjoy relationships that don't totally revolve only around church.

Unfortunately, there are some people who have a strong desire to be on the "inner circle" with the pastor and his wife or other staff team members. Some individuals thrive on this. Maybe that zeal is innocent, but one should see red flags in a relationship based on wanting to know more information than the rest of the congregation or monopolizing and attempting to control time spent with you. Beware of those who instantly swarm you and want to be your best friend. Those people rarely end up being those you are closest to. Ask God to give you great discernment where friendships are concerned. I am not suggesting that you be suspicious of every person who wants to befriend you, just use caution as you develop that relationship. A good thing to remember is, if you have not shared anything confidential, you'll never have to worry about it being repeated.

Confidentiality is a must. Establish boundaries with your husband. By that I mean if you can't keep your mouth shut, don't have your husband tell you everything. Ronnie and I have made it a practice that I not know anything I don't *have* to know. Not because I can't keep my mouth shut, but it's just not necessary for me to know many things that my pastor husband has to deal with. Wives of ministers were not made to bear the burdens of the church. We are to share the burdens with our husbands, but there are times when it is best that you are not aware of everything. Men handle challenging issues better than women. We tend to get our feelings hurt and carry an offense with us. Men speak their piece, deal with the situation, and move on. God wired us differently.

I do not mean to indicate that we live like pie-in-the-sky Pollyannas who don't live in reality, but there are boundaries (again) to what you "must know" and what you "don't have to know." You and your husband need to come to agreement to establish those boundaries within your relationship.

No one is exempt from the temptation to share something confidential at one time or another. You can always count on one thing — if you share something confidential, rest assured, that person will only share it with *one* other person and that person will only share it with *one* other person. . . . Do you get the point I am trying to make here?

Beware of sharing too much with those whom you consider to be your closest friends. They may not end up being your friends after all. We have all experienced the pain of close friends who, for whatever reason, end up not being friends at all. Although this is hurtful and personally painful, if you haven't shared anything of a confidential nature, there will be no concern or regret over having shared confidential information.

I am reminded of a friendship that I had once. We shared prayer requests, participated in children's activities, enjoyed celebrating birthdays and many other fun times. I probably considered this to be one of my closest friendships at that time. There were plenty of times that I could have chosen to share confidential information or concerns, but I chose not to. I knew better than to do that, but sometimes we get comfortable with familiar friends and are tempted to share things we shouldn't. Friendships can sometimes blur the lines and soften our discernment. We all grieve when relationships take a different turn, but if you have "held your tongue" and not shared confidential information, you will not have to worry about the repercussions of them repeating something you might have told them. There won't be anything to repeat!

You never get so old that you don't have to remember to control your tongue and keep confidentiality. It's not an "age thing," and it will always be a temptation to deal with. Beware also of "God talk." You know what I'm talking about — those people who disguise their real motivation of just wanting to be "in the know" by convincing you they will "make it a matter of prayer."

I pray these Scriptures for my life, and our entire family, my husband, my sons, their wives, and our grandchildren:

> *Those who control their tongue will have a long life; opening your mouth can ruin everything* (Prov. 13:3).

> *The tongue can bring death or life; those who love to talk will reap the consequences* (Prov. 18:21).

> *Wise words bring many benefits, and hard work brings rewards* (Prov. 12:14).

> *For the one who wants to love life and to see good days must keep his tongue from evil and his lips from speaking deceit, and he must turn away from evil and do good. He must seek peace and pursue it, because the eyes of the Lord are on the righteous and His ears are open to their request. But the face of the Lord is against those who do evil* (1 Pet. 3:10–12; HCSB).

You will need to become quickly seasoned when you deal with church members who want to share criticism of others or just flat out gossip about others. When you encounter those types of people, you need to be prepared in advance. Know what to say and what *not* to say. A good thing to say when someone else is talking about others is, "I'm surprised by that. I've not known that individual to be that way personally." At times you will need to have the boldness to say, "I'm sorry, I can't listen to that," or, "I'm sorry, I just cannot go there." Have your plan in mind of what you plan to say — don't be caught off guard.

I want to insert here something that I came to realize after many years in ministry. Anytime someone left our church, I was extremely hurt and offended. I always took it very personally, thinking that we as a pastor and wife or our church must have failed in some way. What I came to realize is this: many times people leave our churches and it has nothing to do with us or the failure of our church. Sometimes it just happens. People's lives and circumstances change for a number of reasons. It was very liberating for me to come to that point personally.

When a relationship begins to dominate above your relationship with your husband or children, or pulls you away from your home, your church, or your relationship with Christ, you need to take a hard look and see if you have crossed the boundaries of a healthy relationship. A healthy, godly relationship will push you to Christ and His Church and will encourage you to be a better wife, mother, and staff wife. If that relationship doesn't encourage all of those things, you should take a look at that situation, and I would advise limited time with that person. We must be responsible and mature in our relationships so that our families do not suffer first and foremost, our churches as well.

I must mention that there are times when a minster's wife will sense an improper attraction toward her husband from other women. When this occurs, and true discernment is accurate, your husband will be a wise man to heed the warning and take the proper steps to cease any relationship with such women. I really believe that many times God will give the wife the discernment when the husband may not see it.

It is truly a blessing to find other couples with whom both you and your husband enjoy fellowship. That seems to be a rare find for some reason! Usually it is just a matter of interests shared, or the lack thereof. Once again, I would recommend proceeding with caution, but when you do find a couple who shares a kindred heart with you and your husband, and also has a love for Christ's church and ministry, consider that a true gift of God.

RELATIONSHIPS WITH OTHER WOMEN

One of the greatest blessings you can experience as a woman is the mentoring and influence of other godly women on your staff and also in your church. My life has been blessed, influenced, and enriched not only by women on our staff team throughout these years of ministry, but by other godly women in the church outside of ministry. Prayerfully, the senior pastor's wife sets a wonderful godly example that you will want to follow. On our most recent staff retreat, as I met with the wives on our ministry team, we discussed at length the word "influence." Women have the power to influence other women in many positive ways — from relationship encouragement to skills in the home, raising children, loving husbands, and growing in their walk with Christ. Women are masters at sharing their lives with one another!

I would like to introduce a new definition of mentoring. Charlotte Akin, wife of Dr. Danny Akin, president of Southeastern Seminary, shared with our wives on that retreat that all a woman needs to do to mentor another woman is to "be what God called you to be in front of another woman." What a great contemporary definition of mentoring. What a great challenge to all women without the restraints of age or other defining criteria! I do believe in the Titus 2 principle that encourages "older women to live in a way that honors God. . . . Older women must train the younger women to love their husbands and their children, to live wisely and be pure, to work in their homes, to do good, and to be submissive to their husbands" (Titus 2:3–5). Again, I believe wholeheartedly in the older teaching the younger, but let's not miss out on how another woman can influence your life regardless of her age. If she leads you to be a better woman, stronger in your faith and stronger in your family, that is a wonderful blessing! I can honestly say that in all these years of ministry, my life has been blessed not only by older women, but by younger women as well.

RELATIONSHIPS WITH OTHER STAFF WIVES

Expect to serve with some of God's finest servants. Some of the sweetest relationships I have had with other women have been those we have served on staff with. I have been blessed in every church we've served to have wonderful relationships with other staff wives. Best friends? Rarely, but occasionally that does happen. You will be closer to some than others. That is natural and many times depends on the age of your children and the particular area of ministry you are involved in. You don't all have to be "best friends," but you can be each other's "best supporters."

Ministry can be lonely at times. I remember many times when I felt like "staff was all we had." I am grateful for faithful and loyal staff members that we have served with throughout these many years in ministry. Many times they have made it bearable.

One of the greatest fellowship builders we have practiced for a number of years is a monthly staff wives' luncheon. We meet during the months that school is in session. This is something that our ministry couples are told about when they are hired. A great benefit of our luncheons is helping new staff wives find a nucleus of friends while they are adjusting to a new place of service. We feel it is a very important time to grow and maintain fellowship among the wives on our staff team. Because most wives are involved in their husbands' ministries, if it were not for the monthly time to touch base with the other wives, they could go for months without ever seeing one another. We feel so strongly about this that we provide child care, and there is an expectation to be there unless work or illness prevents it. Throughout the years we have carried this out in a number of ways. Before our ministry staff became so large, we would take turns meeting at each other's homes. The host house was responsible for providing the meal. As time went on and the size of our staff and age of our staff wives changed, I decided that the easiest thing to do for all involved was to have the luncheon at the church and provide child care and meals for the wives. I try to make this as simple as possible for them — and I stay away from planning this time on the weekends when it would interfere with precious family time. We meet the same time each month, and I ask them to put these dates on their calendars several months in advance.

We have done a variety of things at our luncheons, from having a prayer time to having someone come speak to the wives about safety and security. We've learned to make chicken pot pies and have shared burdens of illness among our wives and family members. We have celebrated the births of babies and grieved the loss of babies. We've prayed, laughed, and cried together, encouraged, and shared the load of life and ministry with one another. This is an invaluable time for the wives to get together.

When Ronnie and I came here almost 23 years ago, I was one of the youngest wives. I have to admit when Ronnie asked me to start this monthly luncheon I was very intimidated because of my age. Now, after all these years, *I am the older woman!* I feel a calling to mentor these precious younger staff wives the best I can. It is a joy to pour into their lives. The younger generation is a blessing to my life and keeps me humbled as I have the opportunity to share what knowledge God has allowed me to experience as a pastor's wife. Those young women are fresh and eager to walk by their husbands' sides in ministry. What a great calling and privilege we have to invest our lives, as the older women, in this younger generation of staff wives!

In addition to our monthly luncheons, our ministry staff goes away for a staff retreat each year. This is not optional and is a time that our staff looks forward to each summer. Although a time of work, planning, and challenge, it is also a great time of fun and fellowship for our staff couples. I have special sessions with the wives, and we also have sessions together as couples. This is such an invaluable time with our wives — it is the only concentrated time we have together. It is truly a time when we get to know one another better, and relationships are more deeply forged. Beyond that, it's just wonderful fellowship time with one another. If you cannot go away with your staff team, at least plan some in-house concentrated time.

Conclusion

The bottom line in relationships is this: we need each other. We need friends on the staff team, and we need friends who are church members. It's always helpful to have great family relationships, but it doesn't always happen that way. The best way to enjoy relationships is to remember that any relationship that does not ultimately make you a better individual is probably not the healthiest relationship for you. Those relationships cannot always be avoided completely, but as you consider the time and energy that goes into those particularly, make sure you spend more time in the ones that replenish and less time in the ones that deplete.

All of us have experienced replenishing relationships and depleting relationships. Some of you are probably indentifying some of those individuals in your minds right now. In short — replenishing people refresh your soul and are a joy to be around.

Depleting relationships are the ones that make you want to run the opposite direction when you seen them coming or avoid answering the phone when you see their name pop up on caller ID! A replenishing relationship will build us up personally and in ministry. A depleting relationship will rob you of time, energy, and many other things. We cannot always avoid some of those depleting relationships, but set the boundaries or you will find yourself completely drained by others. There are times in ministry when we make ourselves available to others, and there is also an art to limiting the amount that you allow others to deplete you. It's not a badge of honor to extend yourself for others at the expense of your own family. You must learn the boundaries and how to make the boundaries work for you. By doing this you are not selfishly limiting your involvement with others. Instead you are using great wisdom and discernment so that you are available for God to use you in the most effective way. If we are "spent" from constantly pouring into the lives of others, we will not be effective in ministering to those God particularly wants us to reach. Remember, even Jesus drew aside from the crowds to refresh Himself.

In summary, here is an overview of the things discussed to help with boundaries in relationships.

Be open to relationships, but proceed slowly and cautiously in new ones.

Remain loyal and confidential to your husband, the staff team, and the church.

Relationships make ministry bearable — and even more, enjoyable and worthwhile.

We need others in our lives.

We can gain from others.

We can give to others.

Relationships are how people are won to Christ.

Learn and discern which relationships are replenishing and which ones are depleting.

I hate to be repetitive, but *all* relationships need to have boundaries. The greatest temptation is to let any relationship veer from what it needs to be to remain healthy.

Knowing the boundaries is *key* to having relationships and reducing the risk of those relationships being other than what God intended for them to be in our lives.

Interactive Testimony

Leigh Lowery is a special friend. She is married to Dr. Fred Lowery, pastor of the First Baptist Church in Bossier City, Louisiana. She is the mom of two beautiful and godly married daughters, and is also a grandmother (also known as "Hunny"). Our paths first crossed several years ago when we accompanied our pastor husbands and several others on a trip to Russia. We immediately bonded — mostly because of Leigh's warm and fun-loving personality. As our friendship has grown, I have observed this about Leigh's life — she is a lover of people. She cares about the people in her church and other ministers' wives, and is willing to reach out to others beyond church walls to make relationships. And she is just one of the greatest delights to be around!

Jeana: You and Fred have been in one church for many years now. Knowing that tenure has its own certain challenges, what wisdom would you give other ministers' wives about relationships within your church?

Leigh: As a young minister's wife, I was given the advice: "Don't have friends in the church because it will cause problems. You will get hurt." We do put ourselves in a vulnerable place when we have church relationships, but I would not want to miss the richness relationships bring to life. I chose friends. I have been hurt. . . . I will choose to do it again. I really cherish the relationships that Fred and I have in our church, and I love, need, and enjoy the "girlfriend relationships" that I have with my sisters in Christ. Many of these relationships have been growing since we came to First Baptist Bossier over 25 years ago. These relationships have become the "intimate kind" where we truly know each other and know exactly what to do if a need arises. We know when to talk and when to be quiet. We know when to make a run for nachos and chocolate fudge cake or just cry with one another! These are friends that I do life with. We have raised our children together, entertained each other at boring middle school games, endured the raging hormones of teenage children, cried through empty nest, celebrated marriages, gone absolutely crazy over the births of grandchildren, and wept at more graves than we can endure. We love and accept each other on a deep level. These relationships are the kind built on the pillars of time and perseverance. They are as close as sisters. (I know because I have the most precious sister in the world.)

It would be unrealistic to say every relationship that I have had over the years was as rich and wonderful as those described above. Nothing feels worse than the betrayal of a good friend, and not really knowing exactly what went wrong is especially hard. Many times, Fred and I have lain awake in bed at night talking about relationships and trying to figure people out! Sometimes it really has nothing to do with us but a grievance with the church or even God Himself. At times all you can do is pray through a bad situation, offer apologies, and let the person go. The relationships in the New Testament have helped me move on. Even Paul and Barnabas had a broken relationship over John Mark!

Jeana: How have you practiced relationships beyond the church walls?

Leigh: Relationships outside the church walls are a bit more challenging, but full of rich treasures waiting to be discovered. I have always enjoyed lots of different sports, hobbies, games, crafts, water sports, etc. I love to "play" in general. My family says I am always either having a party or looking for a party. For a sanguine, it is not hard to make friends. The challenge is to be real and glorify God. Being "real" is my heart's desire, but the desire of my flesh; calling out to be liked and accepted is sometimes a battle. I grew up with an alcoholic father and I learned to wear a mask, cover my feelings, and keep secrets. When you think about it, those coping skills can work really well for you as a pastor's wife! But in reality, these characteristics are roadblocks to relationships. I have learned that when my inside and outside don't match, I feel and act like a phony.

Over the last few years I have gotten to know and grown to love a group of women who play golf at our neighborhood golf club. I was intimidated at first because I am a high handicapper, and a beginning golfer, but that is the tip of the iceberg. Many of the women I play with are well-educated, intellectual, professional career women who are confident, strong women. I worried that I would not fit in and wondered how they would feel about a preacher's wife joining their foursome. Of course, every game keeps a score, and small amounts of money are won for low gross, low net, longest drive, and low putts. I well remember the first day when everyone was putting in her "dollar." Do I put in my "dollar" or try to explain why I couldn't? I wanted them to feel comfortable with me and yet I did not want to compromise my convictions. One of the ladies said, "Leigh is not putting in any dollars. We are not letting her"! That was the end of that conversation. At times they apologized for a few colorful words that came out of their mouths, but they kept asking me to join them. One day one of my new golfing buddies said to me, "Leigh, your game would really improve if you said a cuss word or two." I told her I was trying not to cuss, but my brother-in-law Charles Lowery told me I could say "Hoover"! That's the biggest dam in the world. She laughed and laughed and told everyone at lunch!

God allowed me to walk with this golfer friend through almost two years of living with a malignant brain tumor. We prayed for her as she bravely faced her last days on earth. We became very good friends even though we were as opposite as night and day. She was a champion golfer, career woman, had never been married, and had a "bigger than life" personality. I learned so much from my friend. She never came to my church, but I had the privilege to pray with her before her brain surgery, several times during chemotherapy, and the day she went to the Grace Home where she waited to go to heaven. Her big, loving family asked me to speak at her Celebration of Life Service at the golf club. At that celebration service, God gave me an opportunity to share Christ with many people who may never go to my church. I really believe the Lord allowed me to be a part of this experience because I was willing to be real and desired to glorify Him. My prayer is that I can show the love and grace of Christ in relationships as I live and minister, and even through the game of golf.

10

LEARN FROM THE PAST, LIVE IN THE PRESENT, AND TRUST GOD FOR THE FUTURE

I REMEMBER THE MILESTONES of our family life — the births of children and the parsonages we lived in with each church. I also remember individuals from each location — mostly great memories, although I'll have to be honest, I remember a few really mean people in a place or two! Each place we have served has a special place in my heart, and God taught me different lessons in each one.

Four months before Ronnie and I married, he began pastoring at the First Baptist Church of Cherokee, Texas. We were both students at Howard Payne University and drove approximately 1 ½ hours one way each Sunday. This church ran about 50 to 60 people on Sunday mornings. Some of my most vivid memories are of the precious ladies in that church who got together and made a quilt to give us when we got married. I still have that quilt and cherish it to this day. Each Sunday we went home with someone different after church. They went down the alphabet, and that was who we had lunch with. By the time you'd been through the alphabet, you knew who to look forward to and who you hoped skipped their turn! Many Sunday afternoons I took a nap on the church pews. We made many sweet memories during that time of service.

Truly this was a sweet introduction into ministry for Ronnie and me. I still use one of the recipes I copied from one of the precious ladies in that church. It's called "Mrs. Gentry's Chocolate Sheet Cake." Anybody relate? As a very young pastor's wife, I believe the greatest lesson I learned at that wonderful church was acceptance. They totally accepted us — young and inexperienced at being pastor and wife. But oh how they loved us unconditionally. I am amazed to reflect now how willing that church was to follow my husband's leadership — only a college student, but with fire in his heart to win the lost community of Cherokee, Texas. We experienced growth numerically and in additional ways as they improved their building and facilities. What a great launching pad!

After Ronnie graduated from college, we moved to Ft. Worth, where he began working on his master's degree at Southwestern Baptist Theological Seminary. For a while we drove back and forth to the church at Cherokee, but eventually Ronnie resigned, knowing they needed a full-time pastor on the field due to the growth of the church. During this time I was the personal secretary to a man who owned five Lincoln/Mercury car dealerships in Ft. Worth, Texas. They were good to me as a seminary wife, but I longed to be at home. At that time of our married and ministry life, that job was part of God's provision for us financially. The time that we were "in between" churches was a challenge, but in God's timing, a few short months later, the First Baptist Church of Cherokee was able to call a full-time pastor, and we were called to a new field.

Our next pastorate was the First Baptist Church of Milford, Texas. The church grew into an average attendance of about 120, and we lived in the parsonage next door to the church, which was over 100 years old. Ronnie commuted back and forth to seminary in Ft. Worth, and I taught private piano lessons. We "did it all" at the First Baptist Church of Milford. Ronnie preached and led the adult choir; I played the piano and led the children's choir. We also cleaned the church, and I was Ronnie's secretary — for a very brief period of time. I discovered I made a better wife than secretary, so I quit! We turned the air conditioning on in the summer and the heat in the winter. And if it was really cold, we turned the heat on in that old, old building the night before. During this time our first child, Joshua, was born. I was finally able to quit work outside the home!

I believe the greatest lesson I gleaned from our tenure in Milford was the value of other women influencing my life. I became a mother at this church. We did not live close to any of our family, and several precious women poured into my life on how to be a mother. I remember in particular, in the first few days of Josh's life, I was concerned about nursing. Was he getting enough milk? How often should he eat? Lots of questions about this tiny baby pushed me to call on the other women in our church — young and old. A wise woman, not that much older than me but just ahead of me in the mothering stage, told me not to worry, "babies are survivors." At that stage of my life and the life of my baby boy, that was some of the best advice an older woman could have given me. Mrs. Bradley, a widow who lived across the street, was my trusted babysitter when I needed one. She even taught me how to make plum jelly. Those were sweet years at Milford, complete with only one gas station and one small grocery store. No shopping, no restaurants, not even a Wal-Mart within several miles. But I was totally content. I can remember telling Ronnie that if God wanted us to, I would spend the rest of my life there. That was probably out of naivety but also a totally willing heart.

From Milford we went to the First Baptist Church of Palacios, Texas, where Ronnie completed his doctoral work and our second child, Nicholas, was born.

Palacios introduced the Texas Gulf Coast to this west Texas girl. We could hear the sound of the waves crashing on the rocks of the bay if we left the windows open in the parsonage. Of course, along with the coastal waters come huge water bugs that looked like cockroaches, and it seemed that *everybody* had them, or at least that's what they told me. The welcome gift when we arrived was a freezer full of shrimp and oysters — fresh out of the bay. The parsonage was complete with a banana tree in the yard and palm trees surrounding the church lot — yes, right across the street. The mosquitoes were so bad that I couldn't even take Nick (who was just a baby) outside on Sunday night after church when everybody stayed to play volleyball in the church parking lot.

Our life in Palacios was so new and different for me. I had never lived near water and was excited to learn how to "de-vein" shrimp and fry oysters. The people there were loving, just like the people in Cherokee and Milford. Now a new group of people was willing to follow my husband's leadership as their pastor, and we saw the church grow from about 120 to just under 400. We were there for three of the happiest years of my life. Where else but in church ministry can you gather such memories and experiences?

Our next move was to Nederland, Texas. That was an especially unique place of service because that is where I was truly saved. When I was nine years of age, I made a decision out of obedience to my parents. I wanted to do the right thing, but I never really trusted Christ as my personal Savior. I lived for many years with doubts, which I kept to myself because I was the "pastor's wife." I did not mean to live in a deceitful way. I loved God and loved His Church and would always rationalize how could I not be saved? But finally I came under such great conviction and was so miserable that I came to the point where I knew I did not know Jesus in a personal way.

I humbled myself in the church we were in at Nederland, and went forward during the invitation and made a public profession of my faith in Jesus Christ. I gave my heart to Christ on March 20, 1985. I almost let "what others might think" keep me from coming to Christ. I have never regretted that decision and have never had doubts since that time, even though it was a difficult decision to make as the pastor's wife. As I stated, I had always had a love for Christ and His Church, but I had failed to make that all-important decision, accepting Him as my Savior. I continually pushed down the doubts that I was not saved. But deep down in the depths of my heart, I was restless. Satan can use many things to trick us into believing one thing, when the reality is quite different. The reality was, I was not saved when I made that childhood decision at age nine. I am so grateful to have settled that most important decision of my life not only for eternity, but for the many challenges I have faced since that time. Now I know for sure that regardless of what I go through as an individual or pastor's wife, He is with me.

If you find yourself in that situation, don't hesitate to settle the issue. You can know that you are saved and not live with doubts.

I believe it was especially important that I settled the issue of my salvation, as our time at this church taught me much about spiritual warfare in a very real way. I would have to say the greatest thing that happened in this church was definitely my salvation, and after that, learning how to deal with spiritual warfare. There were many great people there, but there were also some very challenging times experienced there. Satan does not like God's Church to grow and advance, and we were met head-on with much warfare and dissension, and a power struggle within the church as we experienced a great outpouring of God's Spirit and many people come to Christ. When we came to the church attendance averaged around 600. We saw many people come to Christ and, during the time we were there, saw the church grow to around 900.

In God's timing, He moved us to the First Baptist Church of Springdale, Arkansas. Having been a Texan all of my life, I figured our time in Arkansas would be a mere "blip" on the screen of our life. Little did I know then that it would be "home" for the next 23 years of our life.

Many significant things have occurred during those 23 years, from raising our children to the expansion of two campuses. We've seen babies born who now have children of their own. We've seen countless people saved and baptized, and lives changed for all of eternity. We've seen marriages healed and marriages broken. We've fed and clothed the poor and needy and traveled around the world to share the gospel of Christ. Tenure in one place has its own specific challenges as well as blessings.

One of the most significant circumstances of my life came just over three years after we moved to Arkansas. That is when I was diagnosed with breast cancer. I was 35 years old. Surely I was too young, too healthy, and too busy to have cancer, but that is what God allowed into my life at that time. Other than my salvation experience, cancer has been the most life-changing event in my life.

Our church family reached out to us in an incredible way. Since our entire family still lived in Texas, the church body became our local family. I include that because significant personal circumstances will always influence your church and church family. It's unavoidable. I believe many times they can weld the pastor and people together.

Each place we have served holds very special memories. God has blessed us more than we ever imagined or deserved. Our desire was never to be in a "big church" but only to be in "His will" for our lives. One thing about my husband is spoken of in Scripture: "He who is faithful in what is least is faithful also in much" (Luke 16:10; NKJV). His life is a testimony of that. Whether it was the First Baptist Church of Cherokee or the First Baptist Church of Springdale, his work ethic and passion for ministry have remained unchanged all these years.

My greatest joy is in being a wife, mother, and pastor's wife. You might say I really "love my job" and have for many years. As our children are now grown, married, and have children of their own, I have no regrets about my children being raised in ministry life. In fact, I consider it to have been a huge blessing and the greatest of benefits to my children.

I feel so fortunate that our children were able to grow up in one place for the majority of their lives. That is rare in the ministry.

I personally attended three different high schools and know how difficult that can be for children.

Our older son, Josh, is now 29 years old. He is married to Kate, and they have two precious little boys, Peyton and Parker. He is a football coach who leads one of the premier programs in our state, has won several state championships, and has been nationally ranked. Josh uses his profession to influence young men to be champions for Christ in football and in life.

Nick, our younger son, is also married and has two children — a girl, Reese, and a boy, Beckham. Nick feels called to full-time ministry and is almost finished with his doctoral degree. Nick and Meredith recently joined our staff team, where he serves as preaching assistant. It is a continual joy to see God's working in their lives as a couple in ministry.

Ronnie and I were recently asked to come back to the First Baptist Church of Palacios for their 100th anniversary. I had such fond memories of serving in that church down on the Gulf Coast of Texas. During that anniversary trip, I took a walk along the bay early one morning. As I reflected on our time there, I also observed some landmarks of ministry that were displayed before my eyes that day.

As I started out on my journey that morning, I couldn't help but recall the feelings I had those years we served in that little community — such passion, such joy, such excitement! Ask yourself this question: do you still serve with the same enthusiasm and excitement that you did when you just started out in ministry?

The bay was calm and beautiful that morning, but I remembered how quickly a storm could come up and how that calm bay of water could be changed by a dangerous squall. "Squall" (a sudden violent gust of wind with rain) was a totally new word to me when I first moved to Palacios, but I soon learned what it meant! It could come out of nowhere. Sometimes ministry is like that too — we're loving the "calm waters" when all of a sudden, without warning, Satan attempts to bring about "squalls" in our lives and the lives of our churches. But God is always faithful, and He is never caught off guard, even when we are.

I noticed a sign there that read *Caution — Oyster Shells*. You see, this bay did not have a beach that you could walk out into the water on. The water appeared to be harmless, but below the surface, the oyster shells were sharp-edged and would cut you if you walked out into the water, even though it was shallow.

As staff members and wives, we must be wise and discerning. What appears to be harmless may not always be. Here's another anaolgy: the oyster shell is hard on the outside, while the good part (if you like oysters!) is on the inside: the shell must be broken open to get the meat out. How like God — He looks on the inside, while man judges the outside. Many of our church members are like that — hard on the outside but needing Jesus to crack open the shell and find the good inside. May God give us patience and acceptance to love those who may not always be so easy to love!

As I continued on my walk that day I passed the home of a dear sweet lady, no longer occupied by her as she now resides in heaven. She was one of my babysitters. Again, we lived away from family, but God providing through others like this dear saint. I was reminded of another important lesson I learned in those early years: when you love others, they will love you back. Don't let the disappointment of a very few keep you from enjoying the love of the many!

Farther down the road, I passed the Texas Baptist Encampment, which is housed at the point of the bay. It was a beautiful, unique location, right on the edge of town. I remembered Easter sunrise services, youth camps, children's camps, church-wide baseball games, but none touched me more than the memory of the loss we experienced there. Oh, the pain of that memory. Our friend, church member, and fellow minister, the camp manager, was killed in a car wreck, leaving a young widow and four small children. Those times that never get easier with the years — the unexplained and tragic loss of life — will always be with us in ministry. Those times when you do not understand the hand of God, you trust the "heart of God."

As I continued on my walk down memory lane, I passed by another sign that read:

ABSOLUTELY DO NOT ENTER THE WATER.
THERE ARE MANY UNSEEN DANGERS IN THIS BAY
THAT WILL INJURE OR ENDANGER YOUR LIFE.
PLEASE DO NOT ENTER THE WATER.

It was obvious from the rusty sign that it had been there for a long time — maybe it was even there when we served as pastor and wife, but I was struck when I read those words. How applicable, I thought, to life in ministry. Satan loves to scare us with the "unseen dangers" of ministry. He also loves to intimidate us and make us live in fear of hurt or disappointment in ministry. Yes, there are "unseen dangers" in ministry, but we must never forget that our victory remains unchanged in Jesus Christ. Jesus Christ lived and died for the Church. Jesus Christ is our deliverer. Jesus Christ is our provider and comforter. Jesus Christ is the reason we do what we do in ministry and endure the trials we go through.

The One who is in you is greater than the one who is in the world (1 John 4:4; HCSB).

If you are unwilling to "enter the waters" of ministry whole-heartedly, you will miss out on some of God's greatest blessings.

Finally returning from my walk, I noticed the historical marker inscription of the hotel that we were staying at. The inscription traced the history of the hotel back to 1903, and the final words read:

. . . HAS WITHSTOOD MANY HURRICANES,
INCLUDING 1961's CARLA.

The Church of the Lord Jesus Christ has withstood many trials and challenges, but God's Word tells us that "Jesus Christ is the same yesterday, today, and forever" (Heb. 13:8; NKJV). What a privilege to serve Him in ministry, knowing that His Church will stand the test of time, now and forever.

Ronnie and I have always tried to live in the present, regardless of the circumstances, or regardless of what church may have contacted us. It's a tricky heart issue to be enticed into thinking the grass is greener somewhere else. It's of great spiritual value to learn to be content wherever God has you. Ronnie has always said that we will live like we'll be there forever, but with our bags packed and ready to go if God calls us away. When you live in the future — or the next place of service — *before* God moves you there, you will never be content to serve where you are. No one can be effective, neither you nor your husband, if you are living in the future. Learn to be content with where God has you *now*.

Godliness with contentment is a great gain (1 Tim. 6:6; HCSB).

Obviously, when God is ready to move you, He will. Or maybe He wants you to stay longer and learn more lessons, or the work where you are currently serving is not done. If we can trust Christ with our eternity, surely we can trust Him with our place of service. Some places are easier to serve than others. I can look back at the different places we've served and know that. I can also remember a time when I knew specifically that God was going to move us — I didn't know where, and I didn't know when, but I knew that He was. After I came to know that, it was of great comfort to me regardless of what was happening at the church. It was God's way of assuring me that He hadn't forgotten us. At that particular time of my life, I needed that!

Rest assured, God has His plan for you and your husband's future. Don't rob God's people whom you serve presently by not serving them wholeheartedly. You also rob yourself of the contentment of resting in the sovereignty of God's hand and working in your life.

"For I know the plans I have for you," declares the LORD, "plans to prosper you and not to harm you" (Jer. 29:11; NIV).

The times when we are discouraged and tempted to think it would be easier somewhere else are the times we need to stay in God's Word and recognize His plan is always better than ours. More than once in our ministry life, God has spared us from "ourselves" — thinking we had a better plan, knew a better place, or desired a different way. Thank God — He is in control of our future and not us.

The following Scriptures should be a comfort to us, knowing that all our days are planned by Him: the churches He leads us to serve at, our tenure there, and ultimately our future in every way!

> *You saw me before I was born. Every day of my life was recorded in your book. Every moment was laid out before a single day had passed* (Ps. 139:16).

> *We can make our plans, but the LORD determines our steps* (Prov. 16:9).

> *You can make many plans, but the LORD's purpose will prevail* (Prov. 19:21).

Have you ever stopped to think that God knows every step of your journey?

> I know every step of the journey ahead of you, all the way to heaven. . . . Don't worry about what is around the next bend. Just concentrate on enjoying My presence and staying in step with Me.[1]

INTERACTIVE TESTIMONY

Charlotte Akin is the wife of Dr. Danny Akin, president of Southeastern Baptist Theological Seminary in Wake Forest, North Carolina. Charlotte is also mother to four boys, three of whom are married, and she and Danny have four grandchildren. Charlotte's journey as a minister's wife has taken her down roads she never anticipated. She always thought they would serve as a local pastor and wife, but God had a wonderful and different plan. Charlotte spoke to our staff wives on our last annual retreat, where I fell in love with her warm transparency and where she served as a great encourager to our ministry wives. I love the definition of mentoring that she gave our staff wives: "Be what God called you to be in front of another woman." Charlotte's ministry life with Danny exemplifies this message of this final chapter: learn from the past, live in the present, and trust God for the future.

Jeana: Have you been able to look back at different times in your ministry life with Danny and see the hand of God in your past even though it might not have been what you expected?

Charlotte: Yes, without a doubt! We entered ministry thinking we would serve as a pastor and pastor's wife, but God changed our direction to professor and professor's wife, then dean and dean's wife, and now president and president's wife. As I look back over our time-line, I see all the wonderful years that the Lord enhanced our ministry through friends and mentors. We can now see how He was preparing us for our current ministry. He truly is an awesome God!

Jeana: Do you think God uses unexpected circumstances in our lives to prepare us for opportunities that we didn't anticipate?

Charlotte: Yes, He does. I believe that God takes us through experiences that stretch us and push us out of our comfort zone. I can now see that He was preparing me for things I would be called to do later in life.

Jeana: How can ministers' wives deal with contentment when they may not always be happy in their present situations?

Charlotte: They must find their contentment in the Lord and not in their circumstances and situations. Those things change, but the Lord never changes. He is the only solid rock and firm foundation upon which we can stand. My life's Scripture is Psalm 91:1–2. It reads, "He who dwells in the secret place of the Most High shall abide under the shadow of the Almighty. I will say of the LORD, 'He is my refuge and my fortress; my God, in Him I will trust" (NKJV). I would also encourage them with the words of the Apostle Paul in Philippians 4:11–12: "I am not saying this because I am in need, for I have learned to be content whatever the circumstances. I know what it is to be in need, and I know what it is to have plenty. I have learned the secret of being content in any and every situation, whether well fed or hungry, whether living in plenty or in want" (NIV).

Jeana: If you were asked to give a one-sentence description that would describe your ministry life in each of these areas, what would that be?

Charlotte: Past — make sure that you make your family a priority.

Present — be open to the Lord's leading.

Future — the Lord has always made us content wherever we are with whatever we are doing, and by His grace, we want that to continue forever.

Endnotes
1. Sarah Young, *Nearer to Jesus* (Nashville, TN: Thomas Nelson Inc., 2008), p. 200.

An Uninvited Guest
One Woman's Journey from Cancer to Hope

Jeana Floyd

"Where science stops, faith begins!"

An inspiring, gentle look at every woman's terror: breast cancer. Written by the wife of one of America's best-known pastors, Ronnie Floyd, this sensitive treatment takes the reader all the way through the stages of cancer: diagnosis, treatment options, emotional issues, and a way forward. Not preachy, but bathed in healing love, this book makes a perfect gift for women from all walks of life.

Floyd takes women through the fears faced by those diagnosed with breast cancer, from losing their hair to losing a breast. Follow her journey as she shares how she learned to face the fears and challenges of breast cancer with grace, hope, and humor.

ISBN: 978-0-89221-664-2 • $12.99
6 x 6 • casebound

10 THINGS EVERY MINISTER NEEDS TO KNOW

RONNIE FLOYD

A survival guide for pastors in a faith-challenging world

From experienced minister Dr. Ronnie Floyd comes this practical guide to ministry for pastors. Dr. Floyd has many years of experience as the senior pastor of churches in northwest Arkansas with a combined membership of 16,000. His insightful advice comes from years of practical ministry experience and is essential for anyone going into ministry. Dr. Floyd goes beyond the realm of faith into the realistic day-to-day challenges and conflicts of church leadership. From pitfalls to avoid to habits to cultivate, Dr. Floyd's guidance is appropriate and timely. With the moral and ethical conflicts that continue to cause those in the ministry to stumble, this book has never been needed more.

ISBN: 978-0-89221-655-0 • $11.99

5 x 8 • casebound

FINDING THE FAVOR OF GOD
RONNIE FLOYD

Hoping to inspire individuals to seek more from all aspects of their personal, professional, and most importantly, spiritual life — Dr. Floyd shares a wealth of wisdom and insight into making the most life-changing discovery you can ever know — when you are *Finding the Favor of God*. Ronnie Floyd explores just how God favors a person. The *how* and *why* and *when* do impact each of us, and this absorbing book will excite the reader who is puzzled about his or her role in the world. From personal experiences to encounters with "successful" people, and his own two-year intensive Bible study in this neglected area, Floyd captures the essence of just what it is God is trying to tell us about the favor that He bestows. This powerful study will serve as a call-to-action for people who wonder if God is really interested in them.

- How can I know God is speaking *to me?*
- Is favor earned, or is it a gift?
- How do I obtain favor?
- Can you position yourself to receive "greater favor" from God?
- What is the *real* meaning of the favor of God?

ISBN: 978-0-89221-619-2 • $14.99

6 x 9 • casebound

Available at Christian bookstores nationwide or at www.nlpg.com

Winning
by Design

Practical application of Lean principles for transforming the speed to market, the quality, and the costs of new product development.

BY **Rob Westrick**
AND **Chris Cooper**

Winning
by Design

BY Rob Westrick
AND Chris Cooper

Contents

Dedications and Acknowledgements

From Rob Westrick

Dedication

To my wife, Jill, who gave me all her support and encouragement when I abandoned corporate life with the conviction that I could make my ideas work anywhere.

Acknowledgement

I would like to thank my co-author, Chris, whose idea it was to turn our consulting material into this book, and to the colleagues at Simpler who motivated us to keep going. Finally, Johan Sedihn, Executive VP at Elekta Oncology Systems, whose editorial insight galvanized our thinking at a particularly critical stage in our writing.

From Chris Cooper

Dedication

To my wife, Nicki, and my children, Elliott and Louis, who are a constant source of inspiration. Without them I would not be an author today.

Acknowledgement

Right back at you, Rob, and likewise to colleagues at Simpler. I would like to thank all the great technical staff I have worked with over the years whose various projects have never failed to get me interested.

John Bicheno

The areas of Innovation, Design, and New Product Development remain somewhat of a "Cinderella" in Lean. A generous interpretation from a sample of four Lean conferences in 2012 revealed a total of seven presentations out of 91 in the area.

This is unfortunate. It is now increasingly recognized that most waste becomes built in during design and development. Moreover there are the huge competitive advantages that reducing development time brings. This was highlighted 25 years ago in Womack and Jones' *The Machine that Changed the World.* Toyota has been very open about the Toyota Production System (TPS), but far more cagey about the Toyota Design System (TDS). Nevertheless, it has been the case that Lean Design has been dominated by texts relating to Toyota. Authors such as Ward, Sobek, and Kennedy come to mind.

Of course, not everyone is in a design situation with highly complex products, large design teams, with many products in parallel at any one time, coordinating with hundreds of suppliers, and working internationally. This is where Rob and Chris' book makes such a valuable, new contribution. The book will be of immediate assistance to those hundreds of companies that should be gaining huge advantage from Lean design but are not doing so due to lack of guidance, or even misguidance.

On misguidance, I have seen several, perhaps scores, of Lean-aspiring organizations attempting to map their design process along *Learning to See* value stream mapping lines. Typically, some waste is discovered and the time line reduced, but the true potential remains under exploited.

So Rob and Chris, both practical design engineers with years of experience, are able to cut through the fog by making the distinction between recurring manufacturing activities and non-recurring NPD activities. Not making this distinction has

led several to the mis-application of Lean concepts and tools that work well in manufacturing, but not in design (or in service!) Nevertheless it is pleasing to see how they have used the Five Lean Principles as a guiding framework, but talking the "gemba" language of designers and managers.

Many who work in design will be aware of the Design Council's "Double Diamond" concept: Discover, Define, Develop, Deliver. But Rob and Chris take this further by extending the concept into two double diamonds, each diamond becoming more focused, before even getting into manufactur. This forms the framework of the book, enabling clear vision of the process with integration of appropriate tools at each stage. Some of the tools described in the book will be familiar to designers, but others such as vertical value stream mapping were new to me, and have great proven potential for many organizations.

What is so good about this book is that it can used by different groups – engineers or managers – on several different levels – from a stand-alone resource to a good introduction for getting into a particular concept. All this is tied in to an integrated framework that will guide you end-to-end through a long-misunderstood area of great potential. I think this book is one of the very few that can help you into a new phase of your Lean S-curve.

John Bicheno
Lean Enterprise, University of Buckingham
Former Director MSc in Lean Operations, Lean Enterprise Research Centre, co-author of *The Lean Toolbox,* and author of *The Service Systems Toolbox.*

New product development: Is this the final frontier of business performance?

Two centuries of industrialization have changed the world beyond recognition. The mass production of goods has transformed the lives of many people to the point where their basic needs are met on a daily basis. The quality movement based on the scientific management of the last century has meant that good quality products are now considered a basic right, not a privilege. In the last fifty years, the Just-in-Time approach to manufacturing and logistics in many sectors has meant that a much wider range of goods and services are available at high quality, low cost, and in many sectors pretty much on demand. That is, as long as it's a product or service that already exists.

Is new product development (NPD) the last great bottleneck of value?

We have become used to the idea in our markets that it is very difficult to gain competitive advantage without creating new ideas and supplying innovative solutions. So how has the NPD process improved over the same two-century timescale? Two hundred years ago the inventor, investor, engineer, and maker all were typically the same person, and hence the NPD process had two very distinct phases separated by the person being in different mental states. He/she may have danced backward and forward between the two states, but broadly speaking the thinking process will have been as shown overleaf.

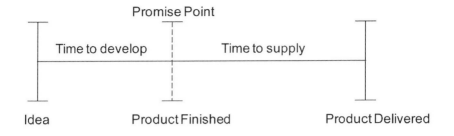

Promise Point

Time to develop | Time to supply

Idea   Product Finished   Product Delivered

In essence there is an idea, but no idea is fully thought through, so some experimentation takes place either cerebrally or physically. Typically this happens in what the British call a "shed" and then learning occurs which is used to refine the idea. The resulting "product" or service would be used in a trial and then possibly refined but only supplied to others (customers) when deemed "ready enough." The pressure on the product development timeline in this era was simple. If you were inventing for yourself, the timeline was based on how long you could tolerate the lack of a solution, or, if designing for financial gain, the lack of income.

In a world without today's competitive pressures, there was no reason to promise a new product before it was finished. For customers there was no need to think they should not have to wait while the inventor/producer did the inventing and producing. As a result, in the past, the bottleneck would only be considered to be in either manufacturing or supply, and hence the focus of the industrial revolution mainly on the means of production. The most famous example of that focus remains that of Henry Ford. His army of "production engineers" toiled for nearly two decades of Model T production simply seeking to satisfy demand. (They never succeeded with the Model T: throughout its life, demand always outstripped supply.) So what has happened since? Where has this world gone? If we are to focus on NPD, what should we do about it?

Let us start with a true story.

A Christmas carol without the happy ending

One October Chris' youngest son was approaching his birthday. Like many his age (and indeed his father), Louis likes computer games, and so "junior" was already making his "business case" for a new console well before it hit the stores.

A certain highly reputable company was designing its next generation of product and Louis was being fed details of its performance by highly reputable magazines relaying the latest official hot-off-the-press specifications and details of the launch titles that would be available. His father duly agreed that the old machine (although still serviceable) would be significantly improved upon, and because the new gaming system would be backward compatible with the significant amount of software they had for the previous generation, Chris promised the gift to Louis as a Christmas present, the timing in line with the official launch date.

That promise turned out to be impossible for Chris to keep because the launch of the console was postponed beyond Christmas and the planned simultaneous worldwide launch was staggered. Louis' American friends, whom he had met on vacation in the US, made his misery worse because they had received their new consoles and were of course eager to talk to him about it via the internet.

Oops. Strike one, highly reputable company...but this was just the start.

In the time following this first failure Louis eventually got his machine, but both father and son have since lost count of how many software titles have been scheduled for release but have never arrived when promised. One such title was actually used to "sell" the console as a launch title and has at the time of writing still appeared so far only in demo mode, three years after it was first promised.

Louis' subsequent birthdays have been similarly impacted, as planned software releases have continually failed to arrive on schedule. The list of broken promises seems (to a twelve-year-old mind) to be endless and led him to reflect one evening

that the company (who shall remain nameless) "tells lies to its customers." Louis's parents have not only had to deal with the frustration of pre-ordering a Christmas gift that didn't arrive on time, but they have also had to manage consistently unmet expectations and deal with disappointments aplenty.

Luckily for the company in question, it seems to be the norm in their industry that software is not released when promised, and the media are rife with speculation about upcoming titles, so his business with this company did not, in this case, go elsewhere. At best, time should have healed things, software partners should have improved their performance, and the ownership experience should have gotten better. It did not.

Soon a hardware failure (known as the Yellow Light of Death), killed the machine less than three years into ownership. As an engineer Chris did some basic research and diagnosed a soldered joint heat-cycle-related failure in design that had clearly not been detected in testing. Instead of the stone-axe reliability of same-brand products which had served the family for over ten years in some cases, there was disappointment over a defective product. This disappointment was further compounded by an official denial of a design defect.

Incredibly, the only solution offered by the company was an extra-cost replacement machine with—wait for it—*less* functionality! It could not play previous generation legacy software like the original machine could, and it had fewer charging and accessory ports.

By any measure the experience has been a disaster, one that has affected the family's previously unswerving loyalty to the brand in question.

So what is really new?

The reason for sharing this story is to explain a key concept and outcomes of the modern NPD process that were not there for earlier inventor/producers.

In contrast to the days of Henry Ford, the games manufacturer was up against real commercial pressure from all angles to promise delivery well before the design was finished. In addition, third-party developers were similarly pressured to produce launch software titles based upon hardware that was clearly not a stable design. Testing of the product during design failed to reveal a heat-related failure that commentators suggest was down to new-generation soldering and bonding materials combined with production processes that were not capable enough to produce the performance required. Officially, this is speculation on our part (and on the part of many others via various internet forums), but what we do know for sure is that we are living in an era when organizations feel like they have to promise new products long before they are ready. What we are witnessing is that an event which we are calling *the promise point* has unconsciously become mismanaged and driven far upstream, making the NPD process the creator of its own bottleneck. We show this situation below and discuss it throughout our book.

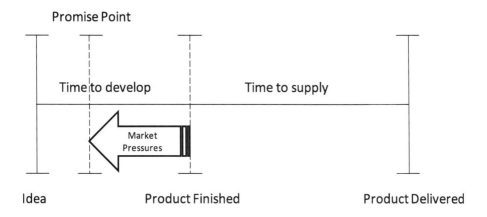

Promise Point

Time to develop

Time to supply

Market Pressures

Idea   Product Finished   Product Delivered

As you read through our book it will become clear that the promise point is a new and fundamental concept for understanding the dynamics of the modern NPD process and thus, we contend, vital for organizations to understand in order to manage and improve the NPD process. Whenever we have done this we have unlocked much higher performance from our clients, but we worry that most technical staff we work

with talk about the constant pressure to do things more quickly. Most apply blanket shame to the project management. We will show in our book how inappropriate project management of NPD creates exactly the opposite effect intended.

In the example of the gaming system, some kind of pressure clearly led to the promise point being given too early. Of course, some may contend that we can only say this with the benefit of hindsight, but in our book we will show how this not only could have been avoided, but clearly predicted. Factually, whatever the cause of the delays and fatal defect, it is certain that at the very least an untested error was designed into the project, resulting in a product that has not met customer expectations. More worrying is the financial impact of this on the organization in question. Analysts suggested that the two year delay in launch and subsequent hardware issue contributed to the company losing their position as the number one in the home games console market; what is currently immeasurable is the impact this frustrating experience has had on a future generation of what should have been loyal customers. That is also one of the issues with NPD: the impact of results is huge, but not always immediately apparent. The Cooper family has switched TV brands as a result.

Is this kind of thing commonplace? Is it happening to all organizations?

The only proof you need that this example is not an isolated case is the inexorable rise of project risk management, stage gate reviews, audits, and a deadline-driven project management culture within the NPD field. Managers and executives have developed these strategies seeking positive impact on NPD performance, but is it really helping? For sure our world is filled with better products each decade, and solutions to life's needs and desires keep improving. But wherever we go we find an underlying sense among NPD professionals that a lot is being left on the table and that the process of NPD has become more complex, more difficult to work with, in despite new technology and management initiatives that were supposed to make things a lot better.

Taking our lead from the founding principle of Lean thinking, we have asked many of those involved in NPD if there is waste in the process, and most quickly agree enough that yes, there is lots of waste. Having said that, soon afterward there is usually uncertainty and debate as to whether waste is perhaps actually necessary for NPD, never mind impossible to remove. We contend that in the modern era, people working in NPD have become so used to waste that most can't even begin to imagine life without it.

In our book we will show how, with a new way of thinking, not only can those involved in the NPD process avoid situations like that of the games console, they can also use their understanding of the promise point and other new concepts to fundamentally transform their NPD performance.

The second major insight we derived from many years of work in the field is that the promise point should be placed in a specific place on the timeline, because all NPD consists of two distinct mental challenges:

1) The Exploration Phase. This is the first part of the project where essentially we *learn* what we don't know.

2) The Execution Phase. By contrast, this is when we apply the learning and *create* the detailed definition.

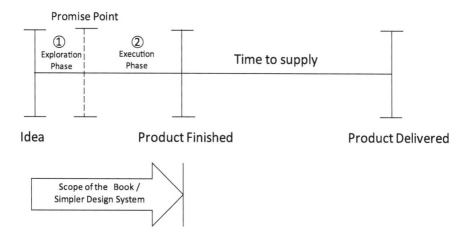

Because these are two distinct activities, we have found that you mix them at your peril. Almost every attempt we have seen to compress the overall timeline by overlapping these challenges ends in worse performance and waste. If not, it is because the project got lucky. These two challenges are in and of themselves fundamentally different and need to be managed as such. We will explain in our book how to do this pragmatically and practically to ensure maximum results.

Our approach (learned after getting it right *and* wrong a few times) has led us to discover that we can always transform the performance of exploration and execution more effectively by treating those challenges separately, rather than trying to integrate and overlap them. Crucially, we get the best results by applying Lean principles in both. Note we said principles, not tools. We have learned that you need two different "medicines" (tools), as the two phases represent completely different "conditions." We realize that this may be in stark contrast to many previous texts which propose to turn design into a "factory," but while this kind of thinking may have some relevance in the execution phase, it always destroys value in the exploration phase.

With the Simpler Design System℠ we can show you how to remove risk quickly from exploration, make a sound promise point earlier than thought, and yet still execute with much less waste. The end-to-end timeline will be much reduced, quality will be higher, morale improved, and cost performance much more predictable.

The good news is that the promise point and the NPD process do not have to return to the days when promises could only be made when a design was finished! Not many of us today have the luxury of the nineteen years Ford had to develop a successor to the Model T (the Model A).

Our third major observation of NPD is that while quality improvements have been great, when looking purely at process

productivity, NPD has not yielded anything like the improvements gained elsewhere in organizations applying Lean principles. Indeed, in many ways it feels like some things have gone backward in terms of efficiency. For example, computer-aided design technology (CAD) was sold hard two decades ago as the great enabler of design productivity. While CAD has improved designs in many fields and has replaced a lot of prototyping, in many cases it has required more and more investment in new product development resources with lower returns.

"Current state" productivity numbers are always hard to determine, and few organizations are able to provide data to "come clean" on this issue. But as soon as you dig, you find a lot of problems.

In his book *Product Development for the Lean Enterprise*, Michael Kennedy anecdotally reproduces the following slide of a company's new product development "performance" over the preceding five years.

From our experience, this is normal with NPD processes.

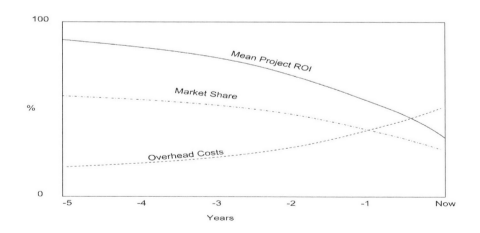

If you have seen this for yourself and wish to reverse this trend, read on.

How to use this book

Early in our writing, we knew our book could have taken two different paths.

1. If this was a primarily academic text, we would take each of our principles, provide plenty of examples of failure, and then advance a hypothesis of how each could be overcome.

2. Alternatively, we could produce a practical book for both the people concerned with the real world of change and its results, and for the people expected to execute this change.

We have learned that those working in NPD want pragmatic advice, so we have chosen the latter option, a practical guide.

Part A is aimed at leaders, so this is a must-read for those who wish to create a vision and initiate the changes. If you are such a leader, read part A, skim part B if you like, and give the book to your NPD professionals as the first step in advancing your vision. Of course, you can read part B, but pay particular attention throughout to leadership tips. What you say and do has an enormous impact.

Part B is mainly aimed at the people who implement and drive the change to a better NPD process and environment. Part B is therefore a very practical guide for project teams working on new products and services. By necessity we have written as if referring to physical products, with occasional references to software development or service development. We have applied our system to all three areas and it works as long as you focus on the principles rather than the specific mechanics. This is true of all Lean transformations in that none are cookie-cutter projects, but within new product/service/ software development, people seem to automatically focus on why things don't work for them rather than exploring what if?

If you are a person engaged in the above, read the whole book and keep thinking about the principles described and how they

would apply to your challenges. We then recommend that you give a copy of the book to your leadership team and have they read at least part A and draw attention to what we say about the way NPD has to be managed in the future.

We believe and hope that this book will initiate a new approach to product development and the way it is managed. We have had many successes with this approach and so want to share it with others.

Only time and your actions will tell, but in any case, we believe it is time for us all to do NPD much better than we are doing it today. All you will need is the ability to believe things can be done better, the humility to read a book about it, and the courage to actually try it.

Some things we say may sound counterintuitive, even heretical compared to today's accepted wisdom, and some things will be downright scary to try, but we encourage you to go for it.

When you have finished reading, keep the whole system in mind and try to apply it in such a way that it practically improves your NPD process from end to end.

The building blocks that we put together to create the Simpler Design System[SM] (SDS) are tried and tested in the field and have proven over decades to get results practically and with increasing success as teams get into the new habits of using them.

If you are curious, then let us show you how you can win by design.

Rob and Chris 2012

Part A

The Business Reason for this Book

> *"The company that delights the most will gain market share. If customers are not delighted they will drop you as soon as they have an alternative."*
>
> —Fred Reichheld

We start our book with the assertion that all enterprise performance can and should be measured in essentially four basic ways:

1. Morale

2. Quality

3. Timeliness

4. Cost

We believe these measures apply whether the enterprise is for profit or not, private or publicly funded, and that measuring these four aspects simultaneously keeps them all honest. As Lean thinkers we believe that it is indeed the only way to tell if improvement is real or not. So whether your enterprise produces products, provides a service, or exists for some other purpose entirely, we ask you to reflect on the following.

Conventional management wisdom seems to suggest that improving one or more of these four dimensions will inevitably lead to a deterioration of the others. This wisdom remains deeply held only in the minds of those sectors that have been able to avoid significant changes in process over the years. For example, the mass production era from Arkwright to Ford brought low cost and repeatable process to the masses. Beyond that, the Deming-inspired total quality movement brought high quality to complex products and services that were expected to remain outside the potential of mass production. The Toyota Production System (popularly known as Lean thinking), consisting of Just-in-Time processes and employee-engaged improvement, has shown that economies of flow far outweigh economies of scale, and that people can effectively have ever higher-quality products and services, in ever-quicker timescales, at lower and lower cost, with fully engaged people involved. How this has been achieved is not fully in the public consciousness, and indeed, many sectors have been passed by, seemingly immune, but for those sectors which have discovered the power of finding and then eliminating waste while engaging and guiding the people currently working within the system, the results have been amazing. In using the Simpler Design System[SM], we have repeatedly improved all four dimensions, typically with the following results:

1. Improvement in New Product Development (NPD) staff morale, evidenced by a 100 percent increase in team confidence in project success and a change from a negative to positive culture.

2. The quality of new designs, evidenced by a reduction in warranty claims and rework by more than 60 percent.

4

3. Reduced project timelines, evidenced by at least 50 percent reduction in time-to-market.

4. Reduced total product costs, evidenced by at least 25 percent reduction of rework costs and design-for-cost thinking.

Importantly, however, we have also observed that neither success nor failure is immediately apparent, as there is always a time lag between cause and effect. As a consequence, many organizations dabble with improvements but do not fully understand both the positive and negative effects of such interventions into the NPD process.

Let us return for a moment to our games console story from the introduction to illustrate the long-term impact of actions without immediate consequences. What has the immediate effect of these problems been? In our example, we can reflect simply on the producer's performance on the "four fundamental" metrics as seen by their young customer. We can see that initially two of the four metrics were compromised from the start:

☐ Morale: "Company X's release dates are lies."

☐ Quality: Initially performed as expected.

☐ Timeliness: Repeatedly poor forecasts for availability both of the hardware itself and then of the software.

☐ Cost: Acceptable; prices high but stable.

The result of the company's poor performance in two of these fundamentals was that the customer reluctantly stayed with the brand but felt very willing to switch to another if any credible alternative became available. Realistically it was only the significant investment in legacy software at this point that was retaining any brand loyalty. This is a very dangerous state for a company to be in, because it may not be aware that its customer is preparing to leave. Note most conventional business metrics would not have picked this up.

So what would it take, when only two dimensions have failed to meet expectations, to push the relationship to a permanent breaking point? We suggest that it would be a third issue such as a price increase in the software or a hardware failure that would probably be the last straw. Ironically this is what actually happened, when the hardware failed after less than three years.

Luckily for the company in question, what appears to have saved them from complete disaster is that the whole games console sector seems to be in the same boat. Indeed, the nearest competitor not only had similar hardware woes but also does not appear to be any better at software at all! Is this a lucky escape? Well, not quite. At the time of this writing, analysts suggest sales of this new generation of console have yet to climb to even half that of the previous generation of machines, which sold over 200 million units worldwide. Analysts estimate that the problems lost the company "at least two years of competitive advantage in the marketplace." Perhaps worse still is to realize that any success they are having is because the market sees them as the least worst!

Throughout this story the customer's morale has deteriorated, and this whole episode has definitely affected intergenerational, long-term brand loyalty for all products, not just games consoles. When it came to replacing the family TV set, despite Company X providing a set that had given ten-plus years of good service, the family switched brands.

Think, could your organization survive a comparable event?

This is not something we have seen isolated to the video game system sector, either. Let us consider an automotive example.

Chris is a serial purchaser of a certain Japanese manufacturer's sports cars, so much so that he placed his name on a pre-order list for a much-publicized new model. Again, reputable magazines working from official press releases set the expectations in this case regarding performance, timescales for availability, and predicted cost.

The first promise to collapse was timescale. Via the press Chris soon learned that the car wouldn't arrive in Europe until some six months later than the Japanese launch. While this hurt, he still wanted that car, and so he resigned himself to the delay even though he felt bad about it. That was until he heard the list price announcement, which had the car selling in the UK at some 1.5 times the expected price being paid in other territories. While some of this could be explained by local tax differences, the residual feeling was not good at all. In a stroke, two decades of brand loyalty went up in smoke as the order was cancelled and Chris bought a competitor's product.

We can again reflect back on the four fundamental performance metrics:

☐ Morale: A lot worse over time as promises were not kept.

☐ Quality: As expected, the car got rave reviews.

☐ Timeliness: Failed to hit expected timescales.

☐ Cost: Price escalated by a factor 1.5x.

Three of the four fundamentals were compromised and the result was again the loss of a loyal customer.

In the case of the car maker's metrics, the company does know that Chris registered interest and then removed himself from the process, so someone somewhere may have a record of the value of lost business. But interestingly, no one ever contacted him to ask why he withdrew his order.

Broken promises are by no means confined to consumer products and services. Rob previously worked in the petrochemical industry with a supplier of oil and gas infrastructure equipment. When a customer such as BP or Shell inquired about a new product, delivery would be promised by sales executives eager to confirm what the customer wanted to hear. Timescales were based on everything going right the first time and engineering capacity being instantly available. The industry is

such that contracts are awarded to those with the shortest promised lead times, even though history shows that those times are hardly ever met. The timing of the contract award is completely outside the supplier's control and there is almost always a delay in starting the project because engineering capacity is already consumed by other projects. Projects therefore invariably start late due to a timescale that has little contingency for any design exploration and things not going to plan as a result of the unknowns inherent in any new product design. In this example most projects involved solutions with different materials, sizes, pressure classes, or features that had not been combined before. As the delivery deadline approached and it became obvious that requirements would not be met, the petrochemical giants would send in any number of trained expeditors who would literally take up residence in the supplier's facility to make sure that their project was being worked as a priority, inevitably at the expense of others. The fact that these customers have whole departments dedicated to expediting is testament to the fact that broken promises are the norm throughout this industry. The result is huge costs and perpetuation of the same situation over and over as other customers are in turn disrupted. This is a paradigm from which those inside the industry feel there is no escape.

Again, let us look at the effect on the four fundamentals

☐ Morale: Becomes worse as the pressure to deliver and do "whatever it takes" increases.

☐ Quality: Usually satisfied to the safety critical standards of the industry.

☐ Timeliness: Failure is built into the process.

☐ Cost: Expediting costs and late-delivery charges are a way of life.

In each of these examples the waste of such failure is obvious when written down, but how much of this is truly visible to most organizations? *Does anyone really know how much is being lost without our even knowing?*

We will go as far to say that if your business has any form of expediting, fire-fighting, or any priority-changing in NPD, then it is a clear indication that your existing NPD process is not capable of performing to your actual needs. In this case one should be asking, "What is the *real* problem here?"

In summary, we would propose that the business reason for this book is that all markets and organizations are doubly exposed on NPD capability, not only from external competition but just as significantly from within.

The bottom line is that anyone, including organizations considered too big to fail, can be seriously impacted by the results of their NPD process, and years of success can be destroyed forever.

The flip side of these tales of woe is the positive that huge gains can be made by excellent performance in NPD. There are many examples of success driven by excellent product development:

The rise of the Japanese motorcycle industry

The resurrection of Apple

The renaissance of Porsche

In each of these examples the organizations in question routinely introduced new products that delighted customers and did it quicker than any of their competitors.

How could you benefit if your organization could consistently develop the right products in half the time, with higher quality, reduced costs, and improved morale?

Think also that in a world where anything can be made anywhere to the same standards, NPD is the last frontier of business success. Get it right and the rewards are tremendous.

In the coming chapters we will show how using a simple, improved system of design will enable your organization to excel in NPD performance.

How Lean Principles can
Transform New Product
Development (Given that Every
Project Is Different)

2

The first thing we need to challenge is a basic belief: "You can't have it all when it comes to designing new stuff."

The following diagram serves as our model for the apparent trade-offs within NPD.

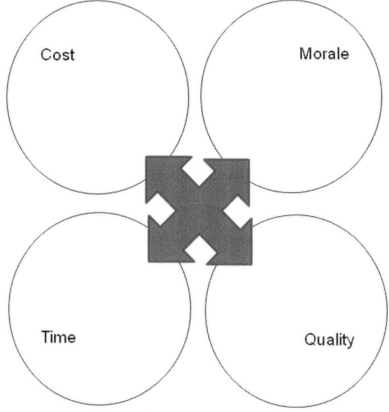

Figure 2.1 The trade-off tension diagram

The fundamental belief many of us have grown up with is that each dimension can only be optimized at the expense of another.

Managers believe it. Customers believe it. NPD professionals believe it. And in most cases, all use it as the first argument of resistance against attempts to improve anything.

"You want it quicker? I need more time and money, and quality is bound to suffer."

"You want lower costs? Morale will suffer, quality will decline, and it will take more time."

In most cases we see, the pressure is typically on time, and specifically it is a shortage of time that leads to some compromise within the other three dimensions. We get called most often by organizations trying to solve problems of lateness in existing NPD projects. Why? We have come to believe this is further evidence of our hypothesis that time-to-market pressures have forced what we call the promise point to be made too early.

As we said in Chapter 1, all things being equal, organizations that consistently have a shorter time for introducing quality new products into the marketplace before their competitors prevail. Sometimes people argue this point with us, but when asked whether a competitor doing NPD faster would hurt their business, the answer is always yes. The true difficulty is having this conversation with a genuine "all things being equal" mindset due to the "trade-off" paradigm above. It is too easy for people to say, "Well, that's life," and accept the compromise without ever questioning the fundamental performance of the NPD process itself.

We have found there is actually a much easier way to have this conversation by simply asking the following:

Would faster be better?

Would faster be better if quality got worse?

Would faster be better if costs get worse?

Would faster be better if morale gets worse (staff or customers leave)?

This does not need to be a difficult conversation. What we really need to break is the trade-off paradigm. This can only occur once people have seen and understand a real improvement in the process. In our book we want to show that improvement *is* possible in all four dimensions simultaneously, and to show how we have done that by learning how to apply Lean principles within NPD. This is the basis of the Simpler Design System[SM], and by using it you can indeed have it all. We call this hitting the design sweet spot, where improvement happens in all four dimensions simultaneously (shown below).

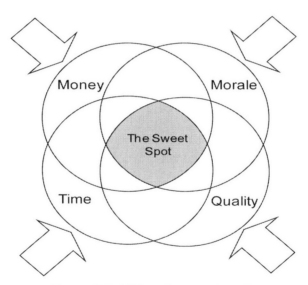

Figure 2.2 Hitting the sweet spot

While it sounds easy to apply Lean principles to the NPD process, we have discovered that it is not straightforward at all, and that specifically, Lean principles for NPD must be done in two steps. First we will present a basic explanation, including the origins of Lean principles, followed by a deeper explanation with specific regard to the application to NPD. This should

destroy the myth of the 'design factory' and also reengage NPD professionals who have become rightfully skeptical in the face of some pretty ham-fisted attempts in the past.

A simple introduction to Lean principles

The book *The Machine that Changed the World* (Womack, Jones & Roos), detailed research that had uncovered a growing gap between Japanese and Western automakers. It revealed a simple but sobering truth. "The best of the Japanese" (as they referred anonymously to Toyota) had discovered a faster, more efficient way of making cars. The Japanese method was so much more successful that the productivity advantage was already four times that of the average Western automakers and was, the authors prophetically warned, "still widening." In an understandable panic, Western industry became (in varying degrees) students of what was then called Toyota's Just-in-Time production system (JIT) and sought to emulate this "better way" of making cars. At first glance the differences in principles between the Western approach of mass production and the Just-in-Time system of Toyota were so subtle that they were difficult to grasp and even more difficult to implement.

In order to help further, Womack and Jones subsequently wrote the bestselling business book *Lean Thinking*. In this second book they sought to reveal the more fundamental principles behind the Toyota system's success. They proposed that the performance gap was ultimately because of the following five principles in use at Toyota:

1. <u>Define value.</u>

Toyota views all "work" as containing two elements:

    a) Activities that add value in the eyes of the customer.

    b) Activities that do not add value. These are also known as wastes.

This is a core pillar of the basic Toyota state of mind. While not described exactly like that in the book, being aware of value and waste encourages us to look at the world of work and to see it differently. The worked example in *Lean Thinking* from everyday life was that of air travel. Readers were given a list of activities to show them that for most people, the only things that added value aboard an aircraft were those that moved passengers toward the desired destination.

The deeper insight from this first principle of Lean thinking is that in all processes that are studied (correctly and with honesty, that is, which is not always the case), the non-value-adding elements typically outweigh the value-adding elements by nine to one. Surprisingly, this remains true after many cycles of study and improvement.

The next three Lean principles describe Toyota's self-improving processes. It is worth noticing that by the time Womack and Jones wrote their second book, Toyota had been improving continuously through these principles for some fifty years. The real insight here is that Toyota's way of thinking has allowed them to enjoy a more fruitful approach to improvement than that of most organizations, never mind their competitors. A relentless focus on waste by all Toyota employees when married to the fifth and final principle of continuous improvement (*kaizen*) in search of perfection has given Toyota a significant and game-changing return for their improvement activities. Getting better at getting better is thus the real secret and goes a long way to explain why the gap in success still exists despite the rest of the auto industry's trying for the last three decades to close it.

2. Identify the value stream.

The second Lean principle describes skills and methods required for the improver to reveal and understand waste in its true end-to-end process context. This is essential to avoid the suboptimal improvement seen when departments improve unilaterally. For example, when an airline defines and studies its end-to-end value stream, it can see their air journeys in the context of the overall door-to-door time. The enlightenment

for all those who choose to see this is that the decades-old pursuit of higher-speed planes may not actually yield a significantly shorter overall journey. Once one is, as we say, "wearing waste goggles" and seeing the end-to-end flow of value, it is usually a revelation to discover that not only is waste everywhere, but almost all previous attempts to improve things before being able to "see" have resulted in little more than an increase in non-value-adding steps somewhere else.

This thinking has direct application in NPD. Witness the rise of bureaucracy in NPD, which is typically well intended but goes something like this:

A process has a problem, so managers instantly ask, "How can we stop this from happening again?" Preventative process steps are added to the main process in order to avoid reoccurrence, and instantly new non-value-added steps (waste) have been baked into the new "improved" process. After enough time has passed, even the best-designed start-up process can be degenerated by layers of management-induced waste built up over years. A key insight here is one of a fundamental leadership approach. The Toyota state of mind is about reveling in problems and highlighting the root cause as a chance to improve and eliminate steps. This of course contrasts directly with the normal state of mind for most managers, which is the containment of problems and curing the symptoms in the fastest time possible. The majority do this by adding steps, checks, and improvements without the context of value-stream thinking.

In our experience, most NPD professionals struggle to truly see their process as a value stream because most of the training examples are from manufacturing, and because most improvement professionals are not experienced enough to help.

So how can we apply value-stream thinking to NPD? If the NPD process is to be thought of as a value stream, we need to consider first how it differs from a production value stream. We have learned to start by simply describing one type of value stream as a recurring value stream (production) and the other as a nonrecurring value stream. This is usually enough

to re-engage NPD professionals so that we can further explain that the two are connected and that the NPD process itself also designs much of the production process.

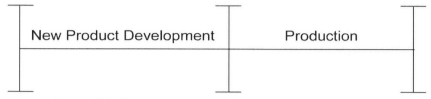

Figure 2.3 Non-recurring and recurring value stream(s)

We have learned that in order to make improvements we must first define that which is truly nonrecurring and that which repeats. In the NPD portion of the value stream it is specifically the exploration phase that is nonrecurring. Also, we need to respect that every development project is different, and we never develop the same product twice. The differences can be significant and difficult to measure, or similar and all too easy to assume as being measurable. As Smith and Reinertsen say in their book *Developing Products in Half the Time*, "Even if the products were the same the projects would not be....Some projects get better people, more time, better information, etc."

We support this view, as we have seen too many failed attempts to create a "design factory," as if projects can be repeated cookie-cutter style. NPD professionals rightly resist such experiments, and process improvers with production backgrounds seem to insist on learning this the hard way.

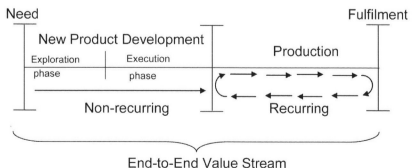

Figure 2.4 The End-to-End Value stream

Yet we have found that as long as we accept this basic truth, we can more readily and appropriately apply the next Lean principle with techniques specific to the world of NPD, thus avoiding the mistake of the more typical approach we see all too often of trying to run the nonrecurring NPD portion of the value stream like a widget factory.

3) Improve the flow of the value stream by eliminating waste.

In organizations that have not adopted Lean thinking, the "waste spotter" will see all sorts of opportunities to improve flow of either craft-based or mass production processes. After all, seeing nine parts waste to one part value-added soon changes the focus of your improvement efforts. The third principle of Lean in conjunction with wearing the "waste goggles" soon causes economies-of-scale thinking to change. This old maxim gives way to economies-of-flow. In addition, the division of work into value-adding steps achieves a consistency of first pass quality that the craft producer can only dream of, or would have to invest huge sums to achieve. Taking the waste elimination one step further by removing batches and their attendant inventory creates single-piece flow cells that produce further economies and quality advantages that even the mass producer can only dream of. In the next wave of waste elimination, strictly feeding items into the flow one-by-one and hence just in time allows real-time problem solving that sees quality levels soar. The real insight here is that waste is the obstacle to flow, so we should pay as much attention to waste in our NPD process as we do to waste in production.

This principle is easily explained but can be counterintuitive. For most, a sea of work in progress makes the uninformed viewer believe that process has a healthy order book and is much more in demand than the quiet Lean-thinking producer. It is vital, therefore, that in order to apply Lean thinking to NPD, one has to first achieve a different state of mind than that of the general population. We need to be able to discern good business from mere busyness.

Lean Thinking proposed that with this waste vision linked to a clear understanding of value streams, producers can consistently make significant improvements year after year of a magnitude that most leaders cannot comprehend. Let us quote George Koenigsaecker, author of *Leading the Lean Transformation*. Koenigsaecker's company, Jake Brake, was also a subject of one of *Lean Thinking*'s case studies. Koenigsaecker writes, "From my experience of over thirty years of Lean implementations within eleven corporations, senior leaders who drive Lean improvement should do so with annual goals of double-digit improvement gains in all four of the fundamental metrics: morale, quality, time, and cost." Doing so "will drive every line item on the income statement and balance sheet in a good direction."

It should be never forgotten that it was Toyota's amazing *business performance* that first alerted the world to the benefits of the Lean manufacturing system. Indeed, it is Toyota's continued and relentless success, despite setbacks, that has aroused the thinking of leaders in many sectors beyond the automotive industry.

Once you are inside the world of Lean, the pursuit of flow becomes all consuming. In fact it was an obsession with flow and exploring what needs to flow in the NPD process that led to our discovery of one of our breakthrough ideas. Specifically we realized that in the exploration phase, what needs to flow is awareness of what we don't know. We realized it was knowledge about knowledge that needed to flow. Hence what we need to remove is waste from the process of discovery, learning, and decision making that is required to build solid foundations for the execution phase. In contrast, what needs to flow in the execution phase is use of knowledge and tasks. This insight has been central to the application of other techniques that we have developed, invented, or borrowed for the Simpler Design System[SM]. An unhindered flow of discovery, learning, knowledge, decisions, and tasks is what makes a project using the Simpler Design System[SM] able to significantly outperform traditionally executed projects. This results in the potential to achieve improvements in all four key metrics.

4) Pull production, don't push.

The fourth principle of Lean is easily understandable by NPD professionals. The idea of pull in a factory context is to remove inventory to its theoretical minimum. This allows defects to be seen immediately and forces correction at that exact moment. While easy to say, most factory managers are terrified at such a prospect. This is because either consciously or subconsciously they believe that the sheer number of underlying problems would overwhelm them. Most factories are designed with buffers and breaks in the flow to enable the managers to contain and deal with problems in a reasonable time without harming continuity of supply. The reality, however, is that most plants are solving problems and fighting fires constantly at the level the buffers encourage. This is because there is no imperative to do any better. What we are really talking about here is another philosophy change. One approach seeks to get problems out into the open and force their elimination; the other does not. The difference in thinking is simple and shown below.

In any factory, the plan is usually sent to all departments, with each working independently. Inevitably variations in time and quality results in inter-process inventory shown below.

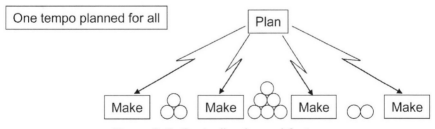

Figure 2.5 Centrally planned factory

By contrast, in a pull-based factory, the plan is instead sent to the very last process step, which then pulls in real time from the next upstream process, resulting in less inventory (waste), lower stress for people, and the ability to automatically cope with variation. This is shown below.

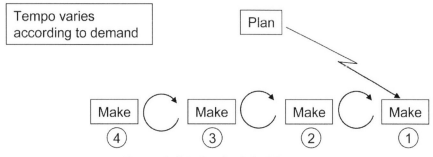

Figure 2.6 Pull scheduled factory

This approach, if persevered with and not fudged into a hybrid, forces a rapid and painful confrontation of the underlying problems that, if addressed, dramatically improves performance. That is easier said than done.

Despite years of progress in Lean manufacturing plants and their associated supply chains, it seems that pull is not yet a universal or founding principle for most managers, for whom the "hurry-up" character trait is the norm. This is despite all of our lives having been changed as our economies have shifted from a mass-production-centric model to a demand-driven one. One of the inspirations for Toyota's Just–in-Time system, the once humble supermarket, with its replenishment approach to supply, has completely transformed both the variety and availability of goods. On-demand thinking is changing many areas of consumption within our society, like pay-per-view TV, yet many other sectors remain unenlightened about this.

In Lean thinking, inventory is seen as the very worst type of waste, as it creates the condition where all the other wastes can appear. Yet most organizations seem to settle at a comfy level and never seek to change it.

This pull principle at least begs the question for people involved in NPD: What is your inventory? Further questions might include: Where is it? What does it look like? Why is it there?

It was questions such as these, driven by habits acquired in previous Lean transformations, that allowed us to explore how the pull principle applies to NPD.

Inventory in NPD certainly prevents us from working on the right things at the right time and, often buried virtually in IT-based mail systems, it quickly covers up the many problems unique to NPD. We will show you not only where and how it appears but how to eliminate it.

5) <u>Pursue perfection through continuous improvement.</u>

The lessons of the Lean thinking principles so far are that:

a. If you understand value from the eyes of the customer, then discover the waste that is making it difficult for value-added tasks to flow, and you will soon see how waste is preventing you from achieving the full potential of your enterprise. With this newfound vision you can see you need to do something that will get results.

b. If you remove waste in sufficiently large amounts, you will create a value stream not only capable of a flow but much more responsive such that you can operate on demand. In addition, if that flow is truly one-item (or decision) flow, then when problems do arise, they will do so only one at a time.

Once you have this kind of operation flowing with very little inventory, the natural human instinct for improvement can flourish and a great many further improvements can be made. The key is getting to a state of mind where "do it now" is the habit rather than "let me take that offline and fix it, then come back to you." This is how such amazing levels of improvement can be made by those doing flow. In short, the more they stop, the more they fix, the better they get. In the very best Lean organizations, such improvement is more a social movement within the organization than a specifically stated objective.

Known in Japan as kaizen, the final Lean principle is that of a relentless and continuous approach to improvement. By using a root-cause-focused, scientific approach with the entire workforce, you will create amazing results. Essential to success is that it must be those who do the work who also do the improvements, not the boss or some other higher-up. Leaders meanwhile have to lead transformation from the top and must do more than simply support the improvements; they must be involved. Over three decades have passed since Toyota first told the world about its amazing annual numbers of fully implemented suggestions per employee per year, and still the improvements keep on coming and they keep progressing despite some significant setbacks. This is because relentless kaizen focus on elimination of waste and elimination defects is a corporate habit that transcends generations.

Lean principles in NPD, despite each project being different

The title we have used here is deliberate and contains perhaps the most important statement to be used when attempting to use the power of Lean principles in NPD.

We have lost count of the times we are told, "Thank goodness you understand our world."

Most attempts to improve the NPD process using Lean seem to be based on the notion of a standard process that repeats. We don't agree and are relaxed enough to acknowledge with most technical staff that every project *is* different. The answer as to why we say this is simple when you can see both the management and the product developer view.

At the level at which managers have to see to do their work, NPD projects *are* all the same, but at the level at which technical staff have to work they are most definitely not. Also, when using Lean to affect business transformation, you have to apply the principles, not solutions that you have applied before.

We come across so many standard NPD processes, each with its tollgates, "user guides," checklists, and subprocess maps. We also come across many technical staff spending their energy describing to professional process improvers and auditors exactly why they didn't follow the process as defined.

We have learned that to engage leadership for this journey you have to promise system adherence and compliance, but to engage technical staff you have to promise creativity and variation.

This dichotomy manifests itself clearly when doing a "value stream map" for the generic NPD project as opposed to an actual map of what really happened on a real project. The generic value stream mapping exercise for NPD quickly descends into an unfathomable complexity of if/or logic that is best abandoned as the task of making the map and accounting for all eventualities gets more and more complex. By comparison, the map showing what actually happened on a real project typically shows a very different picture, as Dimancescu and Dwenger found in their book *World Class New Product Development*: "In our experience almost all employees pay lip service to them [documented NPD processes], and then go around the system to get things done....The reason is that 'the book' never quite responds to the actual circumstances faced by a project team."

We will return to this idea, but let us start a deeper dive by further defining the nature of waste and what it means for culture.

In order to get Lean thinking, one has to be able to see what a "Lean-er" version of today would look like. Human beings need contrast to see, and even then our brains retain patterns and paradigms to inform behavior to the degree that even when seeing "different," we don't always register it. In the early years of visiting Toyota-like Just-in-Time manufacturing plants, many executives returned puzzled and armed only with what they could see was different. Most executives are sufficiently removed from the detail of the value-added processes that seeing for them is not easy. In NPD this is a further challenge, as seeing what needs to flow takes a certain

amount of abstraction, and to give form to ideas of how it could be better, even more abstraction is needed. In our experience, most NPD professionals and their managers are often using the limit of their powers of abstraction to give form to the design in question, never mind "imagineering" a better-flowing process.

As a result, breaking the existing paradigms and culture is not optional; it has to be done. Sufficient contrast has to be created within the minds of the team to make them want to at least try something new. If they are not ready to do this, it will not happen. Most NPD professionals will have to think it through for themselves first and then be pushed into trying it. This reality of culture is that many years of transformation are lost as people seek to cut and paste solutions that worked in previous situations.

Unlike recurring manufacturing, production, or continual service, waste as a concept for NPD is found in two major areas, and in ten separate types. We came to this conclusion after seeing too many attempts to force the classic seven wastes into NPD. To do so misses a great deal of waste.

Area 1: NPD Process Waste

Eight basic wastes are found within the NPD project itself:

      I.   Overproduction

     II.   Transport

   III.   Inventory

    IV. Motion

     V. Waiting

    VI. Process steps that do not add value

   VII. Defects

  VIII. Waste of human talent

Area 2: Product or Service Designed in Waste

IX. *Features* that through either inclusion or omission do not add value to customer needs

X. Function provided at excessive *cost*

Note that while the first eight wastes are the same eight used to improve other areas of the enterprise, the final two are unique to the world of NPD. Moreover, we have discovered that these two are *the* gateway to get Lean thinking into the minds of NPD staff, who will appreciate the notion of "Designed" in waste well before accepting they have any process waste. Indeed, as mentioned before, many believe the first eight wastes to be necessary to a good iterative design process, as most have no contrasting experience of life without these wastes.

In short, when introducing Lean principles into this arena, we must first focus on the thing likely to get buy-in and engagement. For example, it is no good talking about the distance people have to travel from the design office to the marketing department if the design is still failing to fundamentally match customer requirements.

Earlier in this chapter we gave an overview of five Lean principles. We will now go into more detail and highlight how the application of each principle may or may not eliminate each of the ten wastes found in NPD. Note we are writing this from the direct experience of applying these principles rather than the specific application of Lean tools. This "principles before tools" approach allows Lean transformation to work in any setting and ensure that improvement is not overly reliant on previous experience. Most Lean professionals involved in transformation have found that culture change requires a high degree of self-discovery and self-derived solutions that mean that copy-and-paste solutions mostly meet with resistance. This is especially true in the NPD arena. Ultimately the principles-led approach assures long-term success in forever changing the culture and beliefs of an organization. We must stress therefore that the tools we discuss in the following sections were only used to achieve improvement in line with the principles

we sought with our client in their setting and circumstances. Hence we advocate using these tools only in the combinations suggested as examples and to the degree that you get the results you require.

Define value: How is this done in NPD?

In a manufacturing process, defining value is quite quick and simple, as the value is the manufacture and assembly of the products that the customer has ordered. In addition to the product itself, the customer also values it to be on time and free of defects. These elements ensure that the overall experience itself is value-added. In a service environment it is the elements of service that directly supply the customer need that determine whether customers see value, and each customers need is personal and situational. In NPD, however, value is derived from the elements of unmet needs that, if translated into product or service features (i.e., solutions), will deliver the required value to the customer. An easy way to consider this is by asking the question, "What problem(s) is the customer seeking to solve?"

In NPD we have to invest much more time in defining what "value" is because research shows that customers typically only tell you part of what you need to know to create successful products. In fact, we've found that as little as a third of what the customer may really value is communicated verbally or in writing in response to direct questioning. Such voice of the customer (VOC) work is a good thing in lieu of nothing, but we suggest that to maximize the elimination of product or service waste, you have to go further.

The legend behind the original development of the first Toyota Lexus is that Japanese engineers were sent to California to live the lives of their target market so that they could observe the individual lives of people in their target market. After recording their experiences in minute detail they then sought to provide a product and brand that met their needs. Clearly, to our European minds, Lexus was designed as a "brand experience" for American consumers to satisfy a need along the lines of

image-appropriate transportation, as opposed to a simple car for basic transportation. For example, they found that while Mercedes and BMW debated the quality and timbre of their engine note, most US luxury car customers preferred no engine sound at all. In the subsequent pursuit of silence they also identified that variation in panel gaps on competitors' cars were a significant cause of wind noise, so they developed a car with the smallest gaps with almost no variation. This led to a famous advertising campaign that showed a small ball bearing running along all the panel gaps without falling through them. Not only did this reduce noise, it was also a terrific quality statement that could be seen just by looking at the car. This highly successful product differentiator was only discovered by observing customers rather than just talking to them.

We do this defining of value in the Simpler Design System[SM] by taking multidisciplined teams to the actual point of use of the target customer and directly observing the setting or context in which the solution will operate. We call this environment of the customer (EOC) work and place it as the highest priority in the early stages of a project.

During the observations we are looking for:

- **Basic needs** that are believed to be so obvious that the customer never bothers to mention them. For example, a hotel room should have a lockable door.

- **Customer "pain" or hassle** that we can eliminate. In many cases we find that customers accept inconvenience without question because they themselves can't conceive of a better way. For example, Chris worked with a client who produced barbeques designed for backyard use, yet in EOC work they saw customers using them on the beds of pick-up truck and struggling to get them flat and level. The subsequent idea for a built-in spirit level and adjustable legs had never been identified in previous customer surveys.

- **Performance features** that the customer expresses as a way of informing their choice between one solution or another.

- □ **Delighter ideas** that the customer never realized they wanted until they saw them. For example, Rob was offered an extra-hot coffee at an airport coffee bar because it would be just the right temperature to drink after the ten-minute walk to the gate.

- □ **Customer interviews and feedback** to understand their environment better and get their product improvement ideas.

It is hard not to overstress the importance of having a direct two-way dialogue in order to capture the raw voice of real customers free from interference subconsciously applied by any third party or internal department. We accept that for many organizations the notion of "customers" may be difficult without thinking about a variety of stakeholders, but we like to define a customer broadly as anyone who can affect the success or failure of your project.

Clearly, with this definition, this step cannot be done in five minutes. Indeed, this first step really sets the agenda for how much front-loading you are prepared to commit to the project. There are many diagrams (like the one in fig 2.7) which suggest it to be desirable to front-load projects. We need to point out that simply adding more resources at the start is not enough. You must ensure that those resources are doing EOC and "defining value" work. Upfront involvement does not mean everyone must be up front. Be careful not to involve people with a "hurry up" gene at this stage as they will likely accelerate the transition to the execution phase prematurely. Almost all NPD texts encourage more upfront work to avoid subsequent rework, but we have found that to be too simplistic a maxim. In reality there is little guidance as to how much front-loading is actually required. In other words, what proportion of the project time should be given to defining value? Or similarly, what resources are needed? These are perfectly reasonable questions in the eyes of any manager or indeed any person looking into the project, but they always seem to elicit the following response: "It depends."

On what? Well, a number of things, and specifically the answers to the following questions:

☐ Is it a totally new design?

☐ Is it a derivative design?

☐ Do we currently have a process for understanding the environment of the customer (EOC)?

☐ Do we have a process for capturing the voice of the customer (VOC)?

☐ How different is the project from others in your experience?

Essentially, an answer at this point is at best a guesstimate or is based on some arbitrary new timescale demanded by the project in question. At worst it will be allocated a timescale based on a standard process template that generically assigns a time regardless of what is actually needed. However, we can show that we have learned that the profile on a first implementation of Lean in NPD should be as follows and the thinking should be two-thirds more resources in exploration than we would normally allocate, two-thirds of the overall timescales we normally take, and one-third of the resources we would normally allocate to execution (see fig 2.7).

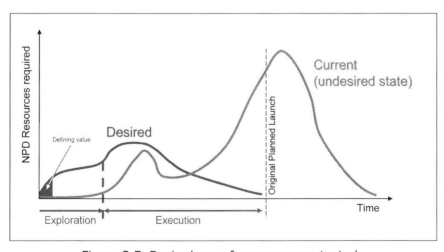

Figure 2.7 Desired use of resources vs. typical

In terms of using these up-front resources effectively over and above just allocating more of them, we have found a way of giving the definition of value work a more structured approach that can be predictably managed. We will show these techniques in Chapter 6 of this book.

1) Understand the value stream.

At its most basic understanding, the notion of an NPD value stream starts with defining the *it* that is trying to *flow*. In NPD we propose that what needs to flow is quite different in the two phases of exploration and execution that was highlighted earlier. (See fig 2.8 for a visual representation.)

> In the exploration phase, *learning*, *knowledge*, and *decisions* need to flow.

> In the execution phase, *information*, *tasks*, and *outputs* need to flow.

For the successful implementation of Lean in NPD we must accept that the exploration phase (sometimes referred to as the "fuzzy front end") is by its very nature nondeterministic and nonlinear. However, this does not mean that it cannot be:

a. Structured OR

b. Have its progress made visible AND

c. Be improved over time

The good news is that the "fuzzy front end" does not have to be so fuzzy!

In fact, we have proved that if we consider the phase as being simply the need to *learn what we currently don't know*, then we can fundamentally change the way this phase is managed.

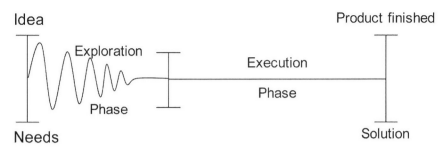

Figure 2.8 Exploration and Execution Phases

A practical insight we have had is that in the exploration phase, instead of the typical task-based Gantt chart approach, we have achieved much better results using a special team-based planning approach, which is much better received and valued by those doing this type of work. By centering on the quest for discovery, learning, and capturing knowledge, we first plan to understand what we don't know, and then set out a path to efficiently learn and close these knowledge gaps. We call this new approach "decision flow" will discuss it further in Chapter 6.

For most traditional organizations, the knowledge gap is traditionally closed as NPD work proceeds in the classic sequential process flow shown in fig 2.9, and the very rework loops traditional Lean thinkers try so hard to eliminate with standard work. Note we are not showing departments here, just logical steps. This is the way the process will flow no matter how you are organized and who reports to whom. It is why changing the organization structure alone rarely makes a difference in NPD.

We show this as a Gantt chart because this is the way 99 percent of NPD projects are managed. Below each phase we list the output expected, but then we show what the reality is, as each process step will go through its own reworking and iterations based upon how much is understood from the previous step and how much the emerging solution can be accommodated with existing knowledge. Known as the over-the-wall approach, it results in multiple feedback/rework loops and creates a collective effect shown in fig 2.9.

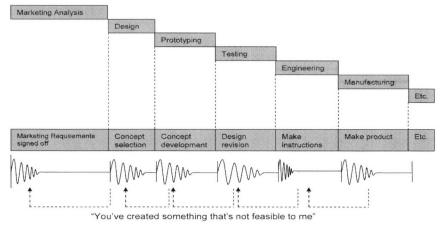

Figure 2.9 Typical NPD project management in view of exploration and execution insight

When combined with a push approach to project management, you can soon see why project performance is often a mess. Even though the most extreme over-the-wall processes have long gone and perhaps even the most highly walled departments have opened their doors to the views of others, do we still have the same symptoms above in the brave new world of so-called concurrent working? If so, why?

The following story is about a client of Rob's and illustrates what is still going wrong despite the fact that they were early adopters of concurrent engineering and had documented what they considered to be a best practice, modern stage, gate-based process. The story also guides us to a solution, which is a central element of our quest to eliminate waste and improve time to market.

The client asked Rob to take a look at a project that was a major product upgrade and had been running for approximately four years. The new machine shared very few components with its predecessor since the overall focus of the project was cost reduction. When Rob joined the team it was in its fourth year and the project was getting close to production launch, which was already a year later than originally promised. From a cost reduction viewpoint, the project was seen as a success with

significant savings being obtained while producing a machine that better fulfilled customer needs. With respect to time-to-market, however, the project was typical of many, and they had a suspicion that they could do much better. Rob analyzed the project with a view to then helping them with future projects to improve their time-to-market performance.

To protect the innocent, we aren't going to reveal the identity of the client, but suffice it to say that they are a large blue-chip company with significant resources. They manufacture vehicles and have invested heavily in Six Sigma quality. Indeed, many engineers had achieved Six Sigma accreditation at a variety of levels, and the leader of this particular project was a black belt.

On the surface the project *looked* efficient. But like many organizations, they mistook process compliance for process efficiency. There had been well-documented design reviews, product marketing had a clear specification, regular meetings were held with production engineers to review 3D virtual models, and drawing efficiency and error rates were about average for the company.

It wasn't until Rob set about looking for the waste in the project's execution that the true picture emerged. He started by assessing the amount of change-driven rework in the project and produced the graph shown below.

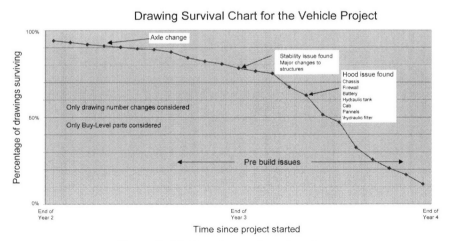

Figure 2.10 Drawing and re-drawing

The x-axis shows a period in time from the end of Year 2 to the end of Year 4 and starts shortly after the first prototype of the machine was built. The y-axis shows the percentage of the drawings created for the first prototype that had survived so far. You can see that at the start of the analysis period 94 percent of the drawings are still in the latest engineering bill of materials and 6 percent have been replaced with new drawings. However, by the end of Year 4, only 10 percent of the original drawings had survived, and 90 percent of them have been replaced with new drawings. Indeed, the team had already produced approximately five thousand drawings for a machine with little over two thousand parts, and changes were still being made.

Just so that we're clear, we're talking about new CAD drawings here, not drawing revisions in which the issue number is incrementally raised to show that a minor change has been made. (If that were the case, Chris can tell similar stories of whole aircraft that in effect have been designed ten times over!)

Next Rob started looking at what had been driving this amount of redesign and found a long list of causes. When studied deeper, however, by far the most significant cause was found to be moving ahead with designing details before the fundamentals of the concept were proven.

This is a key point: don't invest in defining detail before proving the basic fundamentals of the concept. Unfortunately this is so counterintuitive to most "let's get things moving" project managers and executives that most of them must deliberately unlearn this behavior or physically be prevented from doing it.

Three example instances of such overproduction are annotated on the graph. In Month 4 of the study period, the team found out that the specified axles were not going to be available at the low price originally quoted by the supplier. There had been a misunderstanding of specifications and some errors in the supplier's cost estimations. These problems were only found when axles for the first prototype were produced.

Since cost was the major focus of the project, the team made some design changes so that axles that were in line with the original cost targets could be used. This was a minor change compared to what happened next.

In Month 12 of the study period, off-road testing of the vehicle revealed that it wasn't completely stable, and the test drivers managed to overturn the vehicle. This was of course a potentially disastrous design flaw. The dynamic computer simulations that had been completed a little earlier were found to have been run by an inexperienced analyst and were not representative of the way the vehicle really behaved. This caused a major redesign of the vehicle's structures to change the handling characteristics. This in turn had a knock-on effect to many other components which were packaged in and around these structures.

In Month 16, a major distributor was invited to see the machine for the first time. This distributor had the potential to sell around 40 percent of the machines sold in Europe and so would have a large influence upon the success of the project. When they saw the vehicle, they didn't like the engine hood line and the visibility problems this caused for the driver. It was too high, too wide, and too bulbous. Having already redesigned large areas of the machine to solve the stability problems, the team started over to create a hood line more to the customer's liking. This again had a knock-on effect to all of the components so tightly packaged under the hood and around the engine.

In conjunction with the initial study of change and what was driving it, Rob also looked at the way the project had been resourced and created the graph shown in fig 2.11.

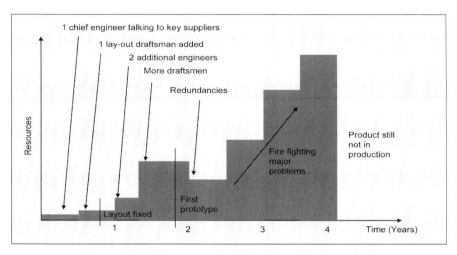

Figure 2.11 Resource chart for the vehicle project

When the project was started there was just one person assigned to it, a senior engineer who worked for six months doing calculations and rough layouts. He talked to suppliers about the costs of the major components for the new vehicle and broadly fixed the specifications. After six months, management thought that the project had some merit, and the senior engineer was given a layout draftsman to create more formal drawings of the new product. The layout geometry was fixed not long afterward, and over the next six months the company assigned two more engineers and then three more draftsmen to the project. This team created more than two thousand CAD drawings, which were loaded into the company's MRP system (so that purchasing could hurry up and order parts for the first prototype).

The organization went through a downsizing as the project entered its third year, and the two contract draftsmen on the project were let go. Once the machine stability and hood line issues surfaced there was suddenly no lack of resources, and the number of engineers and draftsmen was ramped up quickly. This resource profile is typical of many companies and shows that allocating resources to a project in trouble is much easier than to allocate them to the same project at the beginning when all the major decisions are being made.

Note that the organization thought that it *had* front-loaded this project, as their highly documented stage-gate process had held the appropriate reviews and multidisciplinary sign-offs, which had all been achieved. The reality of course was that each sign-off, although executed, was made much like those sign-offs one does before accepting the terms and conditions of downloaded software or in a rental car agreement—which is to say, no one read them.

So what went wrong? In Lean parlance, the team *overproduced* detail before proving any of the fundamentals. As we have said, this is by far the most prevalent waste we see in the NPD process. This was mostly down to traditional program management which treated exploration like execution. Changing this project management approach to program management is fundamental to our approach.

In reality the vehicle company spent two years producing two thousand, drawings before doing any testing at all. In fact the company created this situation itself by closing a prototype-manufacturing area at the site on grounds of cost, thus making it even more difficult for engineering prototype parts to be made to sketches. Prototype parts were now required, as a result of outsourcing to production suppliers, to be produced using production standard drawings for which purchasing was using a three-quote process to select the supplier. Time-wise, this was a disaster in terms of the flow of knowledge required in the exploration phase.

Ironically, the company had invested heavily in a full virtual-reality-based product design suite in which, had the dealer been invited to earlier reviews, the issues could have been found some six months before the study period started. In addition, when challenged about the stability testing, the team soon realized they could have modified the previous model to be adequately representative. This could have been done some nine months before the study period.

Unfortunately, stories like this are the norm, and having the time to map these "current states" is a rare luxury. We have actually concluded that to map an NPD current state in total

detail is a waste of time as it can only be done historically and so holds little relevance to subsequent projects.

Our insight with regard to this principle for NPD is that you only need to map as much as it takes to:

a) Understand and accept that the current situation can be radically improved.

b) Have the team accept this and be willing to try a new approach.

c) Have some sort of baseline measured to be able to "prove" the relative magnitude of improvement.

The power of value-stream thinking for NPD, therefore, is more cerebral when used to realize what is supposed to be flowing in each of the separate phases of exploration and ex-ecution than when used to produce current and future state maps essential for Lean transformation of traditional recurring processes.

2) Remove waste to improve the *flow.*

Earlier in this chapter we listed ten wastes that are applicable to NPD and how they link to what Dr. Robert G. Cooper calls the "two ways to win at new products."

a) Doing the right projects (products)

b) Doing projects right (the NPD process)

Very few people, whether technically oriented or in managerial roles, will argue about the need for the former. This is about having a product strategy that is right for the strategic aims of your enterprise. Selecting projects with good odds of suc-cess and exploiting unmet needs to provide solutions for pent-up demand. Similarly, few would argue with the very practi-cal applications of new technology in order to serve customer needs in a new and interesting way. This is the stuff that gets technical staff out of bed every morning and business leaders

dreaming about the potential of having hot new products. It is the "doing projects right" bit that seems brings out all of the opinions, arguments, and conflicts, yet we must consider both.

We said that product waste (or not doing the right projects) comes in three forms, which we will now explore in more detail.

a. <u>Features</u> that through inclusion or omission do not add value to the stakeholder's needs.

This is all about having both an effective product strategy and developing products that are actually needed. How often do projects begin as the "pet ideas" of technical staff but then turn out to be non-viable? In most commercial organizations the technical staff seem reluctant to ask the "can we sell this thing?" question.

Our favorite example of this is "New Coke" which was launched in 1985. The Coca-Cola Company took the world's bestselling soft drink and improved its flavor. Even though initial sales were up 8 percent over the same period of the year before, as soon as journalists, talk-show hosts, and Coke's rival, Pepsi, got onto the subject, it was doomed to failure. For something marketed for years as "the real thing," it seems obvious that value in the eyes of the customer would include "constancy" and "unchanging nature."

Red-faced executives had to announce the removal of the "new" product just three months after its introduction and the reintroduction of the original formula under the brand name Coke Classic.

Of course, good product strategy relies on good business strategy, and it is easy to argue that New Coke was a "good" product (it consistently won blind taste tests, often to the anger of the participants) and was simply developed to serve what was

actually bad business strategy. We would not agree. We simply conclude it must have been a flawed NPD process because it did not fulfill a true customer-driven "need" in the market. This breaks the first Lean principle of defining value in the eyes of the customer. New Product Development therefore cannot be conducted in a vacuum regardless of strategy and vice versa.

Clearly New Coke did not add value to the lives of its intended customers nor to the stakeholders of Coke who saw the "value" of the stake-holding plummet.

Contrast this with the launch of Coke Zero in 2006. This so-called "Blokes Coke" was targeted at young males who shunned both Coke Classic (unhealthy) and Diet Coke (perceived as a feminine product). Marketed as zero sugar and zero calories, as opposed to "diet," it was also launched as a business strategy to combat a loss of market share to health drinks and energy drinks. Coke Zero is now a successful worldwide product.

This same thinking applies to product features too. Have you ever had a product that was overfeatured and you wished that the producer had spent a little more on the quality of the prime functions? For example, budget automobiles are often loaded with features from up-market models but at a lower specification or quality. Many probably wish that more was spent on noise insulation or the suspension. Conversely, have you ever thought that a piece of equipment would be "great if only it did some additional functions as well"? Remember our earlier example when Chris worked with a barbecue grill manufacturer who added a spirit level and bottle opener as standard features on their product and watched as sales soared.

Our learning is that developing new products, product strategy, and business strategy must go hand in

hand. Otherwise the desire to "do the right project" is compromised from the start.

b. <u>Costs</u> that do not provide function that the stakeholders want.

This waste is prevalent throughout many products and can be made visible by looking at a product design in terms of primary and secondary functions. A primary function is what the customer (or stakeholder) wants and is willing to pay for. Secondary functions are created by the product designers to achieve the primary function, but customers don't necessarily care about them directly. If you map the primary and secondary functions on a "function map," you can start to see the complex structure of secondary functions that have been created.

Let's take a simple can opener like the one shown in the picture.

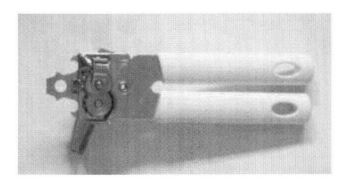

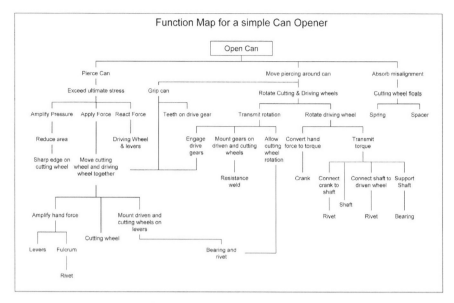

Figure 2.12 Can Opener – Function map

The function map for the opener pictured is surprisingly complex to the beginner seeing such maps for the first time. Indeed, when you first draw it, it naturally leads you to wonder how you can open a can more simply because a customer really doesn't care about teeth on the driving gears or springs absorbing misalignment as long as it works.

There are of course many can opener designs on the market and all of them open cans. Many have function maps that are far simpler than the above example, and consequently they also have fewer components and lower manufacturing costs. Of importance to us is that the producer of the can opener in the picture has launched a new model that has a simpler function map and yet they can sell it at a higher price! This is the great thing about good design. It is often seen as high value when it is actually lower cost.

How does this thinking work for you if you design products?

Imagine now that we are talking about a subassembly within one of your products that your customer doesn't even know exists. How much secondary function complexity has crept

into the design? We find it useful to see this unnecessary complexity as waste and to see its presence in a design as an inefficiency of the design process. Consider that it not only took more effort to create it, it also multiplied costs throughout the enterprise. The Lean NPD person understands that it is better to spend the extra time designing a simple solution than quickly designing a (wastefully) complex one. This is another thinking pattern that is counterintuitive to most and requires deliberate unlearning to overcome and be successful. For those readers who don't design a physical product—perhaps you design software or services—simply ask yourself what would the function map look like, for example, for the various elements of service you intend to provide?

Let us take the example of a general medical health-check. What are the elements of service required to provide the "value"? What things are necessary to satisfy the purpose? What are the unnecessary steps?

Having understood how we get the right products or services, let us now consider examples of the eight NPD process wastes to show how they arise in NPD.

I. Overproduction—We covered this in our earlier example of the vehicle design.

II. Transport—Number of electronic hand-offs, travelling to meetings, going to see tests, visiting field tests, etc.

III. Inventory—Unchecked documents, document queues

IV. Motion—Mouse-clicks, searching for stuff

V. Waiting—Sequential approvals

VI. Process steps that do not add value—Redundant approvals, irrelevant checklist items

VII. Defects—Flawed designs

VIII. Waste of human talent—Training people and not applying the new information

In the Simpler Design System[SM] these wastes are eliminated through a variety of methods, the primary ones being he use of collaborative co-located, team-based working, as opposed to individual, desk-based working, throughout the project. In manufacturing, when waste is eliminated and the value-adding steps inevitably move closer together, the resulting process is known as a *flow cell*.

The NPD equivalent is a dedicated and well-designed project room that allows work to flow between team members from different disciplines with minimal waste, whether they are collectively learning and discovering in the exploration phase, or collaboratively designing solutions in the execution phase.

3) Pull, don't push.

As we mentioned earlier, in manufacturing, Lean thinkers literally reversed the conventional wisdom regarding how material should be encouraged to flow through a factory. The seed for this revolution was when Kichiro Toyoda missed a train on a tour of Europe in the 30s (thanks to an out-of-date timetable). He wondered how long the typical factory timetable (production plan) lasted before it too was out-of-date and things were no longer synchronized. Until this point all factories ran as per the diagram in fig 2.13.

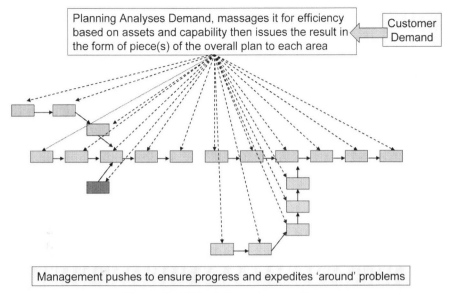

Figure 2.13 Push-based operations

Even today many manufacturers (that have yet to be touched by Lean) use this model. With this push-based model, one needs to invest heavily in planning and expediting resources. The results are that managers that can hurry things up and get things out of the door despite promoting problems along with them. This is no different in most NPD projects where the pushy project manager is seen as the enemy of the technical staff and the friend of the management. Looking closer at most Gantt chart–formatted project plans, it is easy to see why. The plan is created and shared with each "specialty" (analogous to factory departments), and then progress is monitored and chased. If a deviation to plan occurs, regaining the position is typically achieved at the expense of later tasks or at the very least a renegotiation of the allocated time. It is now acquired behavior for many involved in downstream tasks to increase their time estimates safe in the knowledge that inevitably they will be given less time than planned. Curiously, we have yet to meet the project manager who then seeks to improve pro-cesses to ensure that their expediting can actually happen without a negative effect.

By contrast, in the pull-based factory system, all departments are notified of the planned demand so that they can plan ahead for capacity, but the *execution* of the plan is much simpler. The actual customer demand is sent only to the end of the flow and then each downstream area, acting as the next customer in line, sends a trigger upstream for what they need when they need it. This Just-in-Time approach makes for a much simplified system that can self-adjust for problems and requires much less in the way of overhead to operate. Pictorially it is shown below:

Pull based Factory

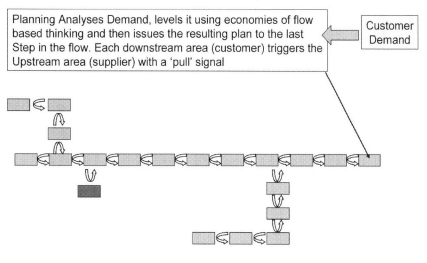

Figure 2.14 The pull-based approach

We draw a clear parallel here between our NPD approach, which focuses on the flow of knowledge within the process, and the efficient creation of solutions to customer needs (value). We place "pull points" and "integration points" into our project plans and organize projects accordingly. If we find problems, we focus on process improvement to regain any lost ground. Most project managers we work with see the benefits in the long term, but short-term they may feel like everything they

know about project management is under attack. For many, going from a push- to pull-based philosophy requires a change of beliefs.

5) Pursue perfection.

In the Lean thinkers' organization, this principle means seeking improvement continually and forever. Having found a superior approach to improvement (the removal of waste within the production or service delivery process), it made sense to the early Lean pioneers to see if there were benefits to be had in repeated application of the principles. They soon discovered the answer was yes, and moreover, it now seems that even six decades after embarking on the path of waste removal, there is no end in sight as to what is possible with continual kaizen (small incremental changes) and kaikaku (large dramatic change). Technical staff, by contrast, have a split personality when it comes to continuous improvement. In the case of improving the actual product or service, most will agree with the idea that everything can be continually improved, and they do this with enthusiasm. When it comes to actually improving the process or their way of doing things they can be as stubborn as a care home resident. Furthermore, many involved in NPD fundamentally believe in the law of diminishing returns, and so the idea of continuous improvement is not always an exciting prospect. These people, if they set their mind and energy to what we call the science of no, can be a formidable roadblock to progress and sap the energy of others. The only way to reverse this is to challenge and engage the same people in the science of yes, and show via contrasting approaches and learning by doing that there may be a better way. There is nothing like trying things and generating some counterdata to move things along. The people interacting to create this environment are key. People in NPD have to be able to trust those helping them make the necessary changes. They are reluctant to do that with anyone unless they believe that person once walked in their shoes. Many regard the science of management like that of homeopathy and distrust it before even starting. Many will have experienced well-meaning but stupid attempts to improve their world before. The bottom line here is to ensure you are accepted as the coach before you start

calling the plays. Unlike the rest of the organization, in NPD, being the boss does not imply you are the coach. So for this principle to be applied in this environment, the challenge is therefore two-fold, to pursue perfection via:

a) Continually enhancing and improving the value proposition of the product, goods, or service design, while

b) Continually improving the NPD process itself through the continuous application of Lean thinking principles.

In our next chapter we will discuss how all of this theory can be put to work.

Many readers will still be curious about what *is* waste in the New Product Development process, as even at this stage of thinking it feels necessary. We will cover this in more detail in Chapter 3, but be assured we have learned that there is more of it in NPD than in any factory, and there are more waste-blind people working in the process. This is good news, really, as the potential for improvement is massive.

Again, the title of this chapter is designed to imply two things about our suggested approach to improving the world of NPD. The first is that the people involved should first see a simple system based on principles and applied at a principles level. Second, the system is seeking commonality only of the approach at the principles level. Each project is by its nature seeking to address different needs, so starting with the idea that they are all the same is just plain stupid and the fastest way to alienate yourself from the technical staff. We have lost count of the times we have had to look interested as we are shown yet another toll-gated "standard NPD" process and its cartload of documentation created by people removed from the actual day-to-day NPD process. Systems are at their most effective when they are readily understood and widely applied. The Toyota Production System is so successful because of the reasons for its success are its relative simplicity:

1. Serve the customer

2. Adopt flow processes based on Just-in-Time thinking

3. Practice *jidoka* (stop and solve problems to root cause as they happen)

4. Pull, don't push, value through the system

5. Forever improve by practicing kaizen

Every employee is shown this as a simple but highly symbolic temple (think about it) from day one. And it is widely practiced at some level by *all* employees. In one sense the real power of

the Toyota Production System (TPS) is that it is better to have the majority acting and regularly improving via a set of simple principles rather than a few superstars using a theoretically superior approach. What is remarkable is that Toyota has been able to demonstrate this for decades, yet emulation of the full system (tools and behaviors) is rare. Why?

Having read this far, it is probable that you actually want to change your NPD process for the better. Given that we want you to succeed, we cannot stress enough the importance of the following new acronym:

K.I.S.S.I.S.O.Y.N.T.T.D.T.O.

Keep It Simple Stupid In Spite Of Your Natural Tendency To Do The Opposite

And yes, the irony of our new acronym is intended!

You need your NPD process to be so simple that everyone can understand it after fifteen minutes' explanation. The foundational principles need to be applied regularly and pragmatically in such a way that they become group habits. For many in the field of NPD, pragmatism and simplicity are not the world they inhabit on a daily basis. Technical work is often by its very nature complex and easy to get lost in. When working with data, specifications, and evidence-based decisions, detail consciousness is highly prized, and many people involved initially struggle with the idea that less is more.

Earlier in his career, Chris, who is by nature a high-level systems thinker, watched in amazement as a new NPD system that he and his team had developed and captured simply on two flip charts and had operated successfully for a year was then "professionally documented" in a virtual mountain of paperwork. It got to the point that the document could not be carried by one person, let alone read! The people on the original project could not understand why this was happening, and having literally been interrogated over months, they could not see how people on subsequent projects could pos-

sibly use the on-line documented "system" practically. Why did this happen?

The problem was that the senior management team understandably wanted to capture the higher performance of the "new way" of working, but in error sought to do that through detail understanding rather than the simple essence of what had made the project a success. We have repeatedly seen the common error that the organizations unwittingly mix the documentation of technical knowledge with that of the NPD process itself. We suggest they be kept separate. We are not saying documenting the process is bad, but the way it is done often is. In these days of information overload, we have to constantly ask how much is really necessary.

When we make this point we are always quickly asked, "So how much detail should we go into?"

We have learned to give a simple answer. Once you get the sense that the documentation is almost turning into training material, you have gone far enough. We recommend a structure that has four levels.

Level 1: Overview of the system and its principles *(should take no longer than fifteen minutes to explain and understand)*

Level 2: Practitioner's level detail of the overall system *(no more than half a day to fully understand)*

Level 3: Recipe cards for the use of tools and techniques *(maximum sixty minutes of study before trying)*

Level 4: Simple capture of design knowledge gained and examples *(A3 paper–based illustrations, text, and data; should be usable on the job)*

This layering approach allows the system to be understood at various depths and ensures that wider appreciation is achieved easily.

Beware the check sheet

The members of the team being interrogated in Chris's example were in hindsight helping to create "check sheets." This form of capturing their newfound knowledge and design decisions was interesting. However, given that the project was a jet training aircraft with an in-service "life problem" with its tail-plane, their findings were only really relevant to another team facing the same or very similar problems. What was unique about their experience and made it valuable to the organization was the way they performed and worked as a team. At this point in the company's history, it was the first time in living memory that the old departmental and functional boundaries had been suspended and a new "concurrent engineering team" had been formed under a single *shusa*-style "chief engineer." If asked about this, the organization would have found a wealth of new learning derived from new working patterns; faster, less wasteful interactions between functions; and a project room design that was the essence of why the project was an unprecedented success in terms of morale, quality, time, and cost. Curiously, like many organizations, the job of the documentation of the process had actually been assigned to nonparticipants, so it was ultimately doomed to be an irrelevant exercise in over-academic bureaucracy. Soon, new project teams found themselves having to spend more time preparing for "gate reviews" and providing evidence that checklists had been followed than doing the actual value-added tasks of designing and engineering the new product! This is a shame, because the thinking behind the check sheet is sound. It is just that check sheets grow and grow, and as time passes, become less and less relevant. This is because, given that each project is different, the things needing to be checked are different. Each new project therefore adds items to the check sheets, and soon they contain more that is irrelevant than relevant. Yet the goal of a check sheet—to capture organizational knowledge and wisdom—is noble. It is just that there are much better ways to do it.

Check are good for training recurring processes until they become habits but soon become counterproductive for nonrecurring processes.

Worship the trade-off curves

Once you clearly understand the needs of the customer, much of the work involved in NPD is creating solutions that optimize the many conflicting requirements. For example, modern cars have complex electro-mechanical suspension systems that can be optimized for different conditions. Each condition will represent a different trade-off of ride comfort and the control of the vehicle's dynamics for optimum performance. In Chris's former world of aircraft engineering, the constant challenge of the airframe designer was that of strength vs. weight. Similarly, for military aircraft, there was the challenge of aerodynamic performance vs. that of radar signature. All of NPD work is a multidimensional balancing act between these known trade-offs, and pairs of trade-offs combine with others. This knowledge and learning is the true "secret sauce" of any organization's capability in NPD, but it is often compromised by organization structures, power, and personalities. Without trade-off data and in NPD teams greater than one member, people are naturally placed in opposition to each other. Various disciplines and knowledge bases are soon in constant negotiation at best and flaming each other in virtual tech wars at worst.

Assuming an organization does not want such trade-off knowledge to leave with people when they go, how an organization captures and presents this for future team members is vital. We have both come to the view that the true size of an NPD team's challenge and the claimed complexity of any project can be critically viewed through the lens of its trade-off curves. How does an organization simply and easily capture its design knowledge? How do team members access an organization's knowledge of the optimum solutions and hence the known compromises they should make along the way? What is the gap between the needs of the customer and current state-of-the-art solutions that should be driving new game-changing breakthroughs that render the old solutions as state of the *ark*? Only when you combine these technical challenges with the process challenges of time, cost, and people do you have your true idea of how tough each challenge is. Without

retaining trade-off knowledge, each project has to start from scratch, and that *is* very risky.

Keeping it ruthlessly simple

As we mentioned earlier, this is vital to ensure success, so we have distilled our knowledge as follows. Above all, consider your NPD process itself as working at different layers of detail and realize that your people will be mixed in their skills and how comfortable they are working at each respective level. There's nothing that slows a team down more than when one member wants to work at a detail level significantly different from their peers. At the highest level we see the NPD process as two distinct phases in the same flow:

1.   Exploration

2.   Execution

These phases are quite different from each other and are often overlapped with the intention of "concurrent" or parallel working in the interests of accelerating the time, but we will argue both experimentally and logically for them to be considered separately. We show this in fig 3.1.

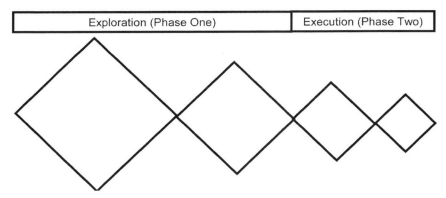

Figure 3.1 Visual Overview of the SDS approach – Detail 1

We show the diagram visually as a series of diamonds because:

a. The overall NPD process needs to be under-
    stood as containing at least another level of detail
    (subphases).

b. They reflect the reduction of uncertainty as the
    project progresses (the area of the diamonds
    decreases).

c. The diamond shape suggests that the work of NPD
    is all about mentally expansive thinking followed by
    contraction.

d. Each subphase is essentially a different mental
    challenge, so it is essential to not destroy mental
    efficiency by mixing them up. We call this to "rush
    slowly."

Having seen the big picture, let us look at what is happening
the next level down. (Fig 3.2).

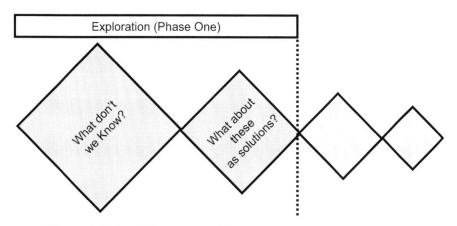

Figure 3.2 Visual Overview of the SDS approach – Exploration

The exploration phase is really the pursuit of answers to the
question, "What don't we know about this project?" This then
stimulates the creation of potential solutions which can be

evaluated against success criteria derived from the "what don't we know" work.

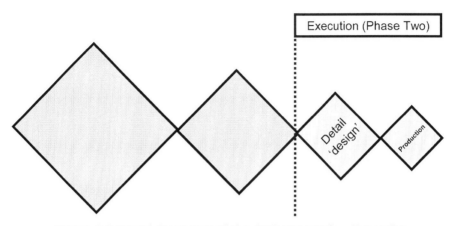

Figure 3.3 Visual Overview of the SDS approach – Execution

The execution phase (shown in fig 3.3), by contrast, is all about detailing the best solution and creating the tangible elements of the product or service.

At this point, a question we always get asked by technical staff needs answering:

"If all the wisdom about improving this process points to more up-front resources, why, oh, why do leaders rarely sanction this?"

We have come to the conclusion that it is driven by leadership behavior and underlying beliefs that in the exploration phase few things seem tangible; most leaders do not like intangibles. Moreover, most of the exploration phase happens conversationally as an exchange or search for knowledge. Even using the best methods, the output will be contained in a few short documents such as experiment outcomes, tables, and trade-off charts. It does not look like much output for the effort put in. It seems that most humans need tangible outputs in order to believe they are actually getting something for their investments. To give leaders the assurance they need, we instead show them a big list of what we don't know, rather than a big

list of tasks. We then follow that with a big list of findings and new knowledge gained from our experiments. Only when you have that can you be confident that the flow of knowledge and decisions has generated solutions that have been correctly explored and then refined into the chosen ones.

In contrast, the execution phase, if approached correctly, will be full of tangible outputs that "realize" in the "metal" the new product or service. Drawings, tooling, production facilities, service manuals, etc.—all of these tangible things feel like progress, and so there is constant pressure in NPD to leave exploration as quickly as possible and start execution in order to do it faster, right?

Wrong.

The importance of the promise point

Over the years we have developed our concept of the promise point. This is defined as the point at which guarantees are given to people outside the project about outcomes. This can be a variety of things such as costs, timescales, capability, availability, etc. Earlier in the book we saw how the games manufacturer made the promise point well before the product launch and got things wrong. We believe that the earliest possible promise point can only be achieved once you have finished the "what don't we know" portion of the exploration phase. In fact we know that if this was done, it would be a rare case where the "what we don't we know" subphase will not have highlighted that the customer needs are things we have seen before and that the project goals can be met with existing solution combinations. We have illustrated the earliest point the promise point should be in fig 3.4 but suggest this would still be a rare case.

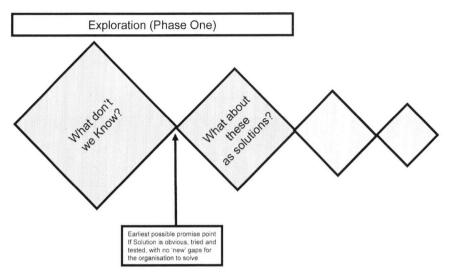

Figure 3.4 Visual Overview of the SDS approach – The earliest possible promise point

Real-world promise point

The reality for most projects is that gaps will exist even when you have a clear sense of "what we don't know" and "what we think the solutions should be." Most organizations get caught out here as those waiting for the next new thing want to drag out of the organization any information they can and a promise point unwittingly occurs during the "what about these solutions?" phase. As we write this, we pay respect to Apple, which is resisting all kinds of clamour to divulge information regarding the iPhone 5 and thus avoiding a train wreck. Many times we have seen the dreaded replan and reforecast due to unexpected test results even when "standard" solutions are combined. So our advice is not only to be aware of the promise point, but also to decide very carefully where you place it, as it will affect your project. We are not saying that there is never a place for JFK-style "this decade, let's put a man on the moon" (if you'll forgive the paraphrase) projects, but don't unwittingly turn every project into one as some kind of motivation because it does not work. Unfortunately we have seen many leaders and marketing professionals do this and it just annoys their staff.

Our advice for a more predictable world is to follow the model below.

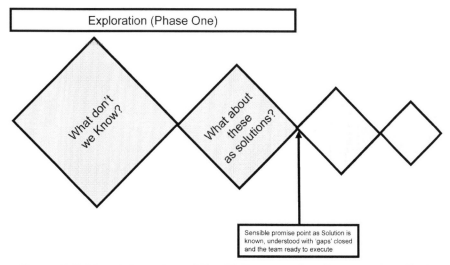

Figure 3.5 Visual Overview of the SDS approach – Suggested earliest promise point

To do otherwise is invariably going to lead to unmet expectations and some form of losses to your organization. As we said, we always watched Steve Jobs with admiration as he resisted all pressure to prematurely reveal the next new thing or when it would be ready. Apple simply announces a press conference and then reveals the new product, and hence they don't play Russian roulette each time they have something new to sell.

In summary, the highest level is the timeline of a project using the Simpler Design System℠. It has two distinct phases, exploration and execution, and each of those breaks down into two diamonds. The promise point is usually never earlier than the end of exploration.

Let us now explore what is happening in more detail.

The Subphases

This next level of detail will be as far as we shall go in describing the overall ideal NPD process. The reason is that

below this level we are typically into using individual tools and techniques and these are described in Chapter 6. We advise similarly making sure that any description of your system is not dragged down into describing the minutiae of tools and techniques. Have people understand the guiding principles first.

So what is happening during the first half of "what don't we know"?

Essentially this is best done as a multidisciplinary conversation of the most experienced technical staff from each area. The initial aim is to understand the needs from the perspective of all stakeholders; we call this approach *Design-for-X* (as different from, say, design-for-manufacture, or design to cost). X denotes any number of stakeholders. Hence you have to be considering all angles from Day One, as the downstream-level risk for getting this phase wrong can be multiplied by X stakeholders. We call this *X-risk*, and we assess project size and degree of challenge based on the size of X. It is a new way of looking at the size and complexity of a project.

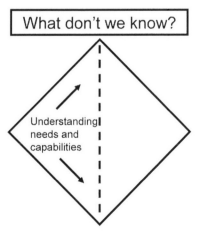

Figure 3.6 Visual Overview of the SDS approach – Next level of detail – Understanding needs and capabilities

As this part of the process is conversational and necessarily multidimensional in its nature, we see many different approaches and wildly varying levels of performance, from the painfully slow email-based discussions across strong departmental boundaries to rapid, face-to-face communications in a dedicated studio designed for such work. The selection of people here is critical, as you need people from all stakeholders who are smart enough to *know what they don't know* and are comfortable enough to say so in a group setting! This by its nature will be an expansive discussion and care must be taken to allow adequate discussion to ensure all issues and unknowns are out in the open. Deliberate effort has to be maintained to avoid closing down the dialogue too early with quick decisions. Human Resource professionals can help here and use personality type tools to identify those more amenable to working at this stage. Those who are not would probably be very stressed by it.

Conversely, in the second half of the "what don't we know" diamond, the team will be starting to fix the focus of their learning and knowledge generation. As needs become refined and better understood, the gaps in current knowledge and capabilities will become clearer.

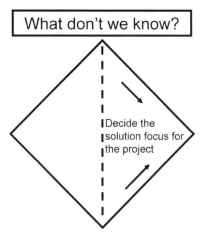

What don't we know?

Decide the solution focus for the project

Figure 3.7 Visual Overview of the SDS approach – Next level of detail – Solution focus

The multidisciplinary team that started this diamond therefore must be the team that finishes it, and they must catalogue three key aspects:

1. Their discussions, rationale, and content.

2. Whether or not they have layered their challenge using systems thinking; if so, they must describe their layering and the reasons behind it.

3. The new organizational learning gained as a result. Note: This is not individual learning we are talking about, but collective learning.

We recommend an internal-team-only review halfway through this first diamond and a wider stakeholder review before moving to the second diamond in the exploration phase.

The second diamond within the exploration phase asks: "What about these solutions?" It is a simultaneous generation and study of multiple solutions aimed at a combination of what best meets the needs of the project and its stakeholders. We suggest that along with the suggested focus on knowledge gap(s) agreed from the previous phase ("what don't we know?"), the key is to avoid homing in quickly on one single solution and to keep the collective mind open to many solutions. It is a difficult discipline for those used to being in organizations that value decisiveness and who managers possess hurry-up genes in abundance, but while still in the overall exploration phase it really pays to "rush slowly" with an open mind. It was by observing this kind of approach in Toyota that early Lean writers triggered the much misunderstood and perhaps in hindsight badly named "concurrent" engineering approach. We simply say keep your options open and alive.

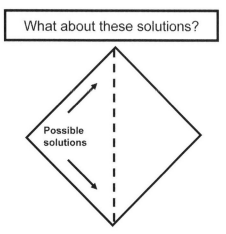

Figure 3.8 Visual Overview of the SDS approach – Next level of detail –
Possible solutions

The rewards for persevering with what feels like inefficiency—pursuing many concepts simultaneously—are not only enhanced organizational learning, but nine times out of ten also is a bigger resulting set of knowledge that will be highly useful for the next subphase. That is why it pays to do the counterintuitive thing.

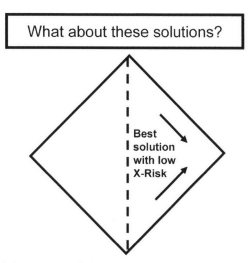

Figure 3.9 Visual Overview of the SDS approach – Next level of detail –
Best solution

By keeping options open when working through the "best possible solution" subphase, the team will invariably narrow collectively to what we call a "super concept." This often has many attributes from the number of concepts explored in the previous subphase. This always results in much richer solutions and greater breakthroughs than the more typical "pick a winner and work it to conclusion" approach. At the end of the second half of this second diamond, the team will have a hybrid solution which is a composite of the best elements from each possible solution approach and hence presents the lowest level of X-risk that we talked about earlier. Narrowing down is pursued until the solution is fixed and all required knowledge gaps have been explored and resolved through breakthroughs, trade-offs, or conscious compromise.

From the outside, a company working this way always seems to have a ready solution no matter what happens. This apparent luck is actually planned and designed into the process.

At this point the promise point can be made, keeping inherent risk in the project to a minimum. Our advice is that these first two diamonds should always be kept in-house, away from the public gaze, with only the involvement of outside strategic partners who can respect your strategic privacy.

If this process is compromised in any way, we always observe that it leads to declaring victory too early and often compromising work yet to be done. The aim is to move into the execution phase such that the team can concentrate on exactly that alone: execution.

The execution phase

This phase breaks down as shown earlier into the subphases of detail "design" and production.

Let us now look into what is happening in each of the two subphases within execution. We have labelled the third diamond detail "design" and definition.

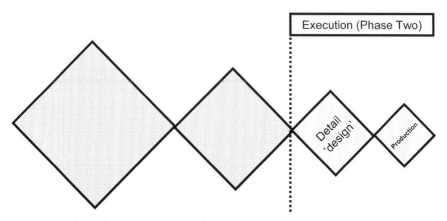

Figure 3.10 Visual Overview of the SDS approach – Execution Phase

All of the big questions have been resolved and we now need to complete all the detail in the project. Depending on your industry, this can include:

1. Technical drawings

2. Computer code generation

3. Supplier contracts and part approvals

4. Production tooling designs

5. Validation and verification testing

6. Production facility designs

7. Manufacturing process validations

8. User manuals

9. Service manuals

10. Logistic support analysis

11. Planned maintenance strategies and spare-part stocking levels

12. Training in the new product

13. Market launch activities and advertising

You can see that the resources required to complete all of this can be much larger than the exploration phase of the project, and so you only want to do all this work *once*. The quality of the decision making in the exploration phase is therefore critical to the success of the execution phase.

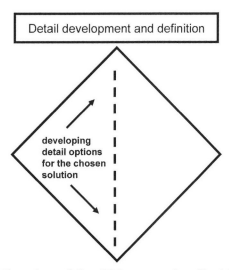

Figure 3.11 Visual Overview of the SDS approach – Next level of detail – Development of detail options

In the old world, "detail design" used to mean creating detail drawings, and in the CAD 3D world this means detailed modeling. But note we are suggesting that this detailing should remain a multidisciplinary activity, and if anything, it should be even more collaborative in nature. The idea is to simultaneously develop detail options for all stakeholders' aspects of the project, so while the designer is modeling their detail options, for example, the tooling expert can be defining tooling detail options; likewise, logistics people can be detailing their solution options, as can service support, etc., etc. Keeping the team in simultaneous working mode is paramount here. After

the exploration phase, the tendency to fall back into "easier," "safer" sequential working must be resisted. Also, the team may get lazy and fixate on single detail options without generating the simultaneous solutions required. The secret is to constantly challenge the team as to "what they *can* be doing" to maximize the potential of working with constant cross-team dialogue, and also to encourage the expansion of detail options, just like we encouraged the expansion of concept options during exploration.

Again, an internal team review is advised midway through the diamond to ensure wide understanding of the whole project across the multidisciplinary team. Having completed the expansive working, the team can then narrow down the chosen details and physically complete their definition. These will be the agreed-upon detail solutions which are the best cross-discipline combination to achieve the project goals. Pressing on with simultaneous working will collapse the lead-time to a minimum. Remember all of the major decisions have been taken in the earlier phase, so the level of risk left in the project should be very low at this point and reworking should be minimal.

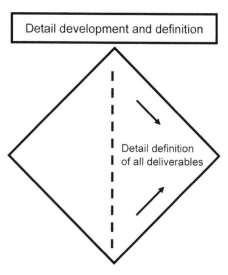

Figure 3.12 Visual Overview of the SDS approach – Next level of detail – Development of detail for all deliverables

The final diamond in our system is that of production itself. Most NPD people mentally switch off at this stage, and more than any other part of the process, this is where the "throw it over the wall syndrome" often appears. Of course, with the multidisciplinary involvement throughout the project as we have advocated, this should not be the case, but still, a planned ramp-up for production is required.

Production ramp-up:

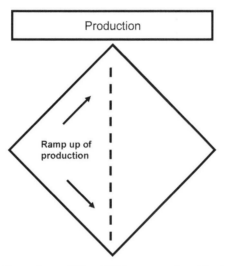

Figure 3.13 Visual Overview of the SDS approach – Next level of detail –
Ramp up of production

Earlier in the book we gave an example of a games console. Products of that nature are subject to massive initial demand that, if not satisfied, turns quickly into unhappy customers. Even if you are not in the mass market world, if you have followed the process as laid out by us, you will be dealing with the positive problems of having a great product. It pays therefore to stay as a multidisciplinary team to plan and execute the ramp-up and again not to slip back into sequential working, or worse still, "just leaving it to production." Sure, resources should be much scaled back by this stage, but that does not mean not being a multidisciplinary team. The ramp-

up plan will be much easier and less error-prone if the team remains multidisciplinary.

Series production and continuous improvement

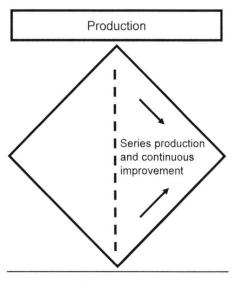

Figure 3.14 Visual Overview of the SDS approach – Next level of detail – Series production and continuous improvement

Given that many of the project's goals will not be fully realized until the actual production and delivery takes place, it makes sense to continue with the presence of a multidisciplinary team to help with the continuous improvement. In NPD terms this phase is also where lessons learned can begin to be fed back into the organization's knowledge base and as input for future projects.

At this point we often face the claim, "Good—we are already aligned, we are already working just as you describe. In fact, take a look at our documented process—it says so." We are then typically encouraged to see how our process fits and vice versa. The problem is when we scratch the surface with a few simple questions to see what people are actually

doing, the claims rarely match the reality. A question we typically ask is, "Okay, how much collaborative working is going on right this instant?" Looking around, do we see small groups of people in high-energy discussion? Are there many groups working across disciplines in real time? We rarely see collaborative work in real time, but we are told often about email threads that stretch over days, months, or even years! In NPD offices we often see individuals working at desktop computers with their backs to others or isolated in a cubicle (a Dilbert den) or an office. Open, interactive, studio-type environments are the exception. As a consequence of in-appropriate office space design, highly collaborative teams have a constant shortage of meeting rooms, or, in the case of over-the-wall cultures, meeting rooms are totally unused, and people see meetings as the ultimate waste of their time. We have found that how people view meetings is a great indicator. Are they a waste of time to be endured, or a place where you go and learn stuff that helps you do your job and the team make the right decisions for the project? Chris calls excellent decisions "the ones that are slightly wrong for everyone" because while win-win is possible, win-win-win-win-win to the x power is unlikely.

In summary then, we recommend that the NPD process not be detailed in any more detail than the principles, phases, and subphases we have listed. The idea is then to use tools and methods as appropriate based on their own "recipe cards" for instructions, combined with the retained knowledge of the organization. Having the team that will do the work fill in the detail of the process is a key cultural step.

In general terms, what we have laid out in fig 3.15 is the typical phase that certain tools may be used, but again we stress *as appropriate*.

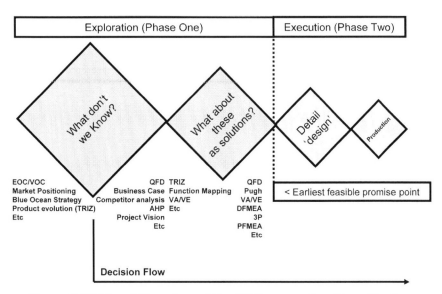

Figure 3.15 Visual Overview of the SDS approach – Use of tools

In Chapter 6 we will talk about individual tools and classify them as:

1. Ones that can be used as-is

2. Ones we have had to modify to work practically in the simpler NPD process we espouse

3. Ones that are used in a very stripped-down or re-configured way to fit the NPD process we have described

As a general overview about tools, we have found that around half a dozen are used throughout the above model, and while a larger number will be used, it holds true that 80 percent of the effect can be achieved using 20 percent of the available toolbox.

Finally, before the chapter on tools, a repeat word about over-lapping diamonds: don't. There will always be a situation where the desire to go faster will effectively result in the overlapping of the diamonds. In our experience, this is where projects get

into all sorts of problems and produce waste of overproduction. If you do find yourself in the situation where it looks like time is running short, it is *always* better to seek improvement in the next subphase than try to overlap the diamonds.

So what is it like to work on a project that has taken this approach?

A case study of applying Lean techniques in New Product Development

Back in Chapter 2, we described how a vehicle manufacturer that Rob worked with fell into the trap of not proving the fundamentals of their concept before investing in a lot of detail work. According to our model, this was a major overlapping of the diamonds. The predictable result was considerable waste as significant areas of the machine were redesigned as a result of fundamental flaws being revealed late in the project. To illustrate how these pitfalls can be avoided, we will use another client who was developing new technology for a sophisticated piece of medical equipment used in the radiotherapy of cancer tumors. As the project team started using the new Lean techniques, clear differences immerged in comparison with previous projects and that of the vehicle manufacturer previously described in Chapter 2.

For example:

a) When Rob joined the medical equipment team, the lead engineer was completely stressed by the task of planning the project and keeping the resulting Gantt chart updated. In this company the lead engineer was a senior engineer who had been given the task of leading the project team.

> *"I spend all my time trying to find out whether tasks have been started, how they are going, and when they might be completed. When I hit the print button, the chart is out of date by the time it comes out of the*

printer. I put a copy of the chart up on the wall but no one uses it but me."

Within three months the team had paused and planned its own "exploration phase" *as a team* and had soon pulled 20 percent ahead of the original Gantt chart. The lead engineer no longer managed a Gantt chart and the team updated its own plan on a daily, weekly, and monthly cycle.*

> *"Now that we are doing team-based project planning, I have time to concentrate on the engineering and solving technical problems."*

b) Team confidence in achieving the project on time increased significantly as the engineers saw that they were now being given the time to really learn what worked and what didn't in a sequence that minimized wasted effort. We have found that a major contributor to low team morale is the fact that engineers can instinctively see when they are investing effort in things that may not work without being given the chance to experiment and learn. Team morale then drops further when changes have to be made because fully developed prototypes are found not to function adequately. You will recall that the vehicle manufacturer described earlier had closed down their development workshop, thereby making any rapid testing of concepts far more difficult. In fact they made things worse by using production standard suppliers as opposed to development specialist suppliers.

c) The team worked on reducing risk from an early stage of the project, and so by the time the second prototype was produced, all of the manufacturing, assembly, servicing, cost, and performance issues had been solved.

So how was all this achieved?

The team had been working for nearly a year when we joined them with the aim of accelerating the project. Even though

*The team used a different method to plan and track projects (see Chapter 6).

a lot of detailed work had been completed (in this case, over three hundred parts detailed and an initial prototype assembled), Rob deliberately took the team back to the voice of the customer and used a modified and simplified quality function deployment matrix (QFD) to highlight what the project team did not yet know. By insisting that the team set targets and measurable values against both the customer needs and the functional features in the QFD, he revealed that many of the fundamental elements of the design had not actually been defined and that the prototype was based on quite a few assumptions. This is typical, and in the new product development environment, assumptions can easily become "facts" with no additional knowledge being learned. As former engineering leaders, we have both learned to be careful not to state assumptions too positively because technical staff readily take them as facts and build the next piece of work based on those assumptions' being correct. Also, the simple act of writing assumptions in specifications or reports can make them become facts if they are not suitably qualified.

Returning to the project example, Rob next had the team complete a function map. This showed how the primary functions were fulfilled by a hierarchy of secondary functions and allowed the team to concentrate on what the design has to do rather than what it is. This is an extremely useful technique which challenges a team to understand the design choices they have already made and the choices they have yet to make. The function map is also good preparation for some of the techniques that were applied later on.

What we were doing here was rewinding the team to earlier in the (uncompleted) exploration phase and the need to identify the gaps in the knowledge. QFD highlighted the gap in the understanding of the customer and in the specification of the design. A function map was used to challenge design choices followed by a modified design failure modes and effects analysis (DFMEA) to identify gaps in the company's design knowledge. (Instead of being used solely as a safety assessment analysis, we routinely use DFMEA to identify what design knowledge the team has that prevents them from leaving failure modes in the final design.) The fact that we had already done a function

map also meant that the team had a good understanding of how functions can be lost. In such analysis, we suggest that a loss of primary function is viewed as equally seriously as a loss of life. Overdramatic, perhaps, but for example, if a car repeatedly fails to start, it is hardly a safety issue, but many customers who are let down in this way will never buy your product again. The failure is the death of the brand or product. For this reason, failure modes that have an effect on functions are also important. The team in our example looked at the failure modes identified and defined the current design experience and analysis capability that they could use to design the failure mode out. For example, the equipment had electronic components in a gamma radiation environment, and the company's long experience of being able to predict stray radiation leakage, shield design, and specifying radiation hard components was determined to be enough to design a system with adequate service life. On the other hand, the proposed design used an optical positioning system with which they had little previous experience. Instead of "hoping it would all work," the DFMEA highlighted the knowledge gaps, and rapidly gaining this missing knowledge was made a priority. How bright should the LED light sources be? How sensitive was the camera? What was the best frequency? And how much light was lost as it passed through lenses and was reflected by mirrors? This knowledge became the "design rules" for designing this and other systems using the same technology and is thus never wasted, providing it is effectively captured for future use rather than residing in the heads of just a few people.

As well as identifying the gaps in design knowledge, the DFMEA highlighted another issue. Against approximately a quarter of the potential failure modes, the team cited the experience of a single expert as the only thing preventing the team from making that error. The expert was not part of the team, and when Rob went to meet him he found that he was within eighteen months of retirement, and much of what he knew was not written down anywhere! Again, this is not an uncommon situation and reinforces the need for effective design knowledge capture.

The team now had a pretty complete picture of all the questions that needed to be answered and the missing knowledge

to be found, and so they were realistically back at the first half of Diamond 1 in our model. Assuring them that this was in fact progress compared to the downward spiral they had got into, we then helped them to build what we call a "decision flow." The unknown targets in the QFD and the missing design choices in the function map are written as decisions that need to be made at some point. Against each decision we write the knowledge and information needed to make a good decision and identify what knowledge and information is missing. This needs to be obtained by research and experiment during the exploration phase. A key principle of a decision flow is that the risk of wasting work in a project can effectively be managed by sequencing the decisions. This is done on the basis that the hardest decisions to change later must be taken first, and the easiest decisions to change later should be taken last. By "hard" and "easy" we mean the amount of effort and expense that would be wasted should the decision be changed later on. The sequence of decisions then informs the sequence in which information and knowledge needs to be learned and thereby the most effective sequence of tasks to achieve the learning.

The sequenced decision flow and the resulting sequence of tasks to generate the appropriate learning can have a profound and positive impact on an engineering team. No longer are they being pushed in the "get a drawing completed by the end of the month" model. Instead they are being encouraged to learn what is important and the drawing or CAD model is reduced to its rightful role as a convenient way of recording the subsequent decisions and design choices once sufficient knowledge has been gained. This is what we mean when we say "change your projects to being learning-based instead of task-based." Also note that subtly the project team are pulling knowledge from each other rather than being pushed by others to complete tasks.

The decision flow has a rather unique quality in that there are no actual tasks listed on it, just decisions and learning against a timeline. You will remember that the lead engineer complained that his project plan was almost instantly out of date. This is because it contained mostly tasks, which change constantly as new information and problems come to light. That

is why task-based planning is inappropriate for this stage of a project. In contrast, the decisions that need to be made and the sequence in which you need to make them are largely unchanged as new knowledge is gained and problems are found. For this reason our decision flows are also known as the "project backbone," as they are a stable reference when everything else is changing. In this particular team the decision flow was still 100 percent valid after nine months.

Based on the decision flow, the team then produced a collaborative plan for the next eight weeks of activity. The plan was highly visible in that it was developed on the wall of the team room using Post-it notes. Each task was written by the person doing the task and so there was significant ownership. The owner also placed the task completion on an eight-week timeline and identified other team members who would be required to eliminate waste and avoid risk. No longer were tasks put in a computer by the lead engineer and then assigned to a team member.

Why do a task-based plan for only eight weeks? The reason is that the plan invariably changes as new information comes to light. To plan tasks in detail to the end of a project is always wasted effort, as it will have to be reworked over and over again. We have found that the decision flow with the timing of key decisions is more than adequate to keep the project on track and managers informed of progress. If we have a planning horizon of eight weeks, we then replan every four weeks, each time for another eight-week horizon. Instead of doggedly hanging on to a plan until it fails, we embrace the inevitable change and build it into the process. The key is that the team always targets completing key decisions on time to the decision flow. The collaborative team in our case study took half a day to plan the next eight weeks when they first started, but after only a few months they had reduced this to just two hours.

Finally, the team created a "team board" which they used for a daily morning meeting that lasted a maximum of twenty minutes. In this meeting the team members wrote on the board what they were doing that day and the next, and whether they

needed help from other team members. There were fifteen members in the team, and as a joke, at the start of the meeting, Rob made them stand on one leg while talking until they got used to keeping the information to that which was important! Instead of the lead engineer chasing everyone for task completion, the team was planning its own project and telling him on a daily basis how it was performing and what problems they needed help with.

You might be forgiven for thinking that the above work took a long time, but everything described above was achieved in two one-week workshops that were a month apart.

In addition there were other techniques that were used in the exploration phase to identify and solve risk. These included creating an effective collaborative working area, value engineering, process FMEA, production preparation process, A3 problem solving, and knowledge capture. These produced a design that has been widely recognized within the company to be the best the company has yet produced for manufacturability, cost effectiveness, reliability, and serviceability.

All the further techniques that made this project a success are described in a little more detail in Chapter 6, but for now the case shows that even projects that are underway can be recovered and improved dramatically.

Managing the Alien Within
Managers are from Mars.
Engineers are from NASA.

There is an old joke that goes: How can you tell the difference between an introverted and an extroverted engineer?

Answer: The introverted engineer looks down at their shoes when talking to you, while the extroverted engineer looks at *your* shoes when talking to you!

Most senior leaders, unless they themselves came from a technical background, would tell you they often find interactions with technical staff to be, shall we say, challenging.

In our travels we have seen a range of variations on a similar theme, but the general feeling is one of us vs. them, management vs. technical staff. They seem to be two different species trying to collaborate. Often technical staffs seem to suffer a lack of social skills seemingly in inverse proportion to their technical skills, and a lot of leaders seem to treat their technical staff with veiled contempt. This attitude exists in so many organizations that we have decided to devote a chapter to it, both in order to cover what causes it and to address how it can be cured. Any improvement starts and ends with people, and in the world of NPD the soft skills are the hardest skills. In this text we will use the term "engineer," but the behaviors are true of most technical types. The disparaging term "geek" is increasingly being worn as a badge of honor and so may be a useful term in the long run, but we believe we are a long way from integration with the rest of corporate society. Effectively managing and motivating the "alien within" is key to the success of any improvement initiative.

In this short chapter we'll first take a look at why technical staffs are different and how to engage them. We'll then discuss the broader difficulties of introducing Lean thinking into nonmanufacturing environments and nonrepetitive processes.

Understanding and motivating technical staff

Both authors are uniquely placed to offer insights to both sides of the divide because:

a) We are both engineers

b) We have both gone to the "Dark Side" as managers and then, worse still, into the parallel universe as entrepreneurs

So what is it about the techno-geek within that makes all others think we are slightly weird?

Reason number one is that we *are* different. We think differently than most "normal" people. Often from early years we have taken extra steps in our learning about the world. When faced with something new, most normal children subconsciously ask:

a) What is it?

b) What does it do?

At this point it is job done, knowledge acquired, let's move onto the next item...unless you have what *Dilbert* cartoonist Scott Adams calls "the knack." If you have the technical "knack," you are also compelled to ask:

c) Yes, but how does it work?

d) Yes, but what does the inside look like?

e) Yes, but is it a good solution?

f) Yes, but how can I improve it?

These extra steps and the insights they bring will mean a highly developed sense of expert opinion by adulthood and the acquisition of knowledge based upon the idea that "he who knows the most wins." Meanwhile, others see your extra "yes, but" inquiries as strange at best and a total waste of time (theirs and yours) at worst. Knowing stuff and knowing how it works is the route to kudos in the engineer's world, and improving things and inventing new innovative ways of doing things is the way to being a superstar geek.

Reason two is that because of their skills, engineers and "techie types" are used to being told *what* to do but not *how* to do it. The *how* is their job. They invent new ways all the time and challenge everything. They like to tell all who appear willing to listen why things won't work. Technical types seem to be pathologically pessimistic about proposals and solutions made by others while being eternal optimists about their own.

Technical staff the world over also have highly developed ideas about the way organizations should be managed and run which, while sounding plausible, seem on further inspection to first require that the whole enterprise think like technical staff.

As engineers ourselves, we had to learn the hard way that it truly does take all sorts to make a world. When we "crossed over to the Dark Side," we could also see the source of the dysfunction.

In contrast to the stereotypical detail-obsessed technical staff, most senior leaders have to manage from the big picture. Wading through detail drains their energy and stops them from exhibiting one of the key skills of leadership: decisiveness. Most senior leaders also seem to have been born with a "hurry up" gene embedded in their bodies which puts them constantly at odds with the careful approach of most technical folk.

Managers want assurances about timescales, resource levels, and budgets, while engineering projects by their very nature are dealing with unknowns. In many companies that we've become involved with, the means with which to do rapid exploration have been removed as prototype workshops have been closed and the willingness to build and test multiple prototypes has evaporated because it looks more like play than value-adding.

Furthermore, managers like to work on planning, countermeasures, and task-based management. Problems and variation in NPD are therefore approached in the same way as in production (i.e., treated as defects). Management typically calls for additional control mechanisms which increase the number of forms, procedures, reviews, tasks, checklists, audits, etc. While this kind of direction controls problems escaping in a recurring process, it is counterproductive in the exploration phase. As we said in Chapter 3, this phase is typically "conversational" and does not recur. A checklist approach can kill the value-adding activities of creativity, learning, and decision making. What is more, they can lead to contempt for management by technical staff. If your process moves more and more toward box-ticking and form-filling, you will soon find you are actually attracting the wrong kind of person to your work.

Technical staff understand this but sometimes lack the social skills to articulate the problem to nontechnical staff. They even have their own cartoon series called *Dilbert*, in which the hero uses a humorous engineering dialect exclusively to lampoon the hapless trio of the managers, HR, and all fellow colleagues. Of course, the whole joke of *Dilbert* is that the world never changes and the same joke runs forever: "I am surrounded by idiots."

Most technical staff not only believe that managers are from a different planet, but more dangerously, they see them as the enemy.

This can have truly disastrous consequences, none more profound than the NASA *Challenger* disaster. The voice of the engineer had become denigrated to such an extent that statements made in "engineering speak" had lost any sense of

gravity and were ultimately ignored when deciding whether the mission should continue.

Both authors have worked during the decades that have witnessed the rise of the professional manager informed by the new power bases of financial controller, project manager, marketing, and H.R. In many organizations it feels to us as though other groups are sending the message that engineering and operations have had their day in the sunshine and "we run things now." It is easy to see how this has arisen through the outsourcing or marginalization of many operations, especially manufacturing.

The trouble with this is without product or service, there is literally no *business*. So how do we re-engage with the technical staff and bring them "back into the family"?

We have found that one of the most powerful causes of low morale in technical staff is the setting of deadlines they have no confidence of meeting. The lack of confidence comes from unknowns in the project that they haven't been able to learn early on. So we are back to the thrust of this book: Do your exploration efficiently and then execute quickly. Every time we've made this happen we've seen morale soar, with dramatic impact on quality, productivity, and project delivery.

We believe that even though a minority of leaders are actively leading the deployment of Lean principles into their enterprises, those who do see a dramatic re-engagement of staff, providing the model for implementation is based on widespread involvement. In the same way we believe that the deployment of Lean principles into the part of the enterprise responsible for development of new products and services will yield similar engagement if leaders accept that it is a different application.

Introducing Lean in nonmanufacturing areas

Even in organizations that have done a good job at implementing Lean manufacturing, we almost always encounter

closed minds in every other function. Whether they like it or not, Womack and Jones' books on Lean have failed to change the mainstream perception that Lean is only for recurring manufacturing processes. To be fair to Womack and Jones, their first book, *The Machine that Changed the World*, genuinely covered the whole enterprise, but since then perhaps the adopters' own paradigms and the rest of the "Lean industry" has done little to sway the thought that Lean thinking is only for manufacturing and perhaps, at a stretch, some other recurring processes such as order processing and running the payroll.

The real question is why?

Most Lean thinkers start from a paradigm that values "process," whereas other people in the world of work do not see process in much of what they do day to day. To most people it is all just work. The Lean notion that work is made up of value adding or non-value-adding steps is not even held in most workers' subconscious.

Most people in developed economies would consider a job done to a standard process as being less prestigious and indeed would argue against their current work being made process-like and repeatable, fearing it would be viewed as lower value skill.

Lean thinking itself is based upon a post "mass production" mindset. As a result it has largely taken hold only in situations where the mass production style division of labor and production-line thinking was the previous norm. In Chris's previous book, *The Little Book of Lean*, he talks about the evolution of an enterprise through the following types of processes as they seek to be more effective and eliminate waste:

1. Artisan approach

    No common standards or formal process. The work is unique to the individual doing it. The artisan does all tasks with no division of labor. This is our two-centuries-ago inventor/producer example.

2. Craft approach

    Generally agreed standards of output with common approaches between similar professionals. No single standard process. Still no division of labor, with the single worker doing all tasks from start to finish. Most office work follows this model.

3. Mass production process model

    Division of labor into a production line/flow configuration. Standard work for each task based upon economies of scale thinking. Management of process by a "push" approach and improvement led by "experts" who can see the whole.

4. Lean process model (flow)

    As above but with one-by-one flow triggered by pull-based management systems (Just-in-Time). Ever-improving standard work achieved through the relentless removal of waste by all. Flexibility of output and configuration via multi-skilling.

The reason for these definitions and the ability to "type" your processes is to understand the starting point of your application and hence the view of those we are seeking to change. We show the likely perception in figure 4.1.

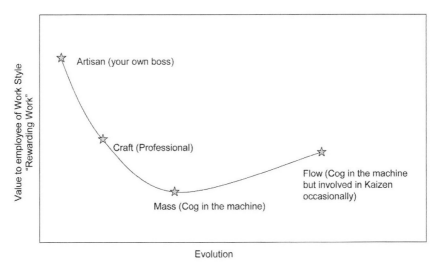

Figure 4.1 How Lean is perceived by different types of worker

Note: Most Lean thinkers, because of their manufacturing backgrounds, seem to believe that flow is always good for the worker without regard to their preferences. This is dangerous.

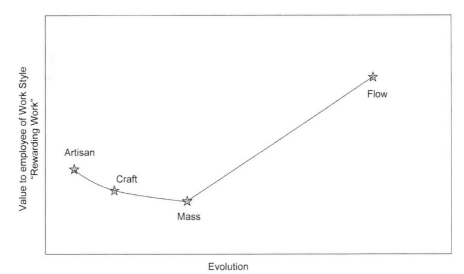

Figure 4.2 How Lean is perceived by those who have tried it

The reality is that neither view is completely correct for NPD work or the people who do that work. How it looks depends on

your point of view. If you are in a craft-like process in which you are doing a task from start to finish and then leap to a Lean- and flow-based process, it is going to be perceived socially as a backward step. Working days will be more boring, tasks will be repetitive, and the assumption is very little brain function will be required to do the job. At the time of Henry Ford's mass production revolution, this was largely irrelevant, as workers came from agricultural jobs and literally stood in line to work in the dry, warm, and more certain employment of a factory. But what about those working right now in our post-industrial society? What if your work is currently craft-like? You will not naturally aspire to flow-line type processes. Consider that almost all work in New Product Development *is* based on a craft approach and you see the size of the cultural challenge.

In a production situation you can, if sufficiently skilled, get craft workers to try a division of labor and flow-based work, but only if the downside is sufficiently offset by a significant or regular upside of improvement events that tangibly improve the process each time. George Koenigsaecker (*Leading the Lean Enterprise*) states that such a culture has to be improving at $X = N/10$, where X is the number of formal week-long improvement events per annum and N is the number of people in the scope of the transformation. This number of improvement events per year is only achieved by a very few organizations, and thus many Lean transformations fade after the initial fanfare. Also, this rate is for formal week-long events moving the organization toward a macro level future state. These *kaikaku* (big revolutionary changes) must also be supplemented by kaizen events (regular, informal local improvements) and *teian* systems (suggestion-scheme-initiated improvements). In a successful transformation within NPD, once the principles are applied, the culture is akin to every day being another kaizen, improving both process and product.

In a support function with recurring processes such as finance (e.g., running the payroll, paying suppliers, etc.), the processes *are* highly repetitive, but because most office-based work is done by a craft-like workforce, each person will point to high levels of variation and profess that "every time is different."

Lean thinkers will have heard it all before and know that when successive wastes are removed and you get people at least ready to try a lower waste approach, the end result is often a huge improvement based upon a highly repetitive flow of work based upon a division of labor. Most Lean thinkers therefore judge the change to be clearly for the better as is fig 4.2 but the same Lean thinkers can easily fall into a trap here because most assume that the same approach works throughout NPD.

The reality is that every project *is* different and that the exploration phase needs to be managed in a way that allows for creativity and changes in plan with the minimum of waste. However, the execution phase of a project can contain many tasks and processes that are repetitive in nature and respond well to the more traditional Lean techniques. The clear insight we've had is that without an exploration and execution phase in a project, even the repetitive processes of creating, checking, and approving drawings are hard to improve because of the disruption of ad hoc trial and error throughout the whole project.

As we showed in our case study, you can get artisans to work in flow as long as you and they:

a) Understand what should be flowing

b) Respect and value their need for self-determination in the way they work

We explore the techniques used in exploration and execution further in Chapters 6 and 7 respectively. In the next chapter we discuss how to change the culture of no into a culture of yes, and how to develop and reward technical staff.

Part B

Entrepreneurial Chief Engineers 5

As engineers raised and living in Britain, we have a common hero who really demonstrates what an entrepreneurial chief engineer is.

Isambard Kingdom Brunel was born over two hundred years ago in Portsmouth, England, and became a civil engineer. In a thirty-year career (he was fifty-three when he died) his designs revolutionized the transport systems of his day. He understood the need for the cost-effective movement of goods and he developed an integrated network of rail, ports, and shipping. Achievements attributed to him are:

- ☐ The first tunnel under a navigable river (the Thames)

- ☐ The first propeller-driven iron steam ship (at the time, the largest ship ever built)

- ☐ The world's longest suspension bridge (to allow tall ships to navigate further up rivers)

- ☐ Many innovative bridge designs

- ☐ Floating harbors that allow ship movements at any tide level

- ☐ Britain's first rail network and the creation of the Great Western Railway

- ☐ A railway line powered by vacuum

Brunel's innovative bridges are still standing today, and his bridge innovation was always driven by the need to reduce

operating costs for the whole rail network through optimum routing for gradient and bends.

Figure 5.1 Clifton Suspension Bridge, Bristol, England, the longest single span of its age

To improve the efficiency of ports such as Bristol, Brunel devised a series of harbors and lock gates that kept the harbor full even when the tidal river that connected it to the sea was not navigable at low tide. This was good for business.

Figure 5.2 Bristol's "floating" harbor

His commercial vision and engineering skill allowed him to extend the Great Western Railway further westward to North America by building huge iron-hulled steam-powered ships that were the largest ever seen but could travel as fast as the tea clippers. The *S.S. Great Britain* was the first. It was again business-driven innovation.

Figure 5.3 The *S.S. Great Britain*, the largest ship of its time

In 2003, Brunel placed second in a BBC public poll listing the "100 Greatest Britons." It's unusual for an engineer to be so lauded, but it shows we are not alone in our respect for the man and his achievements.

Crucially, what made Brunel an entrepreneurial engineer was that he could see and understand a business opportunity. He could also envisage complete systems that would better serve the market, and solve and implement the key technologies required to realize his vision. These are key traits of an entrepreneurial chief engineer and they are behind many product successes. Here are only a few examples of engineers who have created great businesses:

- Ichiro Suzuki, chief engineer for Lexus

- James Dyson, creator of Dyson vacuum cleaners

- Henry Royce, cofounder and chief engineer for Rolls-Royce

- Thomas Edison, founder of General Electric

- George Westinghouse, founder of Westinghouse Electric

- Bill Gates, founder of Microsoft

- Joe Cyril Bamford, founder and chief engineer JCB Earthmovers, Ltd.

- Jerome Increase Case, founder of Case tractors

- Soichiro Honda, founder of Honda

- Colin Chapman, founder and chief engineer of Lotus

We realize that those on the above list are famous, but we have come across entrepreneurial chief engineers in many of our client companies and throughout our careers. Wherever they have been allowed to flourish, they have created value and business success for their employers by creating innovative products that create new market space. Where these innovators are absent, we see companies with "me too" products using price or manufacturing quality as their main differentiator, with some justifying falling sales by declaring that they are content to be niche players. One such company that Rob worked with had told themselves that owner/operators who purchased their own equipment to use themselves were discerning customers who were prepared to pay a higher price for the comforts provided by their product design, which was over ten years old. In truth, the owner/operator sector had shrunk from 60 percent to 20 percent of the market in that same period and the company had no products to enter into the rapidly growing rental and contractor sectors. They lacked

a senior engineer who could conceive new products to solve the needs of the new emerging sectors. Without this, it is always safer to stick to what you know.

In our experience, the majority of companies that develop new products do recognize the value of entrepreneurial chief engineers, but few of them have a clear strategy for developing and retaining them.

In this short chapter we will explore some of the best practices in developing entrepreneurial chief engineers. However, if you don't already have them, they may be difficult to attract to your business and can take a long time to develop from within. So perhaps even more importantly for the short term, we will also show how the role of the entrepreneurial chief engineer can be filled by a trio of experts using the very same techniques we've developed to make Lean principles effective in NPD.

Finally we will talk about the importance of providing career progression for all your engineers parallel to the management career path so that your engineers have reason to keep doing their work, rather than seeking a management position just because it is the only route to higher rewards.

Attributes of an entrepreneurial chief engineer

It is pretty easy to recognize that Isambard Kingdom Brunel was an entrepreneurial chief engineer simply by looking at his astonishing catalogue of game-changing achievements that reshaped the commercial world of his time. But how do you recognize the entrepreneurial chief engineers in your own business?

Answering this question is not as easy as it might seem. At first thought you might think it is a matter of inventiveness. However, invention without a commercial purpose can be wasteful and sidetrack a company into investments that don't give a return. Entrepreneurs not only see how an invention or

new application can lead to commercial success, but also have the drive and leadership to bring that invention to the market in time. In this context we use the term "leadership" in a broad sense, since many entrepreneurial chief engineers do not hold line management positions and yet have tremendous influence over their businesses. In many situations the entrepreneurial chief engineer may not be the inventor but rather the one who saw the opportunity and identified the gaps, and then other engineers with more expertise in a particular engineering discipline did the inventing.

A "can do" attitude to problem solving

A key attribute of an entrepreneurial chief engineer is the approach to uncertainty. They revel in it. While most engineers are thinking about why things are too difficult and how solving unknowns will take too long, the entrepreneurial chief engineer has a "can do" approach driven by the commercial attractiveness of solving the problems. This requires viewing uncertainty and the unknown as opportunities. Entrepreneurial chief engineers know that solving problems that differentiate your products from your competitors' can create profitable market space. More importantly, they can see the critical technologies without which the potential solution would be commercially impracticable, and they go about solving these before investing too much in the project. They understand how to separate exploration from execution.

Creativity

In Chapter 4 we discussed how, as children, there are differences in the way we approach learning, with engineers needing to know *how* things work rather than being satisfied with only knowing *what they do*. Likewise there is variation in our levels of creativity, and these levels also change with age. Most theories of child development view young children as highly creative, with a natural tendency to fantasize, experiment,

and explore their physical and conceptual environment. This high level of creativity is not necessarily maintained throughout childhood and into adulthood. The level of creativity declines when we enter kindergarten and peaks again when we reach puberty. Research has shown that there is a large drop in creativity by the time we've completed our education. In many curriculums we are taught that there is one right answer or one best way. It is important to understand that creativity, intelligence, and talent are not necessarily related, and researchers actually argue that they are independent. For example, talent, in this context, refers to the possession of a high degree of technical skill in a specialized area, and the acquisition of this talent, through repetitive practice, can actually reduce our creativity. And there are many examples of highly intelligent people not being particularly creative at all.

Creativity is essentially a form of problem solving that involves problems for which there are no easy answers. In these cases popular or conventional answers don't work and creativity employs adaptability and flexibility of thought to see past the conventional paradigms.

We need our entrepreneurial chief engineer to be naturally creative, but alternatively, the modern engineer could be familiar with some strategies and techniques that bring structure to creative problem solving, such as TRIZ. For mere mortals not born as inventors, these techniques are explained in more detail in Chapter 6.

Education and life experiences

Entrepreneurial chief engineers need to be able to move quickly with confidence. They can do this because they have amassed knowledge and experience upon which they can build. They don't reinvent the wheel but instead see the gaps in their knowledge which need to be addressed in order to take risk out of a project, and they focus on these. They have an insatiable curiosity and never stop learning.

In our careers we have worked with entrepreneurial chief engineers in many industries, and there is no rule about the level to which they've been educated versus the life experiences they've accumulated. We've worked with engineers who could conceive and predict the performance of entire systems who hadn't attained an engineering degree. They'd worked their way up through the engineering organization from trade apprenticeships and had more than twenty-five years of direct experience. Conversely, we've worked with Ph.D.-qualified engineers who lacked the breadth of knowledge or business sense to be entrepreneurial. What is key in the entrepreneurial engineer role is that a person is at ease with and respected in the company of both, whatever his or her background.

Obviously, the technical complexity of your product will have a great bearing on the level of theoretical understanding and analytical ability required from an entrepreneurial chief engineer. However, our experience in developing very advanced products is that while the very highly qualified engineers are usually deeply expert in a particular aspect of the technology involved, the entrepreneurial chief engineers tend to be more generalists who understand how all the subsystems combine to create the overall product. They know the trade-offs between subsystems, and how system-level performance affects the profitability of the product. At General Electric Aircraft Engines, for example, the more entrepreneurial chief engineers were drawn to the systems engineering organization and aspired to become program managers. A program manager was part of the executive team that negotiated the deal with the launch customers and was then responsible for delivering the product to market, together with the profits that followed. They were responsible for the realization of the whole business case including production, sales, and after-sales support, and so their careers had grown to be far more than just the technical engineering.

Commercial and technical awareness

It would be too easy to say that entrepreneurial chief engineers are also businesspeople. But in reality they need to be

good engineers and have enough commercial awareness to identify the right products at the right time. They don't need to be good salespeople or have the leadership skills required to be a CEO.

Of course they need the communication skills to talk to all the commercial functions in your business, and the knowledge to understand exactly what they are talking about. But more importantly they need to be able to talk to customers, identify unmet needs, and understand the commercial potential of meeting those needs. This needs to be within the context of the maturity of the market and the product. For example, does your business need to find new applications for its existing technologies, invent new "disruptive" ones, or value engineer current products to stay competitive?

In Brunel's time the world was simple enough for a single person to acquire experience in many areas of business and engineering. In today's complex world of diverse technologies and markets, entrepreneurial chief engineers are more likely to be working with a team of technical and commercial functions. However, they will have the broad experience necessary to understand the trade-offs between business case, technical performance, product cost, project timeliness, and project costs. This experience, together with their experience of cross-functional teams, allows them to be effective brokers of consensus and even be the ultimate decision makers.

The ability to teach and develop others

In their book *Built to Last*, James Collins and Jerry Porras show that companies that sustain their success beyond a single generation from the founder have leaders who build organizations that aren't dependent upon their own personal skills, charisma, or ambition. These organizations have a sustaining vision or purpose, shared knowledge, and skills development at all levels.

So too we need the technical capability within our businesses to survive beyond a single brilliant entrepreneurial chief

engineer or technical expert. Our modern entrepreneurial chief engineer therefore needs to be a creator and teacher of knowledge and best practice. However, it is important to recognize that in this role they are not necessarily a preserver of rules and practices but will creatively seek or generate new ones when the old are no longer effective.

We have lost count of the clients we have worked with who had no technical knowledge management or sharing infrastructure and were totally reliant upon a single expert who jealously guarded what they knew because it gave them power and job security. These experts gave answers to questions rather than teaching the understanding of the fundamental knowledge that led to that answer. These same companies had no career path for engineers other than management positions, and they were surprised when engineers who had a desire to be more technically competent but no wish to be managers left because they weren't learning fast enough and there were no career prospects.

Compare this situation with General Electric's Aircraft Engine division (where Rob worked for eight years), which has a number of chief engineers who create knowledge and share it through a knowledge management system that has design rules, all manner of engineering data, and lessons learned. They work closely with new product developments and lead design reviews. In addition, there is a "parallel career path" for technical staff that provides a progression of levels up to the highly respected position of chief engineer, and this doesn't involve any line management positions. Not only do they retain their good engineers, but they actively encourage the development of future chief engineers through learning and the continued development of technical skills.

What if you don't have an entrepreneurial chief engineer?

At Toyota, chief engineers are known as *shusa*, and they have a minimum of fifteen years' experience of technology, market

requirements, production process knowledge, and business acumen. Toyota's shusas are able to progress their projects faster because they embody all three areas of expertise. They provide a consistent vision and direction as well as effective decision making. You can appreciate that finding potential shusas and developing their experience to the required standard is not easy, and Toyota has struggled to create them in pace with their expansion to become the world's largest car manufacturer. Toyota has rewarded technical knowledge and skill for decades, in contrast to many Western companies that have no parallel career path and whose only rewards are limited to management positions for a few.

So how can you fill the role of an entrepreneurial chief engineer when you don't actually have one—for example, when the engineers who invented and developed your products have all retired, taking their knowledge with them, and you've been maintaining the design with minor changes ever since?

The good news is that the techniques within the Simpler Design System[SM] can make the role of the entrepreneurial chief engineer initially into a team-based activity from which future entrepreneurial chief engineers can develop. Many companies already have product managers, technical experts, and project managers as well-defined roles in their organizations. The same effect can be created by using techniques such as voice of the customer, Kano, quality function deployment, design failure modes and effects analysis, etc., within a team which allows a trio of product manager, technical authority, and project manager to act as a tight vision-setting and decision-making nucleus within the project.

An example of this team approach comes from one of our clients, Elekta, for which the trio is a formal role in their project process, and a product manager, technical authority, and project manager are officially appointed to fulfill that role at the start of each new project. To be very clear, it is not the intent to have the trio make every decision. The same techniques allow for the effective communication of the objectives, strategy, and requirements to be communicated at growing levels of detail throughout the project team. It is only when a

decision might affect the objectives strategy and requirements that it needs to be forwarded to the trio.

Where do chief engineers fit into an organization?

In this and the previous chapter we have noted that many expert engineers don't want to be managers or actually have what it takes to be an effective manager. Companies that don't have a parallel career path for technical people or a chief engineer culture will struggle to know where these roles should fit into their organization. In three of his career moves, Rob took the director of engineering role and the management of engineering departments with precisely this issue. In all cases he inherited a situation where excellent engineers with many years of knowledge were in management positions in which their time was sucked away by administrative and management tasks that they neither were particularly good at nor enjoyed. In each case he created new positions for them as chief engineers which were senior but nonmanagerial positions and then empowered them to be both entrepreneurial and mentors in engineering best practice. In each case the "aliens within" started to enjoy their work and the organization could benefit from their core skills.

A High-Level Introduction to the Techniques

6

Introduction

We know that busy executives have a lot of demands on their time. The fact that you are still reading this book is indication enough that you're interested in transforming your new product development performance, but how much of the detail do you really need to understand before you hand this book to your technical people and challenge them to find out more? We've designed this chapter to be in enough detail for you to have intelligent conversations with your engineers (yes, it is possible!) without loading you up with technique-implementation details.

Some techniques, such as value engineering, are well documented, and Lawrence Miles' groundbreaking book on the subject is even free to download. Other techniques such as QFD are relatively common, but we've significantly modified them to facilitate flow in NPD and to right-size the effort of using it for different situations. In this chapter we detail how. Finally, there are techniques such as decision flow that we've created ourselves to fill gaps in the Lean NPD process. All the techniques are listed at the end of this chapter along with how much they've been modified to work in the Simpler Design System℠ process and the difficulty of implementation.

We've presented the techniques in a rough timeline starting with planning the evolution of your products through to capturing the knowledge and learning gained from a completed project. Throughout the chapter we also show roughly where we are in the "four diamonds model" presented in Chapter 4.

For example:

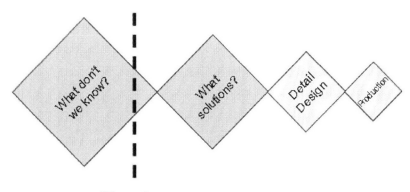

We are here

Figure 6.1 SDS visual overview – we are currently here

Here is a list of what you will find in this chapter.

6.1 Product Planning

6.1.1 Product Cycles

6.1.2 Looking for Market Space

6.1.3 What Does Innovation Really Mean?

6.1.4 Providing a Steady Stream of Valuable Projects

6.1.5 Systems Thinking

6.2 Determining Customer Value

6.2.1 The Environment of the Customer (EOC) and Customer "Pain"

6.2.2 The Voice of the Customer (VOC) Table, AHP, and Project Vision

6.2.3 The Voice of the Engineer and Quality Function Deployment (QFD)

6.2.4 Critical to Quality (CTQ)

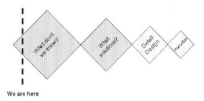

We are here

6.1 Product Planning

We have always been amazed at the lengths companies will go to make new product development projects "efficient" but then never question whether they are working on the right projects. Two guiding principles for both of us have been to make the process as visual and visible as possible and to drive quality as far up the process as possible. Making information both visual and visible is key to effective teamwork and spotting problems early. By "quality" we mean the quality of decisions and choices so that there is no need for changes, rework, waste, and U-turns later on. These principles start with the quality of project selection and the clear communication of the product strategy upon which it is based.

Being in the right market with the right product, at the right time, and at the right price may seem like a black art with the main techniques being the use of a crystal ball in the sales department or reacting to the customers that complain the loudest. However, there are ways of making this a more factual and structured process while still allowing the creative freedom that product marketers feel they need. Better still, the following techniques present product planning in a format which is readily assimilated by engineers, so you are much more likely to get the products you want!

6.1.1 Product Cycles

Before embarking on product planning and deciding how to invest your product development resources, you should consider

where your products are in their product life cycles. This is typically represented by a product "S Curve" which shows how "ideality" typically increases with time.

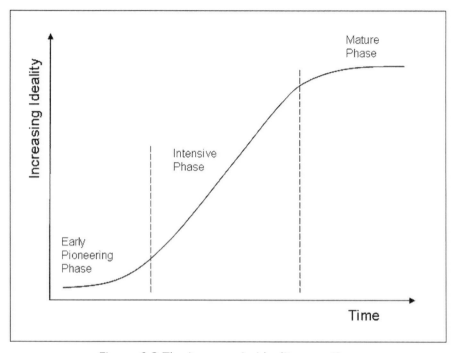

Figure 6.2 The increase in ideality over time

"Ideality" is a measure of the consumer attractiveness of a product. An ideal product gives the highest possible benefit (features and performance) with the lowest combined cost and harm. By "harm" we mean any detrimental effect produced by the product. It can be a wide range of factors from inconvenience, difficulty of use, and energy used to harm done to people or the environment.

$$\text{Ideality} = \frac{\text{Benefits}}{\text{Cost} + \text{Harm}}$$

For our air travel example from an earlier chapter, the ideality equation could look like this:

$$\text{Ideality} = \frac{\text{Speed from door to door + Service}}{\text{Ticket Cost} + \begin{array}{l} \text{Greenhouse Gasses} \\ \text{Waiting \& Boredom} \\ \text{Cramped conditions} \\ \text{Risk of Crashing} \\ \text{Contracting disease while on board} \end{array}}$$

In the early pioneering phase the product is new to the market, and in all likelihood the developer concentrated on producing something that actually works in the race to get to market. Products in this phase provide basic functions. There are usually very few competitors in the market and the competition centers on how well the basic functions are met.

In the "intensive phase," the technical difficulties of the basic functions have been overcome and the focus is on improving the ideality of the product. Performance is improved, cost is reduced, more functions are added, ease of use is improved, etc. Take for instance a mobile (cell) phone. The first units on the market were very large, had heavy batteries, and did nothing more than make and receive phone calls. You even had to punch every phone number into a keypad every time you called it. Over the last couple of decades this product has been successively improved. It got smaller, lighter, went digital, got cheaper, and acquired functions like phone number memory, speakerphone (so you don't irradiate your brain!), camera, text messaging, music player, GPS, web browser, calendars, voice recorders, and many more. All these improvements increase the benefit to the consumer while reducing cost and harm. No longer do you need pockets packed with pads of paper, diary and gadgets. Your phone does it all. In this phase there are more competitors entering the market and the competition is centered on levels of performance, new features, and, to a lesser extent, price. For example, the technology boom in Japan was fueled by Japanese consumers

wanting the latest new feature or improved performance, and the model they bought only a year earlier was now consigned to the attic.

In the mature phase the drive to increase ideality has slowed and may have even halted. There may be many competitors in the market, and competition is primarily centered on price for a given level of quality (reliability) and delivery (availability). Since there is less differentiation between products, brand and styling will be more of a factor. There are plenty of products in this phase and profitable companies supplying them. A client of ours produced railway track switches and the basic design had not changed for nearly a century. For many years the company enjoyed a strong market position in its local market due to customer loyalty. However, when the European Union expanded, lower-cost competition was able to enter their market without restriction and our client was driven to value engineer their product and Lean their manufacturing to first stay alive and then thrive in the face of these new challenges.

If a mature market is large enough to support the producers in it, the situation can continue for many years and even decades. However, the market is always vulnerable to a paradigm-changing innovation which takes everyone back to zero, and the s-curve starts again and ideality increases once more. This is shown in the illustration below. We've shown the new s-curve starting at an inferior point than the one it replaces, which is often the case. A good example is the move to digital mobile phones. Analog phones had been perfected over a number of years and Motorola was the market leader. Then Nokia launched its digital technology, and sound quality and signal coverage were clearly inferior. However, the improvements in function, features, and cost (ideality) made possible by digital technology soon outpaced analogue. In the new paradigm, Nokia rose to prominence. Lately smartphones have created a new paradigm shift and Nokia has suffered.

This paradigm shift can come from any company that understands the product cycle. With the railway track switch manufacturer mentioned earlier, we used value engineering techniques and identified an alternative design that was inherently

60 percent less cost, more reliable, and required no heating to prevent freezing in winter. Typically heating track switches requires about 14kW per switch, and so the reduction in operating cost and carbon footprint (harm) is significant. They started a new s-curve before being a victim of one.

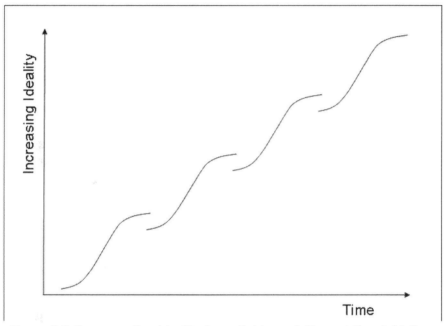

Figure 6.3 Compounding ideality by switching solutions at the right time

How is this useful to product developers?

Ideality as a concept is something that engineers can understand, and the fact that it must always increase is like the second law of thermodynamics. It gives marketers and engineers a common language and it is well proven that products that go against this trend are much more likely to fail.

More importantly, the work done by Genrich Altshuller in his theory of inventive problem solving (widely known as TRIZ, from the Russian *Teoriya Resheniya Izobretatelskikh Zadatch*) has shown that there are clear trends in the way products progress up the s-curve. Spot the trends operating in your market and you are much more likely to make winning choices

in your product planning. Winning by design should be your aim. TRIZ trends, once you can see them and use them, show you the way.

Additional innovation techniques within TRIZ, systems thinking, and value engineering that identify the leap to the next s-curve and progression up the curve are described later in this chapter.

6.1.2 Looking for Market Space

Some companies thrive on aggressive competition and the race to provide more features and performance at ever-lower prices. However, there are usually only a few winners in this race-to-the-bottom environment, and many companies operating in this space have lackluster financial performance. You only need to look at the automotive market to see who is winning and who is merely surviving in this intensive phase of the automobile as a product. Using TRIZ thinking, one alternative is to change the paradigm of personal transport completely and start a new s-curve. However, a less drastic alternative is to seek a market space with fewer or no competitors where your product can provide a unique value proposition. Chrysler did this with the minivan and the success of this vehicle is believed to have saved the company in the 1980s.

So far this sounds like "marketing jargon." How can we make this understandable to engineers and product developers?

The answer is to be able to express market space in terms of trade-offs. A trade-off occurs when an improvement in one performance parameter means compromise of another. On the laptop computers we have used to type this chapter, an increase in battery life is accompanied by an increase in size and weight, or a dimmer screen, or a slower hard drive (because it shuts down after only a minute). In a competitive market space the tendency is to try to match competitors' specifications and compete on price and brand. This leads to a proliferation of features that become more and more compromised

the lower the price. In an expensive hotel, for example, you get a high standard of service and many facilities. Some budget hotels attempt to provide all these same features, but the swimming pool is tiny, the carpets threadbare, the bed old and creaking, and the breakfast selection limited. The trade-offs are created by the price. If you spend more on beds, you have less to spend on reception staff and so on.

The situation is shown in fig 6.4.

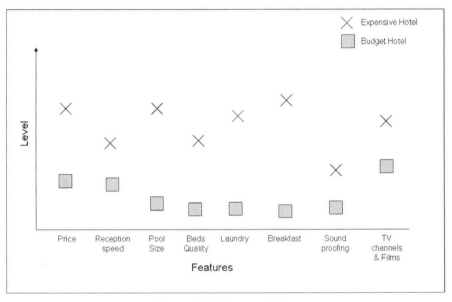

Figure 6.4 Gap analysis

If you overlaid competing hotels, you would find that those in the same price range may differ by a few percentage points on some features, and they will concentrate on this as the differentiator that makes them more attractive to a consumer. In reality, customers hardly notice these differences between competitors.

So how can you create your own market space? The answer is to solve one or more of the trade-offs that are inherent in your industry. This can be done in two ways.

The first is a marketing solution to trade-offs. This comes from the realization that you should concentrate on satisfying customer value rather than trying to match your competitors feature for feature. For example, a survey of customers seeking a lower-price hotel room may show that they have no desire for a small pool, a slow laundry service, or a limited breakfast selection. What they really want is fast, hassle-free check-in, a quiet room, and a new comfortable bed. In response to this, a French hotel chain has been very successful in cornering a piece of the market with a feature map that looks like the one below:

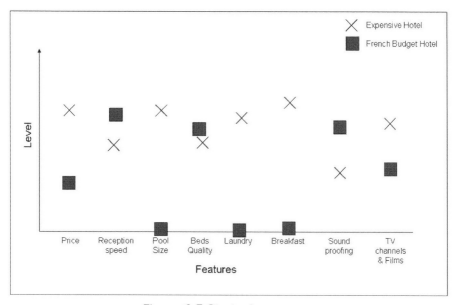

Figure 6.5 Strategic response

By concentrating on what is really important to the budget customer and minimizing or eliminating what isn't, the hotel chain has managed to provide a more comfortable bed, a quieter room and faster check-in than even an expensive hotel. For most of the time the reception isn't even staffed and customers get their room key or code number from a vending machine using their credit card. These cost savings can easily pay for the increase in performance of the features that matter.

If the above graphs look familiar, it could be that they are the same as the "competitor comparison" used in a QFD (quality function deployment), or maybe you've read *Blue Ocean Strategy*, by W. Chan Kim and Renee Mauborgne.

The second approach to solving trade-offs is through innovation and technology development. Here we look at the limiting trade-offs for the industry and select ones that can give us clear market space and competitive advantage. In the example of the battery life of the laptop computer, there are many trade-offs. Battery-stored energy versus weight and size; screen size and brightness versus power consumption; hard drive power efficiency versus cost; and many more. Engineers and product developers can focus on these trade-offs, and there are many techniques to identify innovative solutions. These include TRIZ, function mapping, and value engineering which are discussed later in this chapter.

The French hotel chain had a trade-off of speed of check-in versus the cost of more check-in staff. One technique within TRIZ is to take the trade-off to an extreme and so you ask yourself, "How can I have very fast check-in with no check-in staff?" This thinking led them to the vending machine solution.

6.1.3 What Does "Innovation" Really Mean?

Many company CEOs have told us that they want their company to be "innovative" and that they demand "innovation" from their new product development functions. In many cases this creates a lot of confusion, as the innovation has no immediate purpose except to serve the need to be innovative. Unguided innovation can be costly and many companies have struggled to be profitable with an innovation strategy.

We have found that there are a number of factors that are key to being an innovative company while balancing the risks associated with betting on technologies that aren't as yet widely accepted in the market.

1. Use the techniques discussed in sections 6.1.1 and 6.1.2 to provide a market need for your innovation or to determine the next logical step for the product's development to increase ideality. Apple's iPhone is a good example of a product combining many known technologies and provides a step change in ideality with many functions available in a pocket-sized gadget that is extremely intuitive to use and customizable to the user.

2. Consider being an innovator in a few of the key trade-offs that then define your product. For example, Toyota reached its position as market leader by being a "fast follower" rather than an innovator, but constantly improved the trade-off of reliability versus price. Honda is seen as an innovative company but largely limited the scope of its innovation to engine technology, solving the key trade-offs between performance, weight, and size.

3. Innovation need not be limited to new technology. A novel application for your existing technology can be equally challenging.

4. There is almost always a financial need to provide performance at ever-lower prices (which is yet another trade-off), especially when there are more competitors in the market. This may require real innovation, and yet many don't see this as "innovative" since there is no new feature or product involved. In our experience, projects of this nature can be many times more profitable than those on the "bleeding edge" of technology.

Dr. Robert Cooper depicts innovation as having the three dimensions of technology, application, and market. This is shown in fig 6.6.

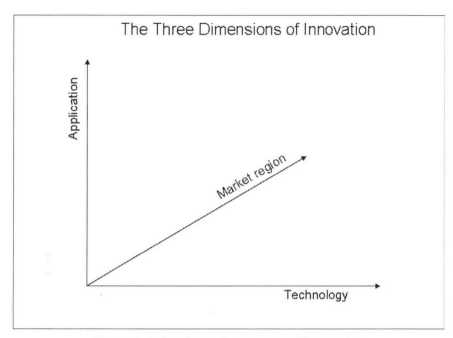

Figure 6.6 The three dimensions of Innovation

Since innovation carries many risks, you shouldn't try to innovate in all three dimensions at once, as this magnifies the risk even more. Instead, why not try new technologies in applications you know well in markets you understand? But more importantly, recognize that using your existing technology in new applications and new market regions can be as innovative as researching new technologies. This is reflected in the work of Genrich Altshuller, the creator of TRIZ, who discovered that only 20 percent of commercially successful patents contain a technology breakthrough. The remaining 80 percent take a known solution from one particular application and then apply it in another application. More importantly, both types of patent can be equally profitable for their creators.

A good example of innovation in product application is Lucozade. The company was founded in 1929 to make a drink designed to give energy and nutrients to sick patients in the hospital. It was successful, but sales stagnated as it saturated its market. There was a limit to the number of hospitals and

sick patients. Many years later the company decided that it was no longer content with this and challenged its own product strategy. They realized that it was not only the sick who needed energy drinks, so they rebranded Lucozade as "Lucozade Energy" and targeted the sports and teenage markets with great success. The drink itself remained unchanged. Once the brand had been established in the new application, the company followed up and released Lucozade Sport, which was a new formulation for its newly opened market.

6.1.4 Providing a Steady Stream of Valuable Projects

The ultimate aim of product planning is to create a stream of NPD projects that create value for the customer, generate profit for the business, and maintain a steady load within the capacity of your product developers. Why? Because NPD is a significant investment, the tendency is to load the developers as high as possible. On top of this the estimates of the workload and timescales are often made before the exploration phase has even started and well before the promise point described throughout this book. As we discussed in Chapter 2, engineers are eternal optimists and will naturally plan for "right the first time." The rest of the business is usually hungry for the new product and there is pressure for even shorter timescales. This can lead to even greater optimism and the blind hope that the first prototypes will work perfectly. Because there is little time, the tendency is to make the prototypes to production standard in the expectation that the design can be released as soon as the design passes test. This has the effect of delaying the prototypes so there is even less time to make changes if the testing reveals problems.

When describing this to clients, we draw on more than fifty years of experience in world-class high technology companies to say that empirically very few prototype tests go exactly according to expectation. Despite experience, education, and access to the combined design knowledge of great companies like General Electric and Rolls-Royce, there are always surprises. This is because the science of Newton, Einstein, or finite element stress analysis can only be used to predict the

exact behavior of a relatively small part of the universe. The rest is influenced by chaos. This is because the exact behavior of many systems is sensitive to factors that are too small to observe or complex to analyze.

For example, an engineering team working on a new hydraulic excavator designed a new hydraulic system for the machine. On the first prototype build, the machine developed hydraulic hammers that threatened to shake the whole vehicle apart. The problem appeared to be instability of load compensation spools in the control valve, but all attempts to solve the problem proved ineffective. After three months of fruitless trial and error, a happy accident led to the discovery that an elbow in a hydraulic pipe was shedding turbulent vortices at the exact frequency at which the spool mass resonated on its return spring. If the distance between the elbow and valve, or the spring rate, or the spool mass, or the oil viscosity, or the oil temperature, or the pipe diameter, or the spool chamber size had been slightly different, then the resonance would not have occurred!

New product development is full of variation, especially in the exploration phase of a project. It is therefore necessary to recognize that the right first time is actually the exception rather than the norm and to load your resources accordingly. To improve this situation, world-class companies value and develop better and better design knowledge that allows them to more accurately predict the outcome of system behavior. This usually takes the form of combining both theory and empirical data together with knowledge of system instabilities that can lead to chaotic behavior.

For example, a new jet engine needs to be proven to be able to safely handle the loss of a fan blade without threatening the integrity of the aircraft. This is done by testing the engine at full power and exploding a charge at the base of a blade. These tests can be hugely expensive since they usually result in extensive engine damage. The purpose is to show that the engine shuts down without ejecting high velocity parts that could puncture the aircraft and without causing vibration loads that could damage the wing or tear the engine off the aircraft. The imbalance forces that result can cause the engine to bend and vibrate to amplitudes well beyond the

capability of normal finite element analysis. Because the test is so expensive, there have been decades of research to improve the predictive analysis of an engine's behavior so that the full engine test is only done once. This involves the testing of pieces of the engine in smaller tests such as only the fan disc and shaft to measure the forces that would be transmitted to the engine structure. This data is then put into a theoretical model of engine structural deflections. The theoretical model may also have data from structural resonance testing of casings and shafts. This mixture of theoretical and empirical analysis is vital to only doing the blade off test the once.

The real question here is: What experience and knowledge capture does your organization have to reduce the time projects need to complete the exploration phase? How does that knowledge get retained for simple recall and reapplication by future staff?

Once you accept that you have limited resources and that these should be loaded to a level that reflects the level of experimentation necessary, you will probably have to choose which projects you are actually going to implement. To do this, the business needs to assess the relative attractiveness of projects that create new products, product features, performance improvements, or cost reductions. Many businesses use a calculation like return on investment (ROI) to judge the attractiveness of a project.

This has the tendency to draw attention to the larger projects since they will generate the largest returns. We have found that a better measure for the purpose of optimizing your investment in NPD is that of net present value divided by the cost of the project:

$$\frac{\text{Net Present Value (NPV) for the project}}{\text{Project cost}}$$

NPV is a commonly used measure of the profit that a project will generate over a certain time window minus the cost of

completing the project. These monies are discounted to the present so that inflationary effects don't skew the calculation. Normal time windows are three to five years. This ratio represents the opportunity cost for the money spent in NPD and a business can seek to maximize this ratio by choosing a portfolio of more profitable projects and by making the NPD process itself as efficient as possible without necessarily driving the business toward ever-larger projects.

Another way of comparing projects is to consider the *financial* benefits, whether they are technically *achievable*, their *strategic* fit, and the *timeliness* with which they can be brought to market. These four elements can be combined into a "FAST rating," which is just one of the many systems used by leading product developers.

Another negative consequence of realizing that your product development engineers aren't a bottomless pit of resources is that the collective mind set develops that a particular project is the only opportunity to change for a long time. This leads to as much as possible being loaded into the requirements for the one project. On top of this there is a tendency for the scope of a project to expand after it starts, a phenomenon referred to as "scope creep." A common cause is that projects usually start with a single purpose, such as adding some new features or improving specifications. After the project starts, more people get involved and special interests such as manufacturing, servicing, supply chain, etc. start adding their requirements to the project. You will find that most engineers are very willing to accommodate these requests because individually they all make sense, and before you know it your small and fast project has turned into a lumbering giant. Remember again the role of the promise point and how public you are with what is coming next. This can make it worse.

By now you've probably noticed that we aren't big fans of large projects that try to provide everything one can possibly think of all at once. We've seen many times that the potential for risk and the creation of waste in a project increases exponentially with size and complexity. Project management can easily become a function in itself, and activities required to

communicate and deal with the project complexity can soon outstrip the value-added effort of inventing and engineering the new product or its features. A parallel in the manufacturing world would be making a hundred parts when you only need ten immediately. This seems like it's efficient because the set-up time for the processes is averaged over one hundred parts instead of ten, and so the piece part cost is less. What has not been accounted for are the costs of holding ninety parts in inventory or what happens if needs change. The cost of producing the ninety extra parts is locked into your balance sheet and you could have used the cash for far more lucrative purposes. The parts cost money to store, keep clean, inspect, and count during stock-take, and take up space that could be used more gainfully or even gotten rid of. Also, when there is a design change, the stock of parts is at risk of being scrapped or you spend additional monies reworking to the new standard. In Lean manufacturing they have learned to only make what is needed, and in many cases this is in single pieces or "one piece flow" using the Just-in-Time approach.

Just as in Lean manufacturing, a Lean NPD process can be far more efficient if there is a steady flow of smaller, right-sized projects. This also makes load balancing much easier to achieve, since you have more flexibility in sequencing the work across different projects. This is rather like getting more material into a bucket, as shown in Figure 6.7.

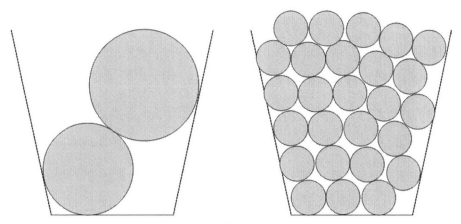

Figure 6.7 Increase flow for more capacity

The smaller balls fill the space in the bucket much more effectively than the larger balls.

This sounds great for a steady stream of new product features and performance improvements, but how can we achieve big things with smaller projects?

There are a number of strategies that can be employed here. One is to have a modular design strategy that creates modules that are independently testable with interfaces that are simple and as robust as possible with other modules. The simplest interface is one that simply bolts two modules together for support. More complex interfaces may have electrical connections, and more complex still there will be things like mechanical movement transmitted, fluid transfer, and data exchange. To achieve this, parts associated with a particular function are grouped together so that as much of that function as possible can be verified by testing a single module. This means that modules can be developed as smaller projects either in parallel or in series, and problems in one module won't impact other modules providing the interfaces are robust.

Modules can also be designed to improve manufacturing and supply chain logistics. The trend over the last two decades has been to source components from lower-cost economies that are often far from the final assembly and test location. With some shipping times being anything up to six to eight weeks, there can be a significant inventory in transit. If you then have a quality problem which only becomes evident when the component is fitted into the whole product, you could have up to six weeks of potentially incorrect inventory in transit that you may need to rework or scrap. What's more, this inventory isn't accessible and so there will be many more weeks of delay. We have seen companies airfreight large and heavy components long distances when such problems are found. A well-thought-out modular design means that the module can be assembled and fully tested in the lower-cost country and then transported safely in the knowledge that it is going to work when it is eventually integrated into the whole product.

Finally, modules can be chosen with your future product development strategy in mind. If the features you want to develop

further are in just a few modules, the speed with which you can bring these enhancements to market is greatly improved because you don't need to chase changes through a mass of interfaces.

The second strategy is to break a large project into smaller pieces through a strategy known as incremental development. This takes specific features and functions and creates them independently of other features and functions. After each "increment" the performance of that feature or function is tested and then integrated into the system that has evolved up to that point. For example, in Chapter 3 we told you of a construction vehicle project that created a vehicle that fell on its side when cornering. The stability of the structures and the universal joint in the center of the vehicle can be verified without the correct engine, cab, hydraulics, etc., providing that these can be represented by masses in the correct place in the structure. The first increment might therefore be the machine structures, and once defined, these are not changed. The next increment might be the engine and transmission, followed by the hydraulics. Each increment builds on the last and the sequence is chosen to minimize the risk of having to go backward. You need to have good preliminary designs of the product that allow you to simulate the functions you haven't designed yet.

Incremental development and modular thinking has also been adopted by the software development community who know it as agile programming. The concept of fully proving a small piece of code before integrating it into a larger package is tremendously powerful. To illustrate this, let's take a simple example of typing a report. I'm sure the majority of us have experience of finding a number of errors per page, whether they be spelling, punctuation, or formatting. Code is no different, and errors can be much harder to find. An error rate of more than one in a hundred lines is not unusual. So we can have a hundred lines of code with maybe two or three errors in it and it probably won't take that long to find them. But what if we had a thousand lines? How long would it take to find twenty errors, and would we find them all? Even worse, what if we had ten thousand lines?

This agile programming method divides code up into "user stories" which are pieces of functionality which can be demonstrated and tested from the viewpoint of the user and is usually a vertical slice through all of the elements of the system. To implement a single-user story might take small changes or additions to the user interface (GUI), the database, and a series of program objects. However, once these small changes have been made, it can be easily verified that all of them work in unison to deliver the function to the user. If they don't, you only have to check the small changes or additions you've made. This has been a cultural revolution in the world of software where traditionally complex code objects would be developed in their entirety before being integrated or tested. Developers and testers would work independently and even on different continents. In agile programming, user stories are planned jointly by the developer and tester, and the formal testing starts when the developer completes the first user story. In agile programming, a group of user stories is known as an "increment," and an increment is typically between one and two weeks of work. Some software developers have taken this concept to the extreme and have increments of less than a day. "Extreme programming," as it is known, works on products that can be easily tested or for which the test can be automated. Typically a day of work is regression-tested overnight. This approach of little changes and often, just like a Lean factory, leads to a huge rise in productivity and reduces the problem solving-load accordingly.

In summary, it should be a goal of product planning to provide a stream of right-sized projects that allow for both speed and efficiency.

6.1.5 Systems Thinking

When planning the development strategy for your product, it is useful to see it in the context of the larger system in which it operates. In many cases this can create new thinking about how you can extract value from a wider scope of

opportunity. For example, remember our client mentioned earlier who produced railway switches which allow trains to move from one track onto another. The system in which this product is a part can be viewed as a people transport system run by a city's administration. In this case they were considering urban tram and train systems. This system comprises trains, tracks, stations, passengers, electrical power supply to heat the switches so they don't freeze in winter, maintenance crews cleaning dirt out of the switches so that they can still move, the actuator to move the switch (supplied by another company), and many more. For all of these elements of the system you can ask why it is needed, what is needed, and how it is done. This then leads to the important questions of how it can be done differently and what advantages that would that bring. This thinking, and the use of creativity techniques such as TRIZ, led engineers to devise the new switch, which had an integral actuator, was self-cleaning, and did not require heating in winter because it could not be immobilized by ice formation. The new design increased the value being supplied since it also provided the actuator. Also, the cost of manufacturing the new design was only 40 percent of the cost of the previous switch and actuator combination. The savings to the railway operator were significant in reduced maintenance costs plus a power saving of around 14kW per switch.

So significantly lower costs, increased scope of supply, and every reason to ask for a higher price: not bad for an industry in which the basic design has been unchanged for over a hundred years.

We have deliberately kept our example of the railway switch vague because it is the subject of a patent application. To give you a little more insight into systems thinking, let's think about a lawn mower. It can be thought of as being part of a bigger system of social rules that provide accommodation for a community of people to a mutually acceptable standard. With this system in mind we can ask ourselves, why do we cut grass? Perhaps the answer is that it is our cultural norm for houses to have gardens that are pleasing to the eye, and

a relatively low-maintenance way of achieving this is to have a neat and tidy lawn instead of a very large (and high-maintenance) flower bed. This may get you thinking about how to make long grass culturally acceptable. Having a meadow garden in which grasses can grow to full height in some areas and ground-covering plants that exclude weeds in others could be an alternative. Perhaps a Japanese style rock garden would be even lower maintenance and provide an immediate creative outlet for the artists among us to create patterns in the gravel. Imagine launching a "rock garden starter kit" for all those tired of mowing twice a week. If this is too radical and society is immovably fixated on seeing a green quadrangle in front of a house, what about Astroturf? If it has to be grass, what about a genetically modified variety that grows at a quarter of the rate or only grows to a height of one inch? If all this sounds a little wacky or too mind expanding for comfort, that is because systems thinking and TRIZ thinking challenge us to attain increased "ideality" and ask how we can solve our problem using resources that are idle or wasted in the system of which the problem is part. For example, decomposing grass can yield biogases that power the lawn mower for the next cut. Imagine that the specially formulated grass-digesting bacteria are so efficient that the composter need be only a quarter of the size and will fit in any urban garden. Now we're into selling composters, composting powder, and gas storage systems as well as lawn mowers. And judging by the sales of the Toyota Prius, there might even be a "green" market willing to pay extra for this technology

If that's too weird, how about seeing the lawn mower as part of a system that includes other garden tools? What about the fact that most households have a "strimmer" that is usually easier to store than a lawnmower? For smaller urban houses and gardens, we could create a strimmer attachment that gives a striped lawn of consistent height.

You can summarize your system thinking on a diagram like the one below. You move up the levels of the system by asking why and down the levels of the system by asking how. You can then move sideways at any level of the system (think

laterally) by asking, "How else?" So instead of just thinking about grass removal, you can explore many alternatives at the garden and cultural levels of the system. Below the lawn mower we could have a "blade with a vertical axis of rotation" and then ask, "How else?"

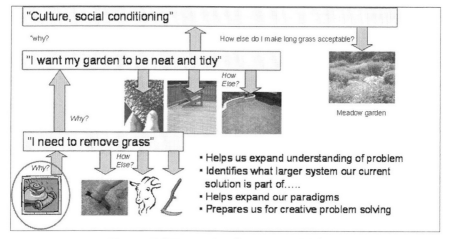

Figure 6.8 Example of systems thinking

Techniques like system thinking and TRIZ give the creative minds in your organization a structure to communicate with and they give the structured minds a method to be more creative. More importantly they give a common language of communication across your organization.

There are many examples of commercial successes that have come from this type of thinking. However, the human brain is conditioned to hang onto the status quo and fears the worst when considering change. In contrast, General Electric Aircraft Engines has a maxim of "try a lot of stuff and keep what works." If Victorian England's Great Western Railroad had realized early that it was going to be an element in a goods and people transit system, we might be flying Great Western Airlines today and paying tolls to drive on Great Western motorways. Instead the company disappeared with the decline of railways in Britain.

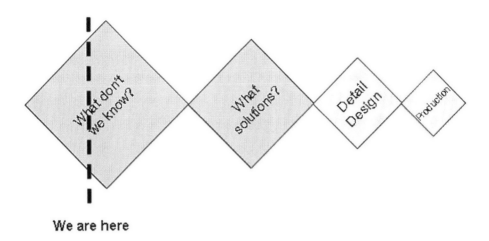

We are here

6.2 Determining Customer Value

One of our favorite examples of *not* thinking enough about customer value comes from the TV show *Dragons' Den*. In the show, inventors and entrepreneurs present business ideas to a panel of investors (dragons). If a dragon feels that the idea has potential, he or she will offer a sum of money toward the start-up capital in return for a percentage of the resulting company. In one particular program an inventor demonstrated a device that could reclaim used paint thinners by separating the dissolved paint back out and returning the paint thinner to a nearly unused (clear) condition. The inventor was clearly a clever man and had succeeded in creating a device small enough for a professional painter and decorator to have to hand for use at the end of the day. However, a few simple questions from the dragons revealed that the suggested price of the device was equal to the cost of many years' worth of paint thinners for even the busiest professional. Clearly the pursuit of the technology had become an end in itself and had become separated from the real need that it was intended to fulfill. Needless to say, there were no offers from the dragons!

Successful products have one thing in common: they completely satisfy a need at a price that is considered to be good

value. This sounds so obvious that it hardly needs saying. But history is littered with products that failed to do this. Some commentators even estimate that one in every three products get this wrong, and less than a third really do it well. A useful way of thinking about a "need" is by thinking about the removal of some "customer pain." The greater the pain that can be removed, the stronger the perceived need and the greater the customer value associated with it. In the case of the paint thinner recycler, the pain associated with consuming a liter of thinners over a couple of months and having to buy more at a relatively low price was very low.

Perhaps the most spectacular example of such a failure is the Edsel motor car, which was a Ford brand with four models launched in 1958. In three years it sold only half the vehicles needed to break even and lost the company $350 million ($1.6 billion in 2010 currency) "Edsel" is now synonymous with "commercial failure" in the USA. The primary reason is that its market positioning was confused relative to other brands and its innovative features, such as self-adjusting brakes, came at a price that no one was prepared to pay. In short, the project failed to identify customer value and to provide unique selling points at a price consistent with that value.

Compare the Edsel to the Dyson vacuum cleaner. The Dyson took away the pain of progressively losing suction until you eventually had to empty and clean the dust bag. This is also a messy operation, and unless you pay extra for disposable bags, which aren't particularly environmentally friendly, it was time consuming. The Dyson was the first to use a different solution of a cyclone to separate air and dust and so there was no need for a filtering bag. This unique selling point, combined with leading quality and robustness, allowed the Dyson to command a premium price which many are more than willing to pay. It also entered a very mature market with long-established brands, such as Hoover and Electrolux, and established a significant market share in many countries, and over 60 percent in some countries, including Japan and Australia.

In this section we will now look at more ways of identifying customer value and converting this into an engineering specification for a product that can most efficiently deliver this value.

6.2.1 The Environment of the Customer (EOC) and "Customer Pain"

As we've already said, it is useful to view needs as problems. Customers will place more value in products and services that completely solve their problem(s) without introducing new problems or waste.

As we briefly discussed in Chapter 3, the key to understanding what customers may value, and are therefore willing to pay for, is in the realization that they will typically only tell you a fraction of what is really important to them. The Kano model (attributed to Noriaki Kano) shown below divides needs into three segments to clarify thinking and is very useful to ensure that analysis is complete.

Kano Model

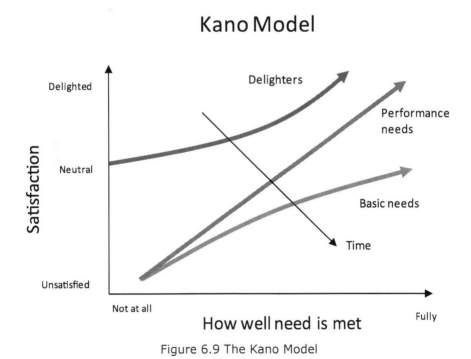

Figure 6.9 The Kano Model

Kano tells us to make sure we don't forget the basic needs that are never mentioned because they are taken for granted.

As such, they may never be explicitly asked for because they are considered so basic. The model also highlights the performance needs that customers use to compare products in the market and which they usually talk about when asked. Finally, Kano challenges us to think beyond mere satisfaction and about how to provide delighting features that the customer couldn't conceive of but are clearly value-adding once revealed.

The chart shows how delighted a customer might be on the vertical axis, and the extent to which a particular need is met on the horizontal axis. What Kano realized is that if a basic need is fully met the best, a customer will be is neither satisfied nor unsatisfied—neutral. For instance, if the sheets on a bed in a hotel are clean when we first check in, we are neutral because we just expect this level of performance without even thinking about it. On the other hand, if they are not clean we can be extremely upset because one of our basic needs has not been met. If we were to ask customers what they want from a hotel, they would probably list things like price, comfortable bed, size of swimming pool, quietness, distance to restaurants, etc. These are "performers" and they are used by customers to compare one hotel with another. Clean sheets are so obvious it does not even merit comment. The Kano model shows us that leaving a performance need unfulfilled causes dissatisfaction, but the more we fulfill the need, the more satisfied the customer becomes. Finally there are needs the customers didn't even know they had. To continue our hotel analogy, Rob visited a hotel and booked the room on the internet. Just before he was due to travel, he received an email giving him the local weather forecast, details of restaurants within easy walking distance, and the option to customize the contents of the mini-bar if he so wished. Until then he never knew he wanted this, but he is now continually disappointed that every hotel he has booked since then doesn't do it! More importantly to our thought process is that of course he would book that same hotel again. The important point about a delighter is that it is seen as high value. If the hotel had charged money to customize the mini-bar, it would have immediately lost its appeal.

Kano insights are best gained through observing customers instead of just talking to them. This can be illustrated by the laser-measuring device that Rob received as a Christmas gift a few years ago. He was restoring a house and had gotten fed up messing about with tape measures to get accurate room dimensions for skirting boards, studding, insulation panels, etc. The manufacturer, Ryobi, had obviously observed people measuring stuff and noticed what else they had to do at the same time:

- Write down measurements

- Add and subtract the results

- Calculate areas and volumes

- Make lists of what to buy at the hardware store

When Rob got his gift he was delighted that it also had a calculator and a voice recorder so he could do everything without pencil, paper, or calculator. These were true delighters since, on researching, he found that the price was less than £30, which was typical of a laser measure without these added features. If this maker is doing this consistently and continually with many new products, it is a very powerful strategy indeed. With a well-structured NPD process using the methods we have described, it can be achieved without massive investment compared to "me too" derivative products. There are many other sectors where this has been a very effective strategy in dislodging the existing power players. The Japanese motorcycle companies did this to great effect in the '60s and '70s and regularly unveiled designs with better features and performance than the then industry leaders.

Ryobi SW204V Laser Pointer
& Project Calculator

with Voice-Recording Function

Figure 6.10 Laser pointer from our example

We have come across many organizations that think that finding delighters has nothing to do with them. However, it is worth remembering the words of Fred Reichheld, the acclaimed business strategist: "The company that delights the most will gain market share. If customers are not delighted, they will drop you as soon as they have an alternative."

So what does that mean practically? Today it is typically the role of just a few specialists to capture the needs of customers and then transcribe them into specifications, or sometimes it is customers themselves who supply a specification directly. Problems start right here as each department reads the specification and interprets it differently. If we consider the Kano model, it now seems obvious with enhanced insight that

at least two-thirds of the requirement will not even be given voice, and hence the need to do an effective environment of the customer observation should be a given. Many specifications by their very nature call for trade-offs and performance breakthroughs that may be currently unachievable with existing designs. Many specifications ask for conflicting requirements that challenge existing paradigms. For this reason it is vital that engineers and problem solvers are always an integral part of EOC.

General Electric's Aircraft Engine business and the United States Air Force recognized this. They sent GE's design engineers to air force bases to experience for themselves the environment and pressures of keeping a fleet of F16 fighter jets at high levels of operational readiness in combat situations. Rob found himself in a chemical warfare suit trying to do preflight checks and maintenance on engines out on a baking hot runway at temperatures of over 86°F while being barked at by a chief master sergeant who thought he was far too slow. Chris similarly took his design team to a working air base to learn exactly what the customer meant by "easy to maintain." Imagine the team's embarrassment when their new prototype could not be worked through its touch screen control in cold weather with ground staff wearing gloves! Such (ahem) firsthand experience of "customer pain" was essential to creating the best design solutions, yet in each case customer liaison staff were offended as they had "already covered everything" with their customers.

Creating a Data Collection plan

Even in organizations that accept the need for more information in this area, we have seen this done as an ad hoc process that at best relies on the knowledge and skills of a few key individuals. For example, the service manager may have been collecting customer experience data beyond simply processing warranty claims. Or the technical specialist decided to visit a customer to expand his or her own knowledge. Or the marketing department ran a market survey a few years previously.

We've learned that a more structured approach is required, and we use a data collection plan. An example for our fictitious can opener, used in earlier chapters, is shown below:

What and why?	Who?	How?
Why do customers buy a particular can opener? What are their performers and basic needs?	Shoppers	Interview of customers in shopping malls using a range of commonly available can openers Comment box on warranty registration form
What is happening while the can opener is being stored and then used? Understand the environment.	All users	Ask employees to video record how they store their opener and to film their family members using their openers. Do the same with various organized groups like the Women's Institute or a student union. Offer a small reward.
What is the condition of old can openers?	All customers	Advertising campaign in selected stores offering a discount voucher for the return of an old can opener and its estimated age.
What would delight a mountaineer who needs to open a can? Can we create an entire new market segment?	Mountaineers	Observe mountaineers during expeditions and look for ideas of how to make the can opener "invisible" until it is needed. Focus group of mountaineers
How do our openers fail to please? What prevents repeat business?	All users	Deeper analysis and follow-up of warranty claims
What promotional material do retailers require? How do we get more shelf space?	Supermarkets and smaller retailers	Supermarket— visit headquarters and look at some of their outlets Small retailers— email questionnaire
What is the preferred packaging lot size? What is economical?	All retailers	Phone call of a representative sample

Figure 6.11 VOC data collection plan

137

To ensure maximum return for this plan, you would also include who should lead and be involved in collecting this data together to have wide understanding.

Documenting the Environment of the Customer

Documenting the EOC can take many forms. It can be notes and video of customers in the target situations for the product's use. It can be focus groups with customers or market research questionnaires. One of our clients chose to hire an anthropologist to help them understand what was truly going on in the minds of customers as they dealt with various problems and situations. These were summarized as "user stories" with photographs, sketches, and notes detailing what was happening and where there were opportunities for removing customer pain. Below is a photograph of just a small piece of the EOC observations "storyboard" captured during this activity.

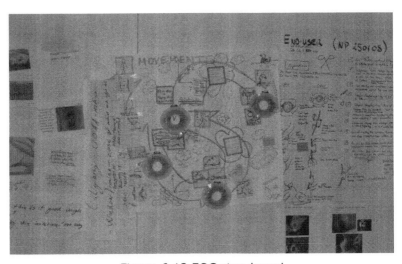

Figure 6.12 EOC storyboard

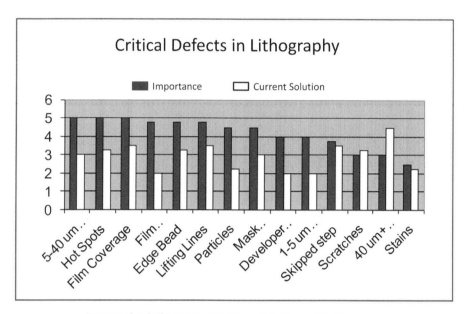

Figure 6.13 Customer pain v solution effectiveness

Another client takes a more numerical approach and creates graphs like the one below that show the extent of customer pain (importance) and the effectiveness of their current solution to the customer's problem.

Most simple EOC studies can be documented by the creation of a table of needs and "customer pain" sorted into the Kano categories. You can then review the list to make sure that all the basic needs are covered, that the performers are putting the product into the right market space relative to price and the competition, and that there are enough delighters to capture customers' interest and make your product or service the only one they want.

Such a table for a can opener could like this:

Basics	Performers	Delighters
Opens can	Safe to use	Hardly any force needed to operate
Dishwasher safe	Ease of use	
	Effort to clean	Doesn't rattle when you shake it
Meets market regulations	Comfort of grip	Retains appearance over time
	Appearance	
	Durability	Smoothness of operation or "feel"
	Price	

Figure 6.14 VOC sorted by Kano categories

You may wonder why "safe to use" is a performer rather than a basic need. Well, if one looks at the can openers available today, they currently range from those that have exposed blades and leave a can with sharp jagged edges to those that are very well shielded and leave the can with smooth, beveled edges. Clearly, the degree of safety is one of the customer's selection criteria among the many choices. However, there is also a "basic level of safety" that is usually specified by government regulations such as the European Union's EC Directives and "CE Mark." This is part of the basic "meets market regulations" need. The level to which your product exceeds this is up to you and is part of your product positioning. A common trap that product developers can fall into is not knowing the difference between "safe enough" and being totally safe. They then get delayed driving for ever higher safety levels (and cost). After all, if we wanted to be "totally safe" we would never drive a car or board an airplane.

This same thought process can also be applied to the need for reliability. Toyota used this as a very successful product differentiator at a time when the majority of cars had reliability problems. However, they made their cars "reliable enough" to be appreciated as better than their competitors but not to the extent that it totally killed their servicing and spare parts revenues.

EOC is a concept we developed with one of our early clients and is something we encourage before the next, more well-known step called VOC.

6.2.2 The Voice of the Customer (VOC) Table, AHP, and Project Vision

You may already have heard the phrase "voice of the customer," and you may have already associated it with quality function deployment (QFD) and the "House of Quality." You will be in the majority if you have also realized that many have tried to use QFD and the House of Quality only to give up because it seems to be more effort than it's worth. Don't worry. We have learned the hard way and simplified these techniques to only use specific elements of them when they are needed to facilitate speed and clarity in our process. In our context, the voice of the customer is simply our analysis of customer needs derived after the EOC study. The relative importance along with specific targets for each of these needs that must be met is the result. The "project vision" is then a clarification of what the new product development project is to achieve. This can then better guide engineers as they make decisions during the course of their project.

Understanding the environment of the customer and the customer pain that can be turned into customer value is an excellent first step to capturing the voice of the customer, and agreeing a project vision. However, before we rush into writing requirements, it is well worth taking a look at the customer's needs that we've identified from a different perspective.

Customers, product managers, salesmen, engineers, and anyone else involved in NPD all have a tendency to create lists of needs which are actually made up of:

- Targets

- Solutions

- Needs

Our clients are usually amazed when they realize that only about 50 percent of what has been listed as customer needs are actually true needs. The rest are stated as targets or solutions. For example, a customer may specify that they need components to be coated with a particular paint to a thickness of 0.1mm. This specifies paint as the solution to a problem and gives a target of 0.1mm thickness. But it is much better to ask, why does the customer want paint? For example, he or she might need corrosion resistance and the target is a life of ten years. Once the need has been stated in this way, you can think about alternative solutions to paint such as stainless materials, plastics, and other coatings such as plating.

An example from Rob's past is that when working on aircraft engines for military aircraft, the United States Air Force specified lower cost type 1 oil on all its contracts. It was assumed that the USAF needed this oil because it was the standard across all military equipment from tanks to ships to missiles. During the negotiation of one particular contract, it was explained that if a modern synthetic oil with good load-bearing properties were used instead, the shafts could run faster, the bearings could be smaller, and there would be a significant saving in weight and cost. USAF replied that the oil was specified only because it was copied from previous contracts and that there was no particular reason why it could not be changed! In our experience, "cut and paste" certainly has a lot to answer for.

This confusion of needs, targets, and solutions happens everywhere. We have clients who had in excess of two thousand customer requirements specified in their projects. When we looked at these again, we realized that the vast majority of these requirements are design constraints (solutions and targets) and only a few are true customer needs. What is more, the true needs are never all specified! In one particular case, fewer than sixty true needs were identified from a starting point of just under 2,500 requirements for a complex piece of military equipment. Perhaps more worrying is that some companies are driven to employ "requirements engineers" to manage (churn) these needs while other engineers write

test cases for them, and yet even more engineers conduct verification and validation tests. How Lean does this sound? What chances for error do these hand-offs generate? Once you realize, for example, that there are less than sixty true needs, and you've set quantified and measurable (and test-able) targets against them, the whole project becomes much more manageable.

So what does a VOC table look like? We've created one for our fictitious can opener in Figure 6.15.

Customer statement	Solution	Measure	Target	Need
Need a guard	X			
Needs to be safe				X
Doesn't rattle when you shake it				X
Large crank	X			
Low operating force				X
Easy to use				X
Must be as small as possible		X		
Must weigh less than 100gm			X	
Need to take on mountaineering trip and not notice its there until needed				X
Rubber on levers	X			
Comfortable grip				X
Positive grip				X
Attractive appearance				X
Needs to be blue	X			
Needs to fit in with my kitchen colour scheme				X
Needs to be easy to clean				X
Must be light		X		
Stainless steel	X			
Dishwasher safe				X
Retains appearance				X
Price less than £1 (Student)			X	X
Affordable to Students on a grant				X

Figure 6.15 VOC table

From the earlier VOC table we have above identified thirteen needs, together with many targets and solutions. Not all of the needs were in the original list. When we have a customer statement or observation that is a target or solution with no corresponding need, we must automatically ask ourselves, what is the need behind that target or solution? The first statement was "need a guard," which is a solution. We determined that the need behind wanting a guard is "needs to be safe," which we added to the list, since there was not already a statement that covered this. Likewise, the statement "needs to be blue" is a solution to "needs to fit in with my kitchen color scheme."

This activity sounds straightforward enough to most product developers until you have to do it on a real project rather than reading about examples like can openers. The immediate difficulty comes from being able to pitch your analysis at the right level. Too high a level and you end up with a very few high-level needs that don't give you any real insight. For example, after asking "why" a few times about the touch guard, you might arrive at "happy customers," and safety, price, color, comfortable grip, etc. all become solutions to this need. Not particularly helpful.

The problem is that there is no magic rule for deciding what the right level is. However, once you know that there is no right or wrong here, teams quickly arrive at a level of detail that makes sense and gives insight into what the customer wants.

For example let's consider the statement, "I want four wheels on my car." Is this a target for the number of wheels to give stability? Is it a solution (wheels) to the need for the vehicle to move with low friction? Or is it a customer need because they won't buy a car with either three or five wheels and they won't consider any other solution, such as magnetic levitation or caterpillar tracks? There is no right answer, but product teams will usually adopt what makes sense to them. In this case usually something along the lines of handling, fuel consumption, appearance, etc.

Another common problem occurs when customer needs and business needs are mixed. It is often impossible to compare a customer need such as "a safe product" with a business need such as "to make a profit" and rank them correctly. Earlier in this chapter we talked about setting realistic targets for some needs and so we may define an "acceptable" level of safety and an "acceptable" level of profit, but it is still hard to weight them relative to each other. We therefore split the list of needs into customer needs that are required to attract them to our product and business needs that are required for the business to invest in this project. Doing this means that we don't need to rank the two groups together and create unsolvable problems, since we have to achieve both. Without the first we won't have a successful product; without the latter we won't even start the project. Another of our clients has called the business needs the "project cornerstones" to differentiate them even more from customer needs.

We will use the needs gathered for the next step of our NDP process, but the identified targets and solutions are not wasted because they can be a useful input to what we call the voice of the engineer, which is described later in this chapter.

Ranking Needs

How can we best rank the needs so we get the right balance of our activities focused on the right areas? Obviously, asking customers directly to rank needs is better than ranking them internally. However, there is an inherent problem with trying to rank a list that contains more than five or six things. In the early days we used to distribute one hundred points around the list as per the textbooks. Bear in mind that the list might contain between twenty and thirty items, and there will be vocal people in the team with interest in specific items. What we found was that this process resulted in the majority of needs being scored around the average of between three and five, with a few scoring less and a few scoring more. The process can also attract heated debate as the special interests of team members are fought for. Actual needs can soon be forgotten as group dynamics take over.

The simple fact is that humans find it difficult to compare long lists of items but are very good at comparing two things one against the other. Is "A" more or less important than "B" and by how much? A lot or a little? Or are they equal?

This is the basis for a powerful ranking tool called a "pair wise comparison" or analytic hierarchy process (AHP). Don't let the technical name put you off. It is simple to use, speeds up the process, and increases accuracy with a surprising lack of argument. Teams comprising members with special interests often look at the results and agree that they are a reflection of the truth, even though the results rarely weigh the needs in the list around the average. Because descriptions of how AHP works are readily available on the internet, we won't go into a long explanation, but here is the essence.

First, before doing the analysis, look at the needs to see if any are actually a repetition of another need. For example, you may have "low running costs" and "fuel efficient." If these are in fact very closely related, you will end up assigning double the importance, since each need will attract its own score. Better to either drop one of the needs such as "fuel efficient," since it is part of "low running costs," or to correctly differentiate them such as by keeping "low running costs" and changing "fuel efficient" to "green" if that was the thinking behind it.

Below is an example for our can opener.

	Needs to be safe enough	Doesn't rattle	Low operating force	Easy to use	Not noticed until needed	Comfortable grip	Positive grip	Attractive appearance	Fit in to kitchen colour scheme	Easy to clean	Dishwasher safe	Retains appearance	Affordable				Weight
Needs to be safe enough	1.00	5.00	3.00	5.00	5.00	3.00	5.00	5.00	5.00	3.00	3.00	5.00	1.00				20%
Doesn't rattle	0.20	1.00	0.20	0.33	5.00	0.33	0.33	0.50	0.20	0.20	0.20	0.33	0.20				2%
Low operating force	0.33	5.00	1.00	1.00	5.00	1.00	1.00	1.00	1.00	0.33	3.00	3.00	3.00				6%
Easy to use	0.33	3.00	1.00	1.00	5.00	3.00	3.00	1.00	3.00	3.00	1.00	3.00	1.00				10%
Not noticed until needed	0.20	0.20	0.20	0.20	1.00	0.20	0.20	0.20	0.20	0.20	0.20	0.20	0.20				1%
Comfortable grip	0.20	3.00	1.00	0.33	5.00	1.00	0.50	1.00	3.00	3.00	3.00	5.00	3.00				10%
Positive grip	0.33	3.00	1.00	0.33	5.00	2.00	1.00	0.33	1.00	0.33	3.00	3.00	3.00				7%
Attractive appearance	0.20	2.00	1.00	1.00	5.00	1.00	1.00	1.00	1.00	2.00	0.33	2.00	2.00				7%
Fit in to kitchen colour scheme	0.20	5.00	1.00	0.33	5.00	0.33	3.00	1.00	1.00	0.50	0.33	2.00	2.00				7%
Easy to clean	0.33	5.00	0.33	0.33	5.00	0.33	1.00	0.50	2.00	1.00	0.20	3.00	0.33				5%
Dishwasher safe	0.33	5.00	1.00	1.00	5.00	3.00	3.00	3.00	5.00	5.00	1.00	3.00	1.00				12%
Retains appearance	0.20	3.00	0.33	0.33	5.00	0.20	0.33	0.50	0.50	0.33	0.20	1.00	0.33				3%
Affordable	1.00	5.00	0.20	1.00	5.00	0.33	0.50	0.50	0.50	3.00	1.00	3.00	1.00				8%
	0.00	0.00	0.00	0.00	0.00	0.00	0.00	0.00	0.00	0.00	0.00	0.00	0.00	0.00			0%
	0.00	0.00	0.00	0.00	0.00	0.00	0.00	0.00	0.00	0.00	0.00	0.00	0.00	0.00	0.00		0%
	0.00	0.00	0.00	0.00	0.00	0.00	0.00	0.00	0.00	0.00	0.00	0.00	0.00	0.00	0.00	0.00	0%
Total Wt	4.87	45.20	13.40	10.20	61.00	15.07	17.87	16.20	20.73	25.23	11.13	35.53	17.07	0.00	0.00	0.00	

Figure 6.16 Completed AHP showing weighted needs

You will see that the needs from the VOC table are listed both on the left and along the top of a matrix. Where the needs intersect there is a number which represents the comparison of how much one need is more important than another. A comparison greater than 1 means that the need on the left is more important that the need on the top. A comparison of less than 1 means that the need on the left is less important than the need on the top. If the two needs are of equal importance, then a 1 is entered. Naturally the diagonal, which is where a need intersects with itself, is scored as a 1.

Again, please don't be put off by the apparent complexity. Only the white squares were filled in and the whole analysis took around twenty-five minutes. We also can report that most technical staff love this kind of tool. We can already hear you saying, "That's for a can opener! How long does it take for a real product?" Having used AHP on a large number of projects at a wide range of clients, we have found that there are typically between fifteen and twenty needs identified, and only rarely more than twenty-five. The longest that we can remember spending on the analysis is an hour and a half.

So what numbers do we put in the boxes at the intersections? We've learned to keep this simple and use the following table.

Intensity of comparison	Left more important	Top more important
Equal	1	1
A little more important	2	1/2
More important	3	1/3
A lot more important	5	1/5

Figure 6.17 Scoring convention for AHP

The key to getting a good result comes from your post-EOC/VOC understanding of your customers. It may sound obvious, therefore, that those in the project team with direct experience of your customers should take the lead in completing the AHP. However, we have often found ourselves having to remind teams of this simple truth when engineers without that direct

customer experience are arguing for their particular favorite. As we keep reminding them, EOC and the voice of the customer come first, and the voice of the engineer comes next.

In practice, the mathematics behind AHP work no matter what scale you choose, provided that it's linear and consistently applied. We have learned the hard way that you have really lost the plot if you're arguing as to whether a comparison intensity is 68 or 69 out of 100! What is useful, though, is the fact that if you find an even more intense comparison halfway through your analysis, there is no problem adding a 7 (or 1/7) to the analysis. Also, you can add a 4 (or 1/4) if you need something between "more important" and "a lot more important," although in practice we've found that is rarely needed.

The relative importance of the needs is shown in the box to the right as a percentage. When the white triangle of comparison numbers is empty, this box will show all the needs as equal—all at 7.8 percent if there are thirteen needs. As you start filling in the matrix you will see the relative importance change. Needs that have strong comparisons in their favor will become more important, and those that don't will become less so.

When a team is new to these techniques, they will often realize—while they are completing the AHP rather than before, as advised—that two or more needs are actually repetitions of each other. This too is not a problem since a need can simply be removed from the analysis without affecting any of the other comparisons.

So what does the analysis tell us about can openers? The graph below allows us to see the data in the right-hand box of the AHP a little more clearly.

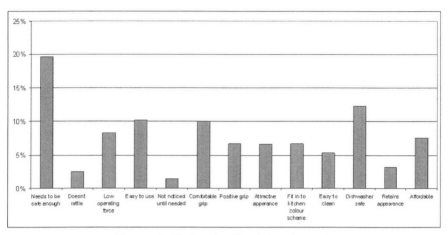

Figure 6.18 Graph of weighted needs

The most important need is nearly 20 percent of the total and twenty times more important than the least important. This is typical of AHP but almost never happens when teams use debate and dialogue alone to distribute points or to argue the relative importance of a long list. More importantly, the engineer who likes mountaineering weekends now fully accepts that the product will not be aimed at that market segment, and the chief engineer who thinks that a nonrattling design would be a "cool engineering achievement" now accepts that it isn't really part of the customer's selection criteria. What's more, if they can't accept this, all you need to do is revisit the comparisons that were made for those two needs and verify that they are still true instead of starting the whole debate over again.

Creating a Project Vision

You would be forgiven for thinking that all this work on customer needs will guarantee that your next project will deliver exactly what is needed. In many cases it will, but we've learned that effective visualization and communication of what is important is essential to aligning the whole team and the wider business.

To illustrate this, let's tell you the story about a quarry truck manufacturer that was related to us by an engineer who wit-

nessed this early in his career. It is so good we have been using it anecdotally ever since.

Imagine the product launch of a new quarry truck range. At the top of a quarry there is a marquee with flags flying. Executives from the manufacturer, major dealerships, and large customers are enjoying the canapés and champagne that followed the marketing director's invigorating speech about the future of quarrying and how the new range was perfectly suited to it. A band is playing.

Deep within the quarry, a truck carrying a hundred tons of stone is crawling up the ramp. Eventually it nears the top and the band strikes up a new tune with vigor, and all the executives come out to see the truck in action. The truck reaches level ground and stops before pulling away at a higher speed.

"Whoa! What happened there?" says the marketing director to the engineering director as they watch from the back of the crowd.

"Well, the driver reached level ground, stopped to change into the high ratio box, and then moved on at higher speed," replies the engineering director.

The marketing director looks horrified and gasps, "I thought we had agreed that the truck needed on-the-fly shifting from low to high, like the last series of trucks."

"No," the engineer says. "It was obvious that the clutch pack would never fit the under the new streamlined engine hood you insisted on. And all the transmission drawings clearly showed a dogtooth clutch at all the design reviews." The marketing director's face is changing to shades of red and purple.

"Dog clutch? What in hell is one of those, and how would I ever know what one looks like on an engineering drawing? The bottom line is we simply can't sell machines with the loss of this very important feature!"

Ultimately, the product launch was delayed by six months as they found a way to provide on-the-fly shifting at great expense and disruption throughout the company.

So what went wrong? In hindsight, the project team concentrated on all the new things that were required: sleek, streamlined appearance; more horsepower; tighter turning circle; improved cab environment; greater reliability; lower running costs. What was never made clear was also *what could not be compromised* as the new design was being created. Obviously, on-the-fly shifting would have been on this list from Day One! But in the absence of this list, engineers had to make trade-off decisions all the time, and as we have said, they will make assumptions if there is no clear guidance.

Equally important but also rarely discussed is what *can* be compromised. We are often surprised about how willing product managers and sales executives are willing to reduce performance or features in one area if it means better performance or features in another. This is in line with the feature map thinking discussed earlier in this chapter and is essential to meeting cost targets and guiding NPD staff as they wrestle with trade-offs and design decisions.

How can this be clearly communicated? A "project vision" is a simple document we have with four headings:

☐   What *must* the project deliver

☐   What *should* be improved if possible

☐   What *can't* be compromised

☐   What *can* be compromised

The name of this document conjures up something much grander than we usually see. Below is a typical project vision on a sheet of flip chart paper with Post-it notes on it. The beauty of this is that this can be hung on the wall of the project room so that everyone can easily see the simple essence of what was agreed at the start of the project.

Below is an example from one of our clients.

Figure 6.19 A vision statement

We are always surprised at just how many items are placed in the "what can be compromised" section. Before the AHP analysis there is usually a lot of debate and people arguing for specific needs. After completing AHP there is usually very little debate about what should be done.

This is a powerful step for the project since it creates the possibilities for trade-offs to achieve the objectives. In many cases the issue is not that engineers make unwanted compromises, like in the quarry truck example, but rather that they assume other compromises aren't possible. This can drive them to over engineer solutions that attempt to satisfy every possible need at extra cost and increased time to market.

One issue to be aware of is just because a particular need scores highly, it does not necessarily belong in the "must be achieved" or "must be improved" sections. For example, being "safe enough" scored the highest in our can opener example, and we would probably choose to put it in the "must not be compromised section."

Very occasionally it may also be necessary to split a need into two parts of the document. Basic performance can be in the "must not be compromised" section, and a higher level of performance can be in the "should improve if possible" section, but this is very much the exception.

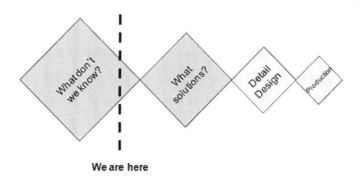

We are here

6.2.3 The Voice of the Engineers and Quality Function Deployment (QFD)

In Chapter 2 we discussed how engineers think a little differently from some of the other disciplines within the business. This is most apparent (and dangerous!) when marketing staff and customers are talking with engineers and it is very easy for ideas to be miscommunicated and for assumptions to be made without even realizing it. We all need a reliable way of translating the language of customers into the language of engineers.

Voice of the engineer

So what is the voice of the engineer? Simply, it's the technical specification for the product (or service). This needs to be stated at a level of detail that allows for the key features and functions of the product to be specified in a way that is quantifiable and testable.

For example, let's consider the need for a car to be stable when cornering. The voice of the engineer that answers this need could be something like:

- Number of wheels and size

- Wheelbase and track width

- Overall weight and center of gravity position

- Engine weight and center of gravity position

- Tire specification

- Suspension type and geometry

- Roll bar stiffness

Don't confuse this list with what some call "requirements." In organizations that have requirements management systems, this tends to include every possible parameter, such as the bend radii on the roll bar together with its material, length, surface finish, diameter, ball joint type, and many more. All of these things are important at some stage of the project, but not at this stage. What is important now is that we specify a roll bar stiffness that will work in the overall product design.

QFD

Quality function deployment originated in the shipyards of Mitsubishi where they were building very large ships such as oil tankers and cruise liners. Their customers noticed that the technical specifications changed depending on what part of the ship they were in, and this was seen as poor quality. They started using a simple matrix to make sure that the specifications were consistent throughout the ship and that they were aligned with customer expectations.

For many reasons, the words "quality function deployment" are unfortunate. They have a different meaning in Japan than in the West, and this has led to some unfortunate misconceptions. For many in the West, the word "quality" creates a picture of quality systems, inspections, measurements, and audits. Often it is something that the quality department does and others don't feel the need to be involved. To Mitsubishi, "quality" simply meant satisfying the voice of the customer, providing exactly the needs they want. We have equally found that there are many interpretations of the word "function" which are usually based more on the functions that the customer sees and uses. This results in an overlap with the definition of quality. The correct and more meaningful definition of "function" is the voice of the engineer discussed earlier. Finally, "deployment" sounds like a military term that means carrying out a plan or fielding an army. But in the context of QFD, it simply means "tell everyone" so that the required quality and function are understood throughout your business.

In its simplest form, QFD, translated by us, is a way of translating the voice of the customer (quality) into the voice of the engineer (function) and representing it in a way that is easily understood by all in the project.

A QFD is in essence a simple matrix that has the voice of the customer listed on the left-hand side and the voice of the engineer listed along the top. In the matrix we then indicate the relationship between the two lists. This can be numerical, but we usually start with an "x" indicating that there is a correlation between a particular need and the features and functions in the voice of the engineer. We insist that every VOC or VOE item on the QFD has a target value.

Here is what our simple QFD looks like:

Simplified QFD

VOC \ VOE		Feature (Target)	Feature	Feature (Target)	Feature (?)	Feature (?)	Feature (Target)	Feature (?)	Feature (Target)	Feature (Target)	Feature (?)	Feature (?)	Feature (Target)	Feature (?)	Feature (?)	Feature (Target)	Feature (?)	Feature (?)	Feature (?)
Need	Target	X	X										X						
Need	?		X		X	X	X			X			X	X	X				
Need	Target			X	X	X		X			X					X	X	X	X
Need	?			X		X					X	X	X		X				
Need	?			X	X		X	X	X					X		X			
Need	Target				X		X	X	X	X					X	X	X		
Need	?				X		X	X		X	X								X
Need	Target			X	X	X	X		X	X		X							
Need	Target				X			X		X	X			X					
Need	Target				X			X		X	X			X		X			
Need	?							X			X								
Need	Target						X		X										
Need	Target						X												

Figure 6.20 A simplified QFD

The true needs are transferred from our VOC Table onto the QFD, but now we add a target for each. In the QFD illustrated above we show one target per need, but in reality there may well be a few targets for some of the needs. Targets need to be both empirical and measurable. This is a crucial step because all too often needs are expressed in vague terms such as "easy to use" or "as high as possible." For example, "easy to use" could be the number of key strokes on a computer interface required to achieve a task, or the force that needs to be applied to a control lever, or the average time taken by a group of ten customers to read the operating instructions and make the product perform a particular function.

This is clearly where the "targets" from the VOC table can be used as a starting point. However, we have often found that this step has the team realizing that the targets from the VOC are too narrow or don't really apply to the needs that have been brought forward.

Target setting can also be extremely useful in making sure that project cost and time don't grow as a result of assumptions. One of our favorite examples is an IT project to roll out a software solution throughout a particular business. In the needs was the statement "global roll-out," and there was a budget of £60,000 assigned to this activity. No one questioned this until we set a target. We asked what "global" meant and found that it actually encompassed just three countries and approximately six key users. The budget was drastically reduced to reflect the real effort needed to translate into just three languages and train the six people—not what many would think of by the phrase "global roll-out"!

A key difference between the QFD above and those we've seen as part of other NPD processes is that where a target is not known exactly, we enter a question mark. This is because of our overriding philosophy of exploration and execution phases. Remember that at this stage assumptions can be the undoing of a project (since they all too easily are perceived as fact), so we only write in a target if we know it to be based on fact. To make this point clear use the well-known play on words that to...

"Assume makes an ass of u and me!"

These question marks against targets are a rich source for understanding "what we don't know" and this in turn helps us to understand "what we need to learn." For us, this is the key benefit for doing a QFD at this atypical early stage in a project, and the questions generated here will be used in one of our other unique approaches to generate a "decision flow," which is described a little later in this chapter.

We believe we are almost unique in starting our QFD as an incomplete document and then driving the project to get the missing answers. We have found that used in this way it works really well. We have worked with many companies that tried QFD when it became popular as a result of Six Sigma. But by comparison, the traditional QFD matrices we've seen that attempt to be complete are either full of assumptions or filled in at the end of a project as some

sort of retrospective record of the project. Further, doing it the more traditional way it can easily become a huge and cumbersome tool with far more detail than is necessary. In hindsight and with our new insights we can see why many of these companies gave up on its use shortly after starting. Problems start with not using a VOC table to separate needs, targets, and solutions, and so the voice of the customer becomes a long list. Then they confuse the voice of the engineer with requirements and this leads to there being hundreds of items on this list too. By then the team are wondering why they are struggling with all this complexity and repetition and morale plummets. So with those insights...

What form should a QFD take?

The QFD can take many forms, and the best is whichever suits your particular situation, project complexity, and team dynamics. We have used Post-it notes to best effect where team interaction is key, but the medium begins to have its limitations with teams much larger than ten people. Here's an example of a relatively simple QFD in Post-it notes.

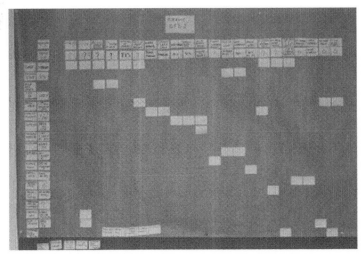

Figure 6.21 A simplified QFD in Post-it notes

You will appreciate that if there were, say, thirty needs in the VOC and maybe a hundred features in the VOE, the piece of paper required could become quite large. Thirty-by-one hundred is the largest we have managed in Post-it notes and still been able to keep it clear enough. One way of keeping the amount of information on a single QFD under control is to create a hierarchy of QFDs, and systems thinking helps here. A purely system-level definition is on the top level (QFD1) and lower-level features for each subsystem are captured on their own level 2 QFDs (QFD2). The photograph above just happens to be a QFD2 for the "frame subsystem" for a machine.

Figure 6.22 is an example of how a system QFD1 relates to a subsystem QFD2.

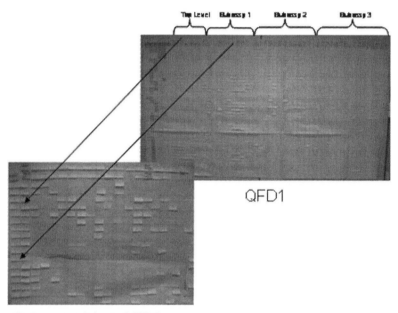

Figure 6.22 A system QFD1 and a second level subassembly QFD2

We have also used QFD with software products and the matrices can be become more complex than in mechanical hardware projects as there are usually a large number of unrelated

features at system level. Microsoft Excel can easily be used to handle these matrices, and the VOC and VOE are managed as lists together with their targets.

Applying QFD to services

We haven't given many examples of how to apply our techniques to services earlier in this chapter because we felt that product planning and VOC would be easily understood by someone with service creation on their mind. But how do you apply voice of the engineer and QFD?

Well, let's take a restaurant as an example. You might have identified that in your market segment people will expect to be served their starter within fifteen minutes of ordering and their main course no more twenty minutes later when the restaurant is handling a capacity of one hundred customers in a sitting.

So what would be the features and functions that provide a solution to this need? We are not expert restaurateurs, but let's have a go!

- Number of chefs

- Number of sous-chefs

- Special-offer dishes that can be partly made in advance because the volumes are higher

- Quick preparation time for starter menu (more time available for main course)

- Relaxed ambiance so that customers don't mind time between starter and main course

- Parties of over ten people can agree to a smaller menu selection when they book in return for speed of service

- Number of waiters (so that food doesn't wait to be delivered to table)

- Servers separate from waiters, who are always out with customers and not running in and out of the kitchen

We know this is a superficial example, but the point is you can see that the QFD is designing how the restaurant operates together with the staff needed and what they should be doing. It is leading toward solutions and combinations of service elements that can meet the needs.

Further understanding targets: Taguchi targets

Our understanding of targets can be further enhanced by using the concept of Taguchi targets. Taguchi found that there is an optimum target for a given customer need and that deviation from that target will cause more and more loss. This loss can be in the form of increased frustration for the customer or in the form of lost sales for the business as customers stop buying the product. Taguchi realized that this "loss function" could be defined and used to make sure that products or services were neither under- or over-designed.

An example of a Taguchi loss function follows. Let's take a pen as an example, and let's consider the fit between the pen top and the body. If you have one to hand, try this as you read. If the fit is too tight it will be a struggle to pull the cap off and push it back on. If it is too loose then it will feel insecure and may fall off. The loss function shows us that a deviation from the target in the too-tight direction is more severe than one in the too-loose direction. We can now create a design and manufacturing processes that assures the fit isn't overly tight and doesn't waste cost on assuring that the fit doesn't deviate a little in the loosening direction. Information that describes the sensitivity of the customer to variation from the ideal is therefore invaluable in assuring that all cost is focused on what is really important.

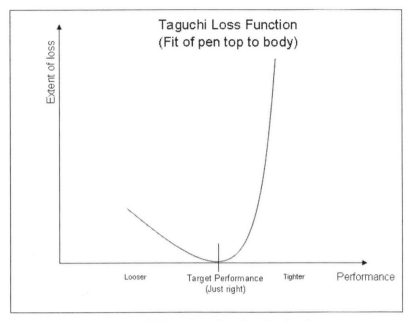

Figure 6.23 Taguchi loss function for the fit of a pen top

There are many other possible shapes to the loss function curve; two different ones are shown below. The curve on the left shows that there is not much point in reducing the measure below the target point. This is because there would be no additional benefit to be gained. An example of this would be the time taken to give the victim of a cardiac arrest medical treatment. If this can be given in around fifteen minutes there is virtually 100 percent chance of there being no brain damage. Any longer and the risk goes up dramatically. Knowing the shape of your Taguchi curves and what data drive them is invaluable to winning by design.

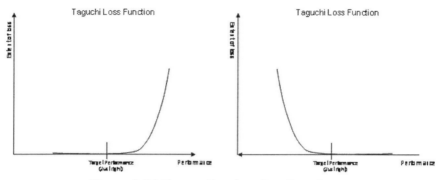

Figure 6.24 Some other loss function shapes

6.2.4 QFD Targets and "Critical to Quality" (CTQ)

Those readers who are familiar with Six Sigma may have come across the term "critical to quality" or CTQ. Ideally, these are the key parameters that ensure that the product or service meets what the customer actually wants. These are used throughout the aerospace and automotive industries, although they may also be known as "classifications of characteristics." They usually appear on technical drawings with symbols next to the features or dimensions that are critical for the product's performing to customer specification.

Both of us grew up with such systems in our aerospace careers where their use was actively encouraged. At GE Aircraft Engines there was even a sign above the exit from the drawing office which said:

"Have you classified the characteristics on your drawing today?"

or words to that effect—it was over twenty years ago!

The unfortunate side-effect behavior that this blanket thinking promoted was that engineers made sure they peppered their drawings with a handful of "critical" and "major" symbols to be on the safe side and to keep the drawing checkers happy with little thought to the quality system costs they had just

invoked. A jet engine has many thousands of components and a huge quality system is driven by tens of thousands of these classified characteristics. This may be appropriate to passenger aircraft, but few businesses can afford to run quality-control systems on this scale. Instead, many do the opposite with a diffused quality control of all characteristics with no focus on anything in particular. Rather like finding a needle in a haystack.

QFD offers a solution to this. The targets set against the voice of the engineer are precisely what is needed to fulfill customer need. For example, instead of inspecting every feature on a car suspension anti-roll-bar, just ensure its stiffness because this is the characteristic that the QFD tells you is vital to car stability. In other words it is "critical to quality." Most of the QFDs we've worked on have less than one hundred items in the VOE section, and these critical-to-quality targets can be used throughout your business to insure that customer needs are being met. We advise the use of the targets from VOE because they are usually measurable and tangible to the products or components themselves. In contrast, targets for VOC items are often only measurable during product use. Kano and the QFD provide insight into the customer needs behind a particular target, so people who weren't involved in the product's design can see quickly and easily why a particular feature is important. This is a key step in "deploying" the QFD beyond the product developers and having the wider stakeholder team more engaged than normal.

6.3 Managing Risk Early in a Project

As we've already discussed, the most significant waste in new product development is repeating work because risk was not taken out of a project early enough. Moving ahead with details before proving fundamentals is the thing we should be avoiding. We label this behavior as x-risk. We call it this because to do so can add risk to any number of stakeholders' downstream work. In the early days of NPD improvement, people used to talk about "design for manufacture." We now say "design for

x." where x = all of the different stakeholders and their needs. It is only this wide-perspective thinking that will eliminate dramatic levels of waste and create better products and services.

As we write this section of the book we are reminded of Donald Rumsfeld's quote from a press briefing during the war in Iraq.

"There are known knowns. These are things we know that we know. There are known unknowns. That is to say, there are things that we know we don't know. But there are also unknown unknowns. These are things we don't know we don't know."

Although the press following this quote was brutal, a lot of NPD staff could and should identify with this. In this section we will look at some simple techniques that identify x-risk by revealing more of the "unknown unknowns." They then give urgency to early learning and experimentation to make good timely decisions before detail work is started and put at the risk of rework. Remember, this is an enormous cause of waste in NPD, so most NPD professionals will be keen to improve this for their projects.

6.3.1 Technology Demonstration

We have some engineering clients whose businesses are still family owned and run by the son or grandson of the founder. A common ingredient to their success was the understanding the founder had for both the needs of the market and the technology behind the product. They were extremely inquisitive and were continually trying new things and running experiments. In one particular company, the founder's office has an adjoining laboratory in which he made and tested new ideas to see what worked and what didn't. Compare this to the vehicle manufacturer used as an example in Chapter 3. They closed their prototype manufacturing facility as a cost-saving measure!

As we discussed in the product planning section of this chapter, there will be market-defining trade-offs that apply to your products. If you were to change the fundamentals behind these trade-offs, you could then change the market in your favor. Many successful companies understand this and have longer-term technology projects aimed at solving or improving these trade-offs. For example, General Electric Aircraft Engines studied the use of ceramic rolling element bearings without there being any immediate use for them. However, as the trade-off of engine temperatures against fuel efficiency drove toward ever-hotter engines, bearings that could survive high temperatures without lubrication became a technology worth pursuing. At any one time, GE might have many technologies being pursued. These were known as the technology demonstrator program, which was linked into the company's expectation of future market trends.

The key to a successful technology demonstration program is not to just prove that a certain technology is feasible. A one-off data point is not a lot of use to a product development team if the conditions don't exactly match their own. Instead, the aim of demonstrating a particular technology should be to explore the design space and develop design rules that would be of use to the engineers who use the new technology in their product. At GE the simple demonstration of ceramic bearings might generate an understanding of the speed and loads that a ceramic bearing could withstand, as well as the details of manufacturing methods required to achieve a ceramic that has a maximum defect size small enough to survive the application. The most useful way of communicating this knowledge may well be graphs of speed against load for a range of temperatures, bearing sizing equations, process methods sheets and photographs of the material microstructure that is created, or any other way of presenting knowledge in a way that is immediately usable to the engineers that need to apply it. Below is an example of what this data could look like.

Technology Demonstration Data that can be immediately applied to new design

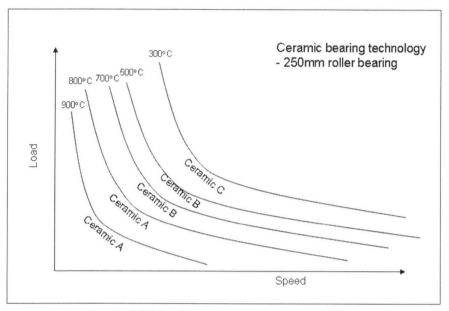

Figure 6.25 Design space for a ceramic bearing

The timescales for this kind of technology research are very difficult to predict (as we don't know what we don't know), and a very common mistake is to include it in projects that have very definite product-launch targets. This leads to perpetual delay as more and more "surprises" are uncovered. It's much more effective to solve the problems relating to a new technology first and then select them for the next product development project. In a company Chris worked for, they decided to promote this behavior by having the R&D function present their breakthroughs and ideas in regular "market stall" events where NPD staff could determine for themselves if the knowledge was sufficiently mature for them to pull it onto the projects they were working on. The inevitable two-way dialogue improved the respective processes of R&D and NPD dramatically.

Many companies already have the equivalent of a technology demonstration program. What varies markedly is the amount they invest in this activity. A pharmaceutical company, for example, may well invest over 50 percent of its budget into R&D.

The economics of the industry are such that there is a large profit to be made for whoever patents a successful drug first. It therefore makes sense in the pharmaceutical sector to explore many new drug technologies even if just one out of hundreds proves to be that winner. Some organizations have been described as seemingly lucky to have just the right technology at the right time. Our experience is that a good strategy based on market trade-offs and the pursuit of enough of the possible technologies means that you will always have something in your back pocket for most eventualities. Most of these "lucky" organizations are no better at fortune telling than their competitors, but they consistently "design their own luck" by covering more of the possibilities.

Not many companies can afford to spend 50 percent of their product development budget or have the resources of aerospace sector technology demonstration programs, so it's important to right-size this activity to your particular situation. When Rob managed the engineering department of a construction vehicle manufacturer, for example, they invested about 8 percent of the department budget in technology demonstration, which was appropriate for a reasonably mature market. Also, the 8 percent was specifically targeted at the medium-term horizon of three to five years. Chris advised one consumer goods manufacturer that had a similar investment level but refocused it into area of products that could drive more share in their mature markets.

6.3.2 Finding Gaps in Design Knowledge

As we mentioned in Chapter 2, engineers are typically optimistic people who are problem solvers and so they believe that their solutions will work. They are also pragmatic and think through what can go wrong, then remove these potential problems from their designs. But because they are "experts" they tend to have blind spots for what they don't know, and they have further blind spots for what can go wrong with their own inventions.

In using our approach to QFD we stripped out much of the complexity of the tool and used it to identify missing knowledge about the product's specification. We now do the same thing with a technique known as failure modes and effects analysis (FMEA). This tool is already used widely as part of a safety assessment, and the analysis focuses on what can occur to threaten the safety of the user of a product. Traditionally this is completed relatively late in an NPD project. Instead, we have brought a modified form of the FMEA technique to the front of the process and we've called it design failure modes and effects analysis" (DFMEA).

The focus of a DFMEA is to search out possible design errors and to evaluate the quality of the design knowledge, analysis, and test capability such that it will prevent these errors from ever reaching the customer. In short, it identifies: "What gaps in our knowledge could lead to design errors that affect the customer and the success of the project?"

As the name suggests, a failure modes and effects analysis lists possible failure *modes* and then considers the *effects* of those modes. This may sound reasonably straightforward but many confuse modes and effects, resulting in an FMEA that can degenerate into something a lot less valuable.

A "failure mode" is what happens to the product (a component, subsystem, software, etc). It is described in language such as:

- Cracked

- Worn

- Incorrect value in data registry

- Seized

- No pressure

An "effect" is what happens to people or what they observe. It is described in language such as:

- Increased noise levels

- Increased vibration

- GUI locks up

- Equipment shuts down safely

- Injury through ejection of failed parts

- Part found degraded at next service

- No effect

Once you have assessed the effect of a failure mode, you can then make a numerical assessment of its severity.

In a traditional safety-focused FMEA, a scale is used from 1 to 10 that starts with "no effect" at 1 and "loss of life without warning" at 10. While this is appropriate for a safety study, it is not helpful in our search for potential design errors since it is weighted too heavily toward serious harm.

In our DFMEA we use four categories combined with a scale of severity from 1 to 5. This serves to simplify the analysis and keep us focused on what is important at this early stage of the project.

The table in figure 6.26 shows how severity is assessed for each of the four categories, which are:

- Item under consideration

- System/assembly

- People

- Enterprise

Severity	Item under consideration	System/Assembly	People	Enterprise
5	Destruction or degradation of other items and equipment	Complete loss of primary function. Non compliance with government regulation	Hazardous to life or severe injury without warning.	Major plant and production loss
4	Complete failure of or damage to item	Operable but at a reduced level of performance	Hazardous with warning. Can be made safe.	Moderate plant and production loss
3	Significant degradation of item or substantial increase in operator workload	Loss of a secondary function or convenience item	Risk of moderate injury with full recovery	Significant production loss
2	Minor degradation of item noticeable to customer	Reduced performance of secondary function or convenience item	Risk of minor injury	Minor production loss
1	Negligible effect on item under consideration	No or negligible loss of capability	No risk of injury	No or negligible production loss

Figure 6.26 Severity assessment for DFMEA

The first column is the level of severity. The next four columns describe the level of severity for failure effects in the four categories. Our clients are usually surprised that we rank a loss of life or severe injury the same as a complete loss of primary function. Remember, this is not a safety FMEA; consider what would happen if you went out to your car each morning to find that it wouldn't start. You would of course be justifiably upset. This is a perfectly safe failure mode because you are in no danger if the car is parked. But are you likely to buy that brand of car again? We think not! The "catastrophe" is not personal to you but it is for the brand.

We think the table is self-explanatory, but the fifth column may need a little more explanation. By "enterprise" we mean either the customer's business or your own. In the oil and gas industry, for example, disrupting the production of an oil rig is a serious event regardless of how "safe" the failure mode is. Similarly, if you supply medical equipment, causing a hospital wing to be evacuated because your machine triggered the smoke alarms is not good either.

The severity level chosen is the highest of the four categories. So if you have a minor degradation of the item, no injury, a loss of primary function, and little effect on the enterprise, the severity level is 5.

We now have a list of failure modes and a measure of their severity, so we can identify the causes of these failure modes. These are the mechanisms that create the failure mode. For example, a "crack" may be caused by fatigue, overload, or stress corrosion, to name but three causes.

Once we have identified the causes of our failure modes, we assess the chance of their occurring on our product. If we are worried about cracking caused by fatigue, we evaluate the effectiveness of our design knowledge. This might include:

- Knowledge of the loads on the part

- Knowledge of customer use (and abuse)

- Knowledge of material fatigue properties

- Knowledge of operating temperatures

- Ability to calculate stresses

If our design knowledge is weak with respect to severe failure modes, then there is a clear reason to rapidly learn or acquire better design knowledge ("what don't we know" again). The answers we get will also require us to make decisions, and so these too should be used in the "decision flow" described in the next section.

There are many other aspects of DFMEA that we have deliberately not gone into here. They would load you up with facts that you really don't need in order to understand our NPD process. However, we would like to list some of the other benefits of DFMEA.

❑ It allows the whole team to assess the emerging design together objectively so we don't allow the inventor to fall victim to what we call "protecting the ugly baby syndrome."

❑ It is an effective earlier starting point for planning the aftermarket support of the product—how it is inspected and serviced, planned maintenance, etc.

❑ It allows you to create an effective validation and verification program that demonstrates that severe failure modes have been designed out.

❑ It allows others throughout the organization to understand why various features of the product or service are more important than at first glance.

❑ It allows you to plan the management of failure modes that you can't design out via other strategies such as:

- Condition monitoring

- Early replacement of critical parts

- Introduction of sacrificial components

- Recommended maintenance procedures

- Recommended spare part stocking levels

- Recommended tooling and personnel training

We also haven't included a completed DFMEA template. The practicality of page size would mean that the font would be too small to read, and it would have forced us to an unnecessary level of detail. Suffice it to say, FMEA has been widely used since its inception during the Second World War and there is a wealth of information available if you are keen to learn more. The key is in understanding how it can identify more of the unknowns and be used for more than just safety.

6.3.3 Manage Learning and Decision Making

We have deliberately avoided calling the exploration phase of a project the "fuzzy front end." That's because we passionately believe that the fuzzy front end should not be fuzzy at all! The logic behind *Winning by Design* is that NPD is not just the domain of superstar inventors or visionaries.

You have already seen that we can improve our crystal ball in product planning and how to make the identification of unknowns a structured process. In this section we will see how the learning gained during the process can be tied to decisions and the delivery of key integration points and milestones to an agreed timeline.

We are well aware that business leaders are nervous of anything called "fuzzy," and we have demonstrated on many occasions that the exploration phase can be structured and managed. The key is to stop asking about what tasks have been completed and to start asking what has been learned, what decisions have been taken, and what rationale was used at the various integration points that have been achieved.

When working with a client in Holland, we quickly found that the site director was a highly driven task manager with a strong production background. In only a couple of months he had learned that true measures of progress in the exploration phase were the speed with which unknowns on the QFD were being filled in and the rate at which key pieces of the system were being integrated on the rapid prototype. No longer did he repeatedly ask for production dates because he realized that they were useless and unreliable until the fundamentals were proven to work. Of course this does not stop manufacturing and supply chain specialists from preparing for the execution phase, but to win by design you need to be mindful of committing too much to detail too early.

The key enabling technique here is what we call the "decision flow," which we believe to be unique to our NPD system. Everywhere we've used it we've seen product developers quickly appreciate its value and use it intuitively. It is simple in

its concept but can provide a more stable planning philosophy to guide the project even though there are unforeseen surprises resulting from the exploration of the technology and market. We arrived at the idea of decision flow by realizing that what needs to flow in NPD is mostly intangible until one looks at what people are waiting for or why they are reworking. We found that unmade decisions, wrong decisions, drawn-out decisions, no decision yet, etc. were the reasons things did not flow smoothly. Once we asked teams to think about the required flow of decisions, cross-functional teams magically started to work closely and in tight collaboration.

So what does a decision flow look like? Fig 6.27 shows an example of a decision flow from one of our clients. The lighter Post-it notes describe the ideal sequence of decisions about the unknowns identified from the QFD and the DFMEA. To the left of each decision are pink Post-it notes that list each learning point required to make a good decision. A blue Post-it note to the right of the decision is the required output from the decision.

For example, a decision might be to agree on the acceptable lever forces for controlling a piece of machinery. The learning required might be legislation, industry standards, a customer focus group evaluating different lever types and loads, measurement of competitor machines, and trials of a new servo-assist invention. The output from this decision could be a reduced list of possible lever solutions for further development.

Once we have identified all the decisions, learning points, and outputs, we need to place the decisions in a sequence that best manages x-risk (for all stakeholders, remember). As we saw with the vehicle manufacturer discussed in Chapter 3, some things are harder to change later than others. The fact that the machine was found to be dynamically unstable caused a lot of drawings to be thrown away and a lot of redesign. You can see that decisions about track width, wheelbase, and the location of centers of gravity would be taken early in the decision flow because they are hard to change later when more detail has been added. You can apply this same logic to all the project decisions and a natural sequence emerges. Learning

rapidly and taking decisions in a team agreed sequence is key to managing risk in your project.

On a really detailed practical note, we've found that a strip of Scotch Magic Tape (made by 3M) across a line of Post-it notes means that they can all be moved as one. This makes getting the decisions into the right sequence, together with the associated learning points and output, much easier.

List of team members showing
who takes the lead for the decision

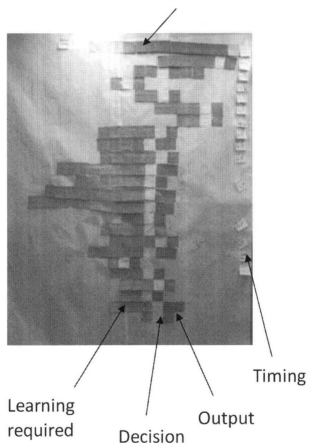

Learning
required   Decision   Output   Timing

Figure 6.27 A decision flow

At the top of the decision flow there are purple Post-it notes with team members listed. The yellow decision Post-it notes are placed under the team member who is to take the lead in making that particular decision.

The blue Post-it notes on the right are key dates for decisions and integration points. These are assessed by starting with the required launch date and subtracting the time needed for the execution phase of the project. This then gives you the true required end point for the exploration phase and you make a judgement of when key decisions need to be made to achieve it. It is important that engineers feel they can report that the target is unachievable if that is what they truly believe. All too often they are told to achieve dates in which they don't believe, and all too often they agree in the hope that "everything will go all right on the night." In reality hardly anything goes exactly to plan because we are "exploring." Discovering things that we didn't expect is in the very nature of the work. If the target isn't deemed achievable, we can now focus on how to use better learning methods, obtain information more quickly, increase resources, etc.

Integration points are a key concept in keeping the exploration phase moving quickly. We have come to learn that teams will pull hard if there is a deadline within four to six weeks ahead of them. As we write these very words, we are acutely aware that we have a book editing workshop in only three weeks and we need to circulate a manuscript to the editors in only two weeks. That is why we're here typing at 9:00 p.m.! If the next deadline is more than eight weeks away, human nature has a tendency to allow us to be easily diverted onto relatively trivial or more seemingly urgent matters until we realize just how much time is left to us. Many creative people actually create and work within much smaller windows, as psychologically they prefer the energy the urgency gives them.

Deadlines are even more effective if they involve a large proportion of the team. There is a lot to be said for peer pressure and not wanting to let the team down. A really effective integration point is one that shows that the product or system

works as a whole and that all the parts can be integrated. This is why we call them integration points.

Examples of integration points for physical products are:

- First space claim model in CAD

- First nonworking prototype

- First cost model

- First working prototype

- Demonstration that computer control successfully operates the hardware

- First customer feedback group

Once you realize the power of integration points, you can make sure that they fall at regular, ideally rhythmic intervals throughout the decision flow with a gap of no more than six weeks. When we have facilitated workshops for our clients, we have sometimes created an integration point specifically to fill a gap that was too long, and the project team welcomed the habit as much as the logic.

As we've mentioned a number of times, in the exploration phase you should try and learn as fast as you can, and devote time and money to developing ways of learning faster. The other side of this reasoning is to delay decisions until they are needed.

Just take a moment to think on that: delay decisions until they are needed. Okay, many of you are probably thinking, "Wait a minute. Delay decisions! Are you crazy?"

Yes, that's exactly what we're advising you to do, and no, we are not crazy. The reasoning behind this is that the time difference between learning something and having to make a decision about it gives you a flexibility of solution that is very useful to you. In a phase where every experiment or learning

point can potentially give you unexpected results, you need as much flexibility as you can get! Let's be absolutely clear. No one is suggesting that decisions should be made so late that they threaten the project. All we are saying is don't purposely make decisions earlier than you need to just to be decisive or for the sake of apparent progress. What we want you to do is give yourself the maximum chance of learning and understanding all the facts before making decisions about them.

A stable backbone for your project

Back in Chapter 3 we said that the decision flow could be a stable plan to guide the project even though there are unforeseen surprises resulting from the exploration of the technology and market. This has proven to be the case on every project we've been involved with. So why is this true, when all our previous experience is that project plans have to be almost continually updated and republished?

The key to this is that the decision flow does not contain any tasks.

When we create a project Gantt chart full of tasks, we find that it needs to be updated with tasks that have been started, tasks that have been delayed, estimates of when they will be completed, and new tasks that have arisen as a result of recent emergent learning events. Every surprise from our learning and experimentation can cause significant change to the Gantt chart. In one extreme example, Chris was part of a multinational project that had ten thousand tasks in a Gantt chart for one subsystem alone! As a result it required an army of staff maintaining it constantly, distracting the hundreds of people who were working on and all but ignoring the chart!

In contrast, the decisions in the decision flow still need to be taken no matter what we learn, and they still need to be taken in the sequence that best manages the x-risk. Because of this, the decision flow rarely changes. We have been involved in a number of projects that worked through their unchanged decision flow for well over a year. Their task-based

plans, however, changed constantly and so we have developed a blended method for creating them and changing them with the least amount of waste. These task-based plans are known as "vertical value stream maps" and are described in the next section.

6.3.4 Creating Effective Teamwork

Despite dramatic advances in technology, we have still found over and over that the most effective way to create teamwork is to give the team the opportunity to work face to face as a team on tasks of mutual importance. You can't achieve this by procedures that demand cooperation or by putting everyone together and simply telling them to work collaboratively. Many people will tell us that modern systems such as desktop video conferencing, Skype, and email have overcome the need for physical face-to-face work. While these advances have improved matters, especially for international teams, when wearing the "waste goggles" it is not always such a rosy picture. Email in particular, unless acted on immediately, is a waste generator as much as a waste eliminator, and the chances for true simultaneous working are low. Webex-type conferences work, but the current bandwidth makes group discussion and debate very clunky and likely to stifle inquiry. This is very dangerous in the exploration phase, for example. We say that the level of waste elimination and mutual understanding falls in direct proportion to the bandwidth available, where face-to-face communication in a studio environment is the highest and micro-blogging like Twitter is the lowest. As we said earlier, we do not know what can be achieved using Facebook-like social networking, but what we do know is that although technical staff are early adopters of technology, they are not a naturally social bunch (as a stereotyped whole) so the jury is still out on this.

What we do know is that working together on the VOC table, AHP, QFD, DFMEA, and decision flow are an excellent start to forging an effective team, but how can we sustain this? We have discovered three techniques that can keep a team

working together throughout the exploration phase even if they are from a wide range of diverse functions. And we know you will be impressed if we reveal that this also includes many projects involving both mechanical engineers and software developers!

The four key techniques are:

- ☐ Team-based project planning (vertical value stream mapping)

- ☐ The team board

- ☐ Creating the project room

- ☐ Tactile, low-tech, group-working methods for the above

Let's have a look at each in turn.

Team-based project planning (vertical value stream mapping)

Vertical value stream mapping (VVSM) is a rather clumsy name for a very effective tool. It is also called vertical value stream analysis (VVSA) by those early Lean thinkers who have used it. The reason is that it is seen as analogous to regular value stream mapping used to create a vision for transforming operations but quite distinct from the world of nonrecurring processes, i.e., projects. With hindsight we have started calling this activity "team-based project planning," but the majority of our clients have already become used to calling it VVSM or VVSA. Team-based project planning is a much more descriptive name for this activity and has been adopted by our newer clients. It builds on a little-known Deming technique exumed by Dan Dimenescu in his book *The Seamless Enterprise*. It was then further developed by us into comprehensive project management system for NPD and other nonrecurring projects. We have modified it specifically to eliminate waste and to optimize team-based collaborative work. We have not had a single team use it to date who do not agree that it is far more

appropriate for managing the flow of a project than more traditional techniques.

Curiously it is best done via Post-it notes in an open-plan studio environment because the level of team interaction is higher, and we specifically want team members to create their own Post-it note content. It also means that the resulting document is highly visible on the wall of the project room and is easily updated and changed in real time. Here's an example of one:

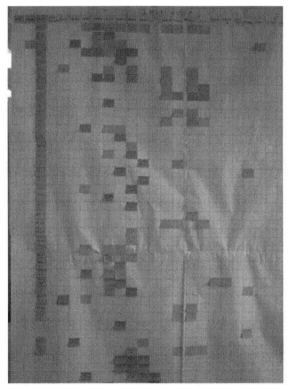

Figure 6.28 Vertical value stream map showing tasks, responsibility, the support required, and timing

The yellow Post-it notes across the top are the functions or disciplines of the team member, e.g., sales and marketing, engineering, and software programming. The orange Post-it notes on the left-hand side are week numbers. (In projects with a different "time signature," these could be hours/days/

minutes.) The pink Post-it notes on the grid are tasks if they have writing on them, or supporting tasks if they are blank. Only one task is permitted per line, and the Post-it note describing the task is placed under the name of the person who is responsible for completing it. A key to the success of this technique is that the task is written by the responsible person and placed on the grid by him or her. This person then indicates what they he or she needs in terms of assistance from other team members by placing a blank Post-it note on the same line as the task under the people or expertise type who needs to help. This action immediately gets verbal teamwork going and can highlight, for example, a team member who has few task responsibilities but is overloaded in supporting others. We have found that facilitation is crucial here to encourage the teams to work in a truly collaborative and high-bandwidth manner. One unfortunate by-product of the IT age is that people all too readily gravitate back to their desks or cubicles and seek to work via email with all its inbox delays and rework. When this happens, it is not long before all of the departmental walls that people fought so hard to tear down have been rebuilt virtually. The prize achieved by the low-tech approach is that more collaborative, face-to-face working takes place, more waste is avoided, and more value is added to the working results. We have seen this so many times we are actually a little zealous and insistent about it. Imagine gathering two families to plan a wedding, with all the attendant politics and perspectives. Now imagine doing that via email! It sounds impossible because it probably is. With the low-tech method, the team members can trade Post-it notes to better balance workload across themselves, and all without a project manager directing them!

The tasks are generated by the team looking at the learning points on the decision flow and deciding when decisions are required to be made. This is done as a team-based activity and there is always a lot of team interaction and support in identifying what should be done to learn and who should be doing it. However, it is not until the person responsible accepts that responsibility that a Post-it is put on the grid. No longer is planning the work of the project manager who creates a Gantt chart on her own by assigning tasks and then following it up

with individuals. This approach is a team thing and it alone develops an all-in-it-together culture.

The picture below is a team in the midst of team-based project planning at one of our clients'. These are technical staff of all disciplines working together on a single plan. Note how up-close and involved they are. Whatever next!

Figure 6.29 Team-based project planning in action

Again, resist all attempts to high-tech this approach into soft-ware. If you want to share it electronically, attach an HD we-bcam to the ceiling and let people see it in real time. We have experimented with doing this high-tech, from simple spread-sheets to web-based applications, and every time, as one per-son inevitably has to do the typing or people take turns, ev-eryone else disengages by degrees until people are suggesting it be completed offline.

Only plan tasks as far as you can see

Back in Chapter 3 we discussed the waste in planning projects in great detail and then constantly revising and changing these plans. As we exampled in many projects, this can become a full-time job for a skilled engineering leader who has so much

more to offer the project. Eliminating this waste is vitally important in the exploration phase of a project, since new learning and surprises may be constantly changing the plan. The dates against key decisions and integration points are usually more than adequate for planning purposes, and adding more detail to the plan will not necessarily achieve greater accuracy in this phase of the project. For this reason we learned in this phase only to complete the VVSM for no more than the next eight weeks, or the amount of time that will get the team beyond the next integration point. Because the situation is constantly changing, we replan after four weeks for a further eight-week period.

To most trained project managers, this is counterintuitive. Many of the project management tools we traditionally use come from execution-focused phases in industries like construction. Here the design is frozen and the challenge is to coordinate the activities of hundreds of contractors and thousands of workmen who do not typically communicate with each other. Resource and time requirements are relatively well known. For example, four men can build a brick wall of a certain size in five days, and bricks of a certain type need to be delivered to site at a rate of ten thousand per day during that period. The project manager acts like the conductor of an orchestra, tapping out the rhythm and signalling the timing of all the individual parts. Are the bricks in the warehouse? Is transport booked? Are the bricklayers available? Do we have cover for sickness? What's the weather forecast?

This approach and thinking falls apart in the exploration phase of NPD where the resources and times taken aren't well understood. It also leads to stress and breakdown when the now "failing" project is reworked to some suboptimal conclusion.

To illustrate this, let's imagine a typical conversation between a project manager and an engineer standing by the side of the first working prototype. It might go something like this:

Project Manager: "Why are those servo motors oscillating like that?"

Engineer:	"We don't know, but we're rigging up a watchdog program to give us real-time software status data."
Project Manager:	"I've got transport arriving this afternoon to take the prototype to the testing facility that I booked five months ago!"
Engineer:	"Well, it can't go like this."
Project Manager:	"How long will it take?"
Engineer:	"To implement the watchdog or solve the problem?"
Project Manager:	"To solve the problem, of course!"
Engineer:	"I have no idea what's wrong. We'll know more when the watchdog software is running tomorrow afternoon—assuming it's a software issue. It could also be instability in the motor drive boards. If it is, we may need to make some firmware changes. We should know more by Friday."

No wonder project managers in new product development seem to age faster than the rest of us! Project managers in NPD are currently cast head first into an impossible task. By asking them to show deterministically a process which by its nature is exploratory and emergent, we ask the impossible. We often face the assertion from many project managers that they have the necessary experience and knowledge to know how long things typically take based on similar projects or past experience and therefore don't see the need to do the session. Conversely, the very technical staff members they have been managing often say, "This team-based approach is the best day's work I have ever done." In one extreme case we had a project manager listen to everyone give feedback

on what amazing value and understanding they now had and then proclaim, "I don't see anything new, I have all this info in *my* plan already."

While we are stressing a much-made point here, quite personally we have found that although open-minded project managers will see this as a way to more effectively manage NPD, many have to first cross a mental barrier, after which they become more skilled and valued by the team. We find that the best project managers, with seemingly less of a role as the team takes on more of the planning, soon become a kind of project stenographer, recording and collecting documents, proceedings, documenting decision rationale, and coordinating reviews.

Some teams we have worked with have struggled to predict tasks even eight weeks ahead, so we had them plan for only four weeks and replan every two weeks. Doing anything more would have created far more waste than any benefit gained by the extra work. The key, as always, is the timing on the decision flow. What we have found is that even teams that start off with a four-week planning horizon get better at planning and will be able to work with a longer horizon next time.

The team board

We have shown how the decision flow can define high-level project timescales and how team-based project planning can define tasks for a short time-planning horizon. What we now need is a means for making sure that the team is focused on the right activities on a daily basis.

During the exploration phase it is quite legitimate to ask, "If what you are doing right now isn't providing the learning to make a decision, why are you doing it?"

You are probably as aware as we are that technical staff love to mess about with details, and software developers equally

love to mess about with coding. Service designers love coming up with different concepts, but the result is that time passes without any learning or decision making at all.

Think about it like this. You have a report to write and so you open Microsoft Word and start writing lots of words. However, at some point, well before you've finished, you decide to do a formatting job to make what you've done so far look presentable. You make sure all the fonts are the same, that there are no orphan lines going across pages, and that illustrations appear on the same page as the text that refers to them. During this time no new thinking is going into the document, it's just detail work. You then start creatively writing again and start making changes to what you've done earlier. Now all the formatting goes wrong and you're continually messing about with fonts, paragraph lengths, page breaks, and illustration sizes to keep it looking nice as you go. We hope you can all spot the waste in this way of working and the fact that it can creep into many activities in NPD. As Lean thinkers know, not all work is value added. For a typical example, consider a client of ours who was a defense contractor that made systems for submarines. While there, Rob found that an engineer had spent a day detailing the cooling fins on a motor so that he could work out how to route pipes around it. The problem was that the motor hadn't been sized yet, and the one in the CAD model had been plucked out of the air just to show that a motor was needed in the space!

The most effective tool we've found to bring the tasks on the team-based project plan to a daily level that promotes team value-added work is what we call the "team board." Here is what it can look like.

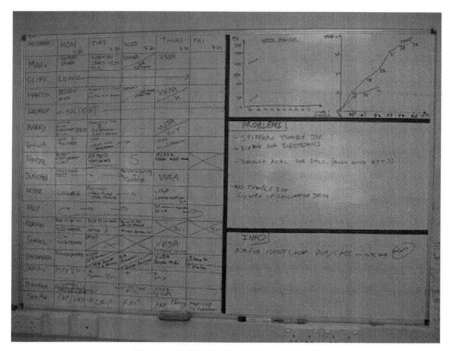

Figure 6.30 Project team board

The board is constructed by the team and is a whiteboard that can be written on and then wiped off. The grid is constructed from "gridding tape" so that it remains while you wipe off the ink. On the left are the names of the team, and across the top of the left-hand side are the days of the week.

A "stand-up team meeting" is held every morning to update the board. The team using the board in the picture numbers sixteen people, and this meeting never took longer than twenty minutes. The marker is passed from team member to team member, and each in turn goes up to the board and writes on it what they completed yesterday, what they are doing today, and their key activities until the end of the week. If a team member has not completed that which was planned for the day before, they can ask for help. If they need help today, they can ask for that too.

If the submarine system project team mentioned earlier had operated a team board, an engineer would have said that he was

going to spend a day working out where the cooling fins on a motor were located, and one of his teammates would have told him that the motor hadn't even been designed yet. Now that's waste-saving through team work. This happens constantly throughout our approach and the benefits that accrue can be enormous.

A key to operating the team board is to have the vertical value stream map hanging right beside the board and to constantly check that the tasks are being completed. This point has been missed by some teams, and in these cases the tasks on the board always start diverging from the plan as engineers start dreaming up lots of other interesting things to do, not all of which are value added!

The duration of the daily meeting is also important. If it goes much beyond twenty minutes, team members can start to see it as more effort than it's worth and will stop supporting it. To facilitate this there is a space in which to write "problems" on the right-hand side of the board. Problems can be noted here for later discussion rather than turning the stand-up meeting into a live problem-solving discussion. In extreme cases, we have insisted that the speaker at the board stand on one leg. This usually keeps what they have to say focused on the key facts!

Other spaces on the board shown in the picture are team performance measures at the top right and shared information at bottom right. The performance measures can be used to great effect. The graph on the right shows the cumulative number of tasks that were planned to be completed (in black) against the number actually achieved in red. Not many weeks have go by before you know whether the plan is working or not. The photograph was taken when the team had just started using a vertical value stream map and a team board. You can see that after three weeks they had achieved less than half what they had planned. At this point the team searched for the root causes and put a new plan together. After six months they were attaining 70 percent to 80 percent of the plan. This is typical of a successful team.

"Wait a minute," we can hear you saying. "A successful team that only achieves 80 percent of the tasks it planned? How can that be acceptable?"

We were as surprised as you when we first started observing teams and their performance-to-plan down at this level. The reason for this apparent paradox is that between 20 percent and 30 percent of tasks originally identified in the exploration phase turned out not to be vital to the project after all. "That supplier visit wasn't needed because we decided to make that part in house." "The plastic prototype wasn't needed because a stress analysis showed that the concept wouldn't work anyway." Soon we learned that 80 percent is a good rate. Chris remembers a large multinational military project which was, according to plan, on target and successful. Successful, that was, until a routine design review invited manufacturing experts for the first time. They highlighted that a manufacturing technology used on the prototype did not in any way prove that the technology would be successful at the production volumes already sold. If the team had ploughed on regardless, they could well have been 100 percent on target to the project plan, but of course this new knowledge demanded a countermeasure plan and all sorts of rework too late in the day. That's the unfortunate nature of exploration if you have not thought collaboratively enough about "what don't we know."

Creating the project room

Creating a space in which the team can work is also vital to collaborative teamwork. We should make the space as visual as possible with the aim that within just a few minutes of entering the room, anyone can have a pretty good idea of how things are going and the status of the project.

In Japan these project rooms are called *obeya*, which literally means "big room." Companies like Toyota pay a lot of attention to these rooms and fill them with the latest technologies to facilitate fast data retrieval and visualization of all aspects of the project, including 3D CAD images. They will have multiple projection screens, prototype models, and even virtual reality capabilities where needed. If you are the sort of company that can afford this type of investment, you probably already have project rooms like this. Good, then, but do not avoid asking yourself how they are used. Are they used habitually

for teamwork and dedicated for each project, or are they only used for reviews?

Figure 6.31 The modern obeya

With our NPD approach, this studio-based working enables the maximum levels of collaboration. The good news for the majority of organizations that can't afford such high-tech facilities is that you can create an effective space almost anywhere and without a huge investment.

Below is a photograph of a typical project room. You can see that many of the tools we've presented are working documents on the walls for all to see, refer to, and update. This project room is actually at the Dutch facility with the very demanding task-focused site director we mentioned earlier. Because he could visit this room at any time and see decisions being ticked off on the decision flow, answers being entered on the QFDs, and the work the team was doing that week on the team board, he didn't create lots of extra work through wanting reports and updates all the time.

The one thing missing from the photograph is a prototype of the new product. Ideally this would be in the room too because something to touch, point at, and play with is hugely effective in improving communication and bringing people together. The product that the team was working on is too large and heavy to bring into the room. The prototype-building and test laboratory, however, was on the ground floor below the

project room no more than two minutes' walk away. This kind of thinking seeks an environment that is:

☐ Highly visual

☐ Co-located

☐ Collaborative

☐ Encourages true team working

This is what is required to really maximize the potential of our NPD approach, and while for many it seems like a big risky leap from the comfort of the cubicle and email-at-the-desk routine, for the majority it becomes the preferred way of working. For us to win by design we have to tear down the cubicles, let go of the individual desk, and create an environment that is serious about working in teams. There is nothing like being part of a highly performing, successful team for morale. The team working room is a must-have enabler.

Most of the items labeled in the room shown have already been described with just a few exceptions.

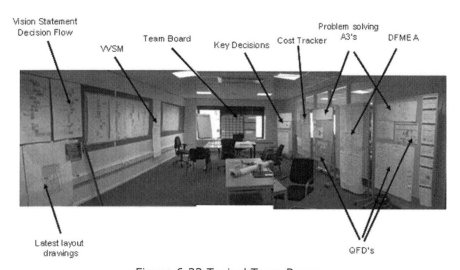

Figure 6.32 Typical Team Room

The vision statement is just out of shot on the left. The "key decisions" sheets at the end of the room on the right are a great way to document the decisions taken as the project progresses. Each decision has its own sheet which shows the decision taken, the rationale for making it, and all the learning points that allowed a good decision to be taken. "Problem Solving A3s" are described later in this chapter in the section on learning and knowledge capture. The "cost tracker" is showing the estimated product cost against the target of a 30 percent cost reduction over the previous product. This was a major project objective and the team applied many value engineering techniques, is a subject we cover in the next section. As you can see, the room is not high-tech, but it has all the key elements required to make it a great project room to work in for a team.

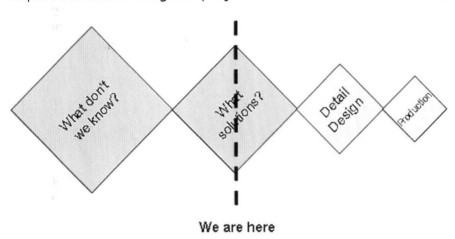

We are here

6.3.5 Set-Based Thinking

The idea of "working in sets" can be used in two different ways. The first is to manage technical risk, and the second is to facilitate concurrent engineering to accelerate your project without the risk of wasted effort.

Unfortunately, set-based concurrent engineering (SBCE) has been misconstrued by many NPD staff to be the pursuit of multiple alternative solutions across their entire project. They

may have heard benchmark stories of organizations starting three totally independent project teams to solve the same problem with the aim of using only the winning solution. Not surprisingly, SBCE is seen as hugely expensive and is hardly ever adopted. But as we shall see, SBCE can be very effective if used in the right way and at the right time.

We will illustrate both the uses of set-based thinking by telling you three stories from our past. Rob was part of the development team for a new gas turbine which had the aim of being lighter and more fuel efficient, but the overriding goal was that it should be ready for the launch of a new aircraft. Timing and synchronization with the larger project was therefore critical.

One of the technical strategies for making the engine more efficient was to use less compressor bleed air for energizing a particular oil seal. Any air that is bled off the compressors for uses internal to the gas turbine means less air going through the combustion chamber and turbines; hence, less thrust. A new oil-seal technology was being developed which used less air and was up to 80 mm shorter, which in turn would save weight.

Because time was critical, the project team decided early that there was too much risk of the new technology being late since it had only just started its rig test program. They therefore decided not to make the rest of the engine 80 mm shorter and to create instead an interface that would suit either a conventional seal or the new seal technology. If the new technology was ready in time, they would simply add an 80 mm spacer.

This example demonstrates what we mean when we say, "Don't plan for right first time."

We have seen many project teams make the assumption that a new technology will be ready and then happily paint themselves into a corner. If the new technology is not ready, they have a huge and wasteful redesign on their hands.

The jet engine team moved forward with a "set" of two seal designs until they chose one of them. The key to successful SBCE is that *at least one of the options in the set going forward is low*

risk. If the project had chosen two high-risk seal designs and precluded a conventional seal, then their risk of failure and not being ready on time may still have been too high. Many project teams miss this point too and think that SBCE is the pursuit of many new alternatives in the hope that one of them will work.

As it happened, the new seal technology was successful and the engine was launched on time with the new seal and the 80 mm spacer. The spacer was removed and the engine shortened during a later product upgrade.

Our second story is from a team Chris inherited that was designing a module for a new generation of aircraft structured primarily from carbon composite, a technological leap from aluminium alloy–based platforms. The prototype module was successful in the bulk of the specification given by a very technically aware customer. Shortly after critically reviewing the project using a SBCE approach, Chris and the team revealed that it was fundamentally flawed with regard to the overall weight target due to a number of key components. Chris separately diagnosed that the team make-up itself was flawed, as it was made up of many young members with a low level of experience and little knowledge of historical design rules and trade-offs. This was due to the transition from 2D CAD to 3D modeling. The young, eager staff had made themselves ready for the new 3D-modeled project in terms of their computer-modeling skills, but not in their level of design knowledge. What had happened then was that a blanket assumption—that carbon fiber composite material was always lighter than aluminium alloy—became embedded in the work. At a simple material level this is of course true, but at the beginning of this technological breakthrough many of the early primitive manufacturing methods used for composites led to some key complex components actually being heavier than the aluminium alloy equivalents that had in contrast benefitted from many decades of process optimization. The work soon started a rumor and led to the highest level materials scientist in the company storming into the team room to demand answers as to "why we are going backward" in terms of material technology. Upon seeing the team rationale and data and the perspective of more than eight different areas of expertise, he had to

agree that the material in a number of key components would indeed have to be "changed backward." SBCE was then used to work up different design approaches to the same structural problems and each was assessed according to its current merits. The knowledge generated by the team allowed them to rapidly advance carbon composite knowledge and future production techniques, leading to multiple patents and applications into other sectors such as F1 motor racing.

Our third SBCE story concerns an aircraft engine manufacturer that developed a gas turbine from a blank piece of paper in a much shorter timescale than that achieved previously. The gas turbine was divided into over ten modules, and these were developed concurrently by a team of around five hundred engineers and specialists.

At the start of the project things were quite vague. There was a clear specification for the Gulfstream aircraft that would be the engine's first application, but the details of the engine itself were not so clear. For example, the fan module team needed to know the weight of the accessory drives module that mounted to the fan case. However, the accessory drives module team needed to know a lot about the engine to determine the power density and therefore the weight of their gearboxes:

- Fuel flow and pressure

- Hydraulic fluid flow and pressure

- Oil flow and pressure

- Electrical power needs

- Engine speeds

This information needed to be provided by the other module teams who, in part, needed data from the fan module team. These information circles existed everywhere, and the project used SBCE to navigate their way through them.

Early on, the specifications and interfaces of modules were expressed as ranges or "sets." For example, the weight of a gearbox

wouldn't be specified as just a single number but as a range based on an assessment of the smallest and largest pumps and generators that could possibly be needed. This was based on set-based data from the other module teams. The fan module team could then move ahead with their design knowing that the final gearbox weight would be somewhere in this range. When they needed a more precise range, they would stop and ask rather than continue with work that would potentially be waste.

All the module team leaders met every two weeks throughout the preliminary design phase of the project to talk about the sets and ranges that defined the engine. The golden rule was that the ranges could only decrease in size because to expand a range would potentially threaten the work already completed by other module teams. As the teams worked on exploration and learning, the sets were progressively reduced and the final specification with the optimum design for all the modules emerged from the process.

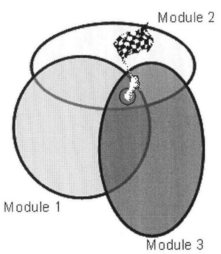

Figure 6.33 SBCE is looking for the optimum overlap of all requirements

In this way the project was completed in three years from start to flight certification, when previously the norm was five years.

In previous projects, designing all the modules at the same time became wasteful as module teams moved ahead based on

assumptions about the other modules. For example, the accessory drives module team might say that their gearbox weighs 322 pounds based on everything they know today. The fan module team then designs the fan case to support a 322-pound gearbox. A month later the combustion module team learns that they need a higher fuel pressure to get the required fuel efficiency and so they need a larger fuel pump. The gearbox weight is increased to 401 pounds and the fan module team has to redo all the stress calculations and add extra material to the fan case design.

This way of working is commonly known in the literature as "point-to-point concurrent engineering." A starting specification is chosen quickly based on many assumptions and then changed iteratively as new learning is discovered until a successful design is reached.

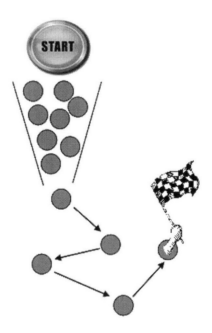

Point-to-point concurrent engineering selects a specific solution and then redesigns it until a successful solution is found

Figure 6.34 Point-to-point concurrent engineering

The problem with this approach is that the starting point is rarely the optimum and the redesigns are usually a series of

compromises under time pressure. The result is a design that is the "best that can be done in the timescale" and never the optimum that could have been achieved. It is hard to resist this model; it seems to be intuitive to most human beings as the natural order to simultaneously achieve economy of effort and trial-and-error-based design. SBCE is counterintuitive because it sounds like a lot more "work," but once experienced it is obvious as another example of rushing slowly. Leaders and NPD professionals alike have to be both brave and humble enough to try it.

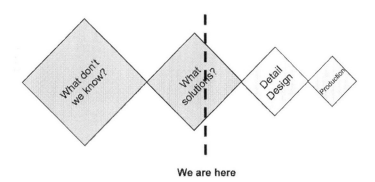

We are here

6.3.6 Making Decisions using Pugh Selection

With a decision flow as the spine of our approach and SBCE recommended, there are many times when a project team will need to choose between various ideas that may each have merits as well as weaknesses. If the team can't agree simply and obviously, then a technique known as Pugh selection may be useful to reveal the strongest solution and to challenge the team to make it even stronger.

The technique uses the customer needs identified in the VOC together with their importance weightings and then compares the ideas in a matrix like the one below.

Concept Selection Better ✚ 1 Same 0 Worse ▬ -1	Idea 1	Idea 2	Idea 3	Idea 4	Idea 5	Importance
Open can		✚			▬	10
Open bottle				✚	✚	0
Safe			▬		✚	10
Doesn't rattle			▬			5
Ease of use		▬			▬	5
Hardly any force to operate			✚	▬		13
Smooth operation		✚			✚	13
Comfortable/positive grip					✚	8
Attractive appearance		▬		✚	▬	10
Dishwasher safe		▬	✚			8
Easy to clean				✚	✚	5
Retains appearance		✚			▬	8
Durable – 10 years			▬			5
Production volume					✚	5
Cost		▬		✚		15
Must be made in China			▬			10
No factory packaging				✚		5
Fewer components		✚		▬		10
Score		3	4	7	8	

Figure 6.35 Pugh selection table

One of the ideas is chosen to be the "baseline" to which all the other ideas are compared. If they are equal, a 0 is entered in the matrix. If the idea is stronger than the baseline, a 1 is in- terred. If the idea is weaker than the baseline, a -1 is interred. In the example, Idea 1 is the baseline and so is scored zero. The product of the number in the matrix and the importance score is totaled for each idea, and these are shown at the bot- tom of the matrix. You may notice that the left-hand column

contains the voice of the customer from the can opener QFD used earlier in this chapter.

You can see that Idea 5 is the strongest idea, but it does have some weaknesses.

Instead of just picking the strongest idea and moving on, Pugh challenges the project team to try to make Idea 5 even stronger. For example, all the other ideas are stronger at "opening a can" than Idea 5, and Idea 2 is the strongest. Can we use this feature of Idea 2 in Idea 5 and create a "super idea"? If that is not possible, then what about Idea 4? It is one point behind Idea 5. Can it be made into the strongest super idea?

In our experience Pugh can be time consuming and so should be used only when there is genuine disagreement and no obvious choice.

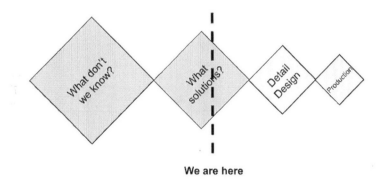

We are here

6.4 Maximizing Value

You should be in no doubt already that a large percentage of your cost base is decided on the drawing board (CAD screen for those of you who aren't as old as we are!). The number of components, their complexity, and their interfaces are key factors in many of your costs:

- ☐ Assembly hours

- ☐ Factory size

- ☐ The number of buyers you need

- ☐ Warehouse size

- ☐ Test time

- ☐ Capital tied up in stock

- ☐ Tooling costs

- ☐ Skill levels

- ☐ And too many more to mention here

The question all organizations need to ask is: "How many of our technical staff appreciate the consequences of their actions as they draw lines, set tolerances, and add more and more complexity to their designs?"

In modern times, value engineering has become a way of life for many industries. In the computing industry, for example, we have seen a constant stream of ever more capable machines at ever-lower prices. In the automotive industry, car ownership has never been cheaper in real terms than it is today, and the levels of performance, safety, and quality are constantly improving.

Many industries pride themselves on cost reduction programs of between 4 percent and 5 percent a year achieved through supplier negotiation and operational efficiencies. The enlightened few know that far greater savings are possible if you are prepared to "start again" with relooking at the design of your product or at least major subassemblies. The worst we have achieved to date through value engineering effort is an 18 percent reduction in the total cost of manufacture, and this was on a mature design already made in Poland because it is a low-cost economy. Realistically, 25 percent and higher is quite achievable,

especially if the basic design is relatively mature and engineers have been tinkering with and fixing it for many years. When running a large engineering department in a large company, Chris never had less than 10 percent of the total headcount dedicated to value engineering. The leader of the team used to easily produce a 20X ROI of their costs and of course guided less experienced staff in their designs. In time the whole level of the team was raised to embed the following philosophy.

Value engineering was developed into a discipline in its own right by an engineer working for General Electric during the Second World War. Lawrence Miles had spent the war supplying equipment for aircraft in the face of severe component shortages. Being an innovative engineer, he started substituting available parts for those he couldn't get. In many cases he had to start making sophisticated aircraft parts out of everyday items and anything he could get his hands on. Being a good engineer, he made sure that there was no loss of either performance or reliability.

By the end of the war he had become very successful at keeping planes flying with components that cost a fraction of the originally specified equipment. As a result he began to question why aircraft components should cost so much in the first place and developed a way of thinking about value that is still very relevant today.

His underlying philosophy is captured in a quotation from Miles himself: "All cost is for function."

By this he means everything that incurs cost in your product design should provide function for your customer. Costs that don't should be eliminated. The parallel with the Lean thinking notion of elimination of non-value-added work is clear.

Today the electrical components Miles made out of knitting needles and the like wouldn't be acceptable in peacetime commercial aviation, and it was only the threat of losing a war that made these substitutions acceptable in the early 1940s. However, Miles found that instead of trying to cost reduce an expensive component, it was much more productive to ask

what cost needed to be added to the knitting needle to make it acceptable.

Value engineering is a huge subject on its own and has been well documented in many texts. Our intention here is not to fill many pages with detailed explanations but to give you a brief overview of the key techniques we use most often in value engineering. These are:

- ☐ Reducing functional complexity
- ☐ Assessing the worth of functions
- ☐ Value analysis matrix
- ☐ Combining or eliminating parts

When practiced repeatedly as in Chris's example, the thinking becomes a habit and teams infused with this way of thinking produce amazing results.

Before we explore these techniques in a little more detail, let us just cover a few basic points, starting with a definition of "value" in the context of value engineering.

6.4.1 What Is Value?

Value is the amount of function you get relative to the price you pay. By function we mean things like:

- ☐ Performance
- ☐ Utility
- ☐ Features
- ☐ Durability
- ☐ Styling

Value is therefore a comparative quality and so is constantly changing. There is no absolute measure of value as it is personal and situational.

For example, paying $50 for a calculator that only performed multiplication, division, addition, and subtraction was good value thirty-five years ago. Today you wouldn't pay more than $5 for one that performs a vast number of mathematical functions.

Value can also change much faster than that! You might have gotten a great deal on a new car and your sense of having received good value is high. This can be instantly destroyed when you find out that a colleague has bought the same car for a thousand dollars less.

The important message here is that value continuously changes and you can't afford to be complacent. A good value today won't be good value tomorrow, and markets can move quickly when a better-value alternative becomes available.

6.4.2 Value Engineering Is NOT Cheapening the Product

When we first work with a client, we sometimes get resistance from product managers and salespeople who think that all we are going to do is strip out features and make the product "cheap and nasty." They assume that quality will inevitably be sacrificed for cost reduction.

Let us be absolutely clear. Value engineering is about delivering all the function your customers need at an acceptable level of quality at the lowest possible cost.

As you read the next few sections you will see how much cost is typically wasted in a product, and that achieving higher performance and quality while also reducing cost is a very real possibility and should be a foundation of every project.

To illustrate this, let's return to our can opener. Figure 6.36 has pictures of three can openers we bought a few years ago.

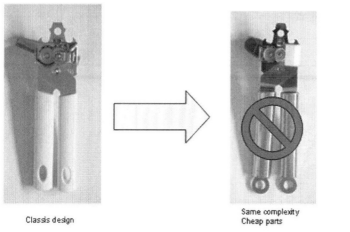

Classis design

Same complexity
Cheap parts

Simplified design
Better performance

Figure 6.36 Can opener comparison

The one on the left is a quality product made by Brabantia and we paid £4.99 for it at Amazon.co.uk.

The one in the middle is clearly a copy of the Brabantia, but all the parts are "cheap and nasty." It flexes when you use it, the gears are cheap pressings and grate and snag against each other, the plastic guard keeps falling off, and the cutting wheel quickly goes blunt. Unsurprisingly perhaps, this one was purchased at a so-called bargain store for £2.99.

In contrast, let's look take a look at the one on the right. The critical components that do the work, the gears and wheels, look identical to the Brabantia and are definitely of the same quality. The rest of the opener has been simplified in design so that it has fewer parts. The levers are now very elegant drop forgings, and the rubber inserts feel very comfortable. Because the fulcrum is now at the top of the opener, it has actually achieved a greater mechanical advantage and so operating forces are lower than the Brabantia. This product was bought in Manchester, UK, for the same price as the cheap-and-nasty bargain at £2.99. The same price, yet the performance and quality are both better than the benchmark Brabantia.

That is what value engineering is all about! This is a way of thinking about design that you need almost as a badge of

kudos among technical staff. They need to see beauty and elegance in simplicity. Technical staff with a VE background would instinctively see this as great design, and it is how brands are made and destroyed. When better designs compete at lower cost, or shall we say better value, it is hard for even the most brand-loyal customer to stay faithful.

6.4.3 Making Things Simple Is Actually Quite Hard

NPD experience soon teaches you that creating a complex product is actually quite easy. The real skill is making a simple product that still achieves the required function and value in the eyes of the customer. This might sound counterintuitive, so we'll illustrate this point with a Lego-based simulation we use to teach value engineering.

We set the class the task of making a parking garage security barrier using Lego Technic, which has pneumatic pumps, valves, and cylinders. It would be too easy if we allowed them to just make an arm that went up and down, so we imagine that the barrier is in a multistory garage with a low ceiling. This requires a little more thought about how to span the road but not hit the ceiling. The conventional solution is a barrier like this:

Figure 6.37 Typical car park barrier for a low ceiling

We give each group of engineers in the class a large box of Lego pieces and one and a half hours to create their inventions. After a frantic period of building they always create wonderfully complex designs using a large number of components. Among these people there often seems to be a pride in the esoteric, and out-of-the-box solutions are much admired. Here are some of the typical solutions from our workshops:

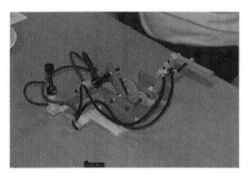

Figure 6.38 Initial Lego solutions

Scary fact: we have trained over two hundred engineers with this Lego simulation, and to date not one of them has ever asked for a price list for the Lego pieces. All just dive straight into building, even though the title of the workshop is value engineering!

As you might have guessed, the engineers are given a second chance at creating a value-engineered barrier later in the workshop and are armed with a price list. Below is a typical result that is usually a circa 90 percent cost reduction over their first attempt.

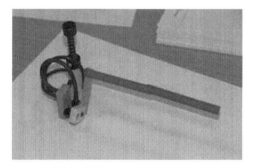

Figure 6.39 Value engineered Lego solution

So why is creating something simple so hard? Time pressure is a factor. It is also easier to keep adding components until you have something that works. Realistically there is very little incentive to really stretch the brains of the type of people in the workshop to create something simple. Why should they? What parent would give a child a Lego or K'nex set and slowly reduce the number of parts to increase skills!

Socially the effect of creating a complex piece with more parts is that people will say, "Wow! That's complex, you must be really clever!" Without a psychologist handy to explain why, we have had to conclude that there is something deep and hardwired at work here. It gets worse for the efficient designer, as when you do work very hard to simplify the product, many even say, "That's so simple! Why didn't I think of that?"

If business leaders are aware of this skill, they can start to pay attention to how you reward your product developers and engineers for maximizing the value (function and cost) of your products.

6.4.4 Reducing Functional Complexity

Back in Chapter 3 we introduced you to a function diagram as a means for visualizing functional complexity, and we saw that it could be quite complex even for a simple can opener. We also mentioned that the manufacturer of the early benchmark can opener had simplified it with their latest product offering (perhaps in response to competition). Below we show the changes in the function map and the old and new products.

The new Brabantia can opener is clearly a lower cost to produce and yet it is better styled and more comfortable to use, and it has the same quality as the previous model. Ironically we had to pay 40 percent more for the new "improved" one.

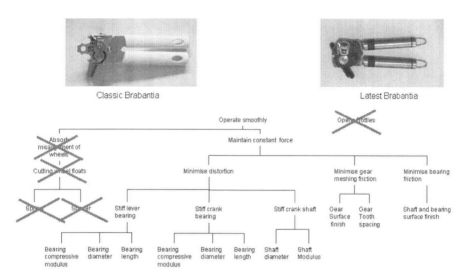

Figure 6.40 Suggested function map for latest Brabantia can opener

6.4.5 Combining Functions

Another powerful technique is that of combining functions into as few components as possible. There are examples of this on the new Brabantia can opener, but we thought it would be much more interesting to use a classic English sports car from the 1960s and '70s. Below is the Lotus Europa.

Figure 6.41 A Lotus Europa

The reason for this selection is because of another of our heroes. Lotus' founder, Colin Chapman, had the goal of producing a car with "super car" performance at a price that the man on the street could afford. The most expensive component in a car is the engine, and it was immediately obvious that the man in the street could not afford to buy a Ferrari with its powerful but complex V12 engine. Instead Colin used a Ford four-cylinder 1,600cc engine because it was mass produced, within the budget, and Lotus found he could get 115 HP from it by modifying it to have double overhead camshafts and by fitting larger valves.

Still, he only had an engine with 115 HP and yet he still wanted the performance of a car that has over 300 HP! How could he possibly achieve that?

The answer was that the rest of the car needed to weigh almost nothing, and so the Lotus Europa was designed with a steel backbone frame resin-bonded (later bolted to allow repairs) to a fiberglass body molding. However, Chapman knew that this technology alone was not enough to achieve the curb weight he needed. He then famously declared:

> "Every component in a Lotus must have at least two functions"

To illustrate this, let's take a look at the Europa's rear suspension and the drive to the rear wheels.

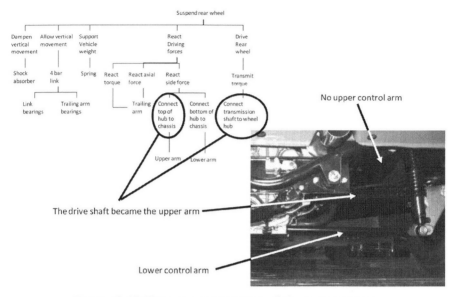

Figure 6.42 The rear suspension of the Lotus Europa

Above is a function map showing that the upper control arm of a traditional suspension has the function of "connecting" the transmission to the wheel hub to keep the hub vertical when cornering. Another part of the function map shows that the drive shaft also has the function of connecting the transmission to the wheel hub, but this time it's to transmit torque. Both parts have the function of "connecting." Lotus saw the opportunity to eliminate the upper control arm and make the drive shaft take over its function. The photo shows that there is no upper control arm securing the hub, as is the case in virtually every other car suspension design on the road today. Colin Chapman's design philosophy of "design the car and then add lightness" was what enabled the company to produce cars with amazing performance for their price and size.

6.4.6 The Worth of Functions

Value is a comparative quality and situational, as we've already discussed. It is therefore reasonable to say that the

value or "worth" of a particular function is the lowest cost alternative way of achieving that same function.

After the excitement of sports cars, we're going to have to go back to can openers to illustrate this point because they're nice and simple.

The lowest cost way we have found to open a can is to use a rock and a nail!

Figure 6.43 Rob opening a can with a rock and a nail

The nail cost £0.01 and the rock was free because we found it in the garden.

So if the worth of the "open can" function is £0.01, why would we buy the latest Brabantia can opener for £6.99? What are we spending the additional £6.98 on?

There are a number of additional functions that leap to mind that would start to justify a price higher than £0.01.

- ☐ <u>Safety</u>: The can quickly became like the mouth of a shark with sharp jagged teeth everywhere when opened in such a rudimentary manner.

- ☐ <u>Speed</u>: It is a struggle to pierce a hole, then elongate it into a slot, and finally fatigue the metal between this new hole and the previous one. Repeating this process around the can took approximately ten minutes.

- ☐ <u>Reliability</u>. While opening a second can the rock split in two and we had to go and find another one!

- ☐ <u>Aesthetics</u>: Both of our partners were not keen to keeping a rock and nail in the kitchen drawer with their other utensils.

- ☐ <u>Food quality</u>: Bits of grit from the rock became mixed with the contents of the can.

The fact is that a rock and a nail do not make a can opener that is very far up the ideality curve. But what can we learn from this exercise?

As Lawrence Miles learned, it is sometimes best to start from a low-cost starting point and ask what cost you need to add to make it acceptable.

Clearly the rock has to go. It's not reliable, it contaminates the food, and there is no way you would put it in your kitchen

drawer. So what can you put in its place that can provide the force needed to pierce the can?

How about a hook that fits under the rim of the can and acts like a fulcrum?

Also, the nail can't be round. Piercing a hole and then wiggling the nail to make a slot takes time and creates a dangerous jagged edge.

Let's flatten the end of the nail and give it a sharp slicing edge.

To make our new can opener comfortable to use, we should add a handle to the nail.

These changes to our rock and nail won't have cost that much and may result in an acceptable can opener. In fact can openers like this are commonplace, like those found on a Swiss Army knife.

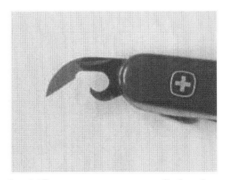

Figure 6.44 The can opener on a Swiss Army knife

Maybe you still wouldn't want this to be your preferred can opener at home. But the point is that there are many components inside products and services that the customer never sees and may not even know exist. It won't matter to customers if you replace an expensive part with one that has been value engineered and still performs all its functions. The same goes for service, as there are many different ways of

varying levels of expense to provide the same thing equally well.

Another way of looking at function worth is to put costs against functions on a function map. In the photograph below, the function map is in yellow Post-it notes. The costs associated with each function are in orange, and ideas for value engineering are in pink.

The purpose here is to *stop thinking about what it IS and concentrate on what it DOES.*

Figure 6.45 Function map with cost information and value engineering ideas

A great example comes from a recent project. The subject was a service tool used to measure backlash in a complex mechanism. The example actually comes from the box that the equipment was supplied in. It was ABS plastic, hermetically sealed, waterproof to 10 meters, and would protect the tool from a fall from a height of 2 meters. It was aimed to be used in the field where things can be accidentally damaged. It normally cost £90, but purchasing had done an excellent job at negotiating a price of £78. On the face of it this was a good price for a box that could do all these things. However, thinking about functions and directly observing the EOC caused us to discover that the service engineers didn't like to have lots of tools all in their own individual boxes. They much preferred to have a single box for all their tools so that they could carry them more easily, so the box was never used. Reflecting on the reality in the EOC, the £78 box was

now used only to transport the tool to the service engineer, after which it was either thrown away or given away. After asking whether this was good value, the clear conclusion was no. The alternative solution was simply to shrinkwrap the tool to a wooden board and ship it with standard packaging materials for less than £1.

We hope you can see that value engineering is a potential goldmine of savings once your team becomes practiced and the natural fit to Lean thinking is clear. By reducing waste in the process *and* in the design itself results can be dramatic.

6.4.7 Value Analysis Matrix

A value matrix is useful to identify areas of a product that have the most cost-reduction potential. It is a tool which is a little like a QFD in that it has the VOC on the left together with the weightings from AHP. This time, however, we have subassemblies or components across the top, and the aim is to show how much they contribute to customer value. If a subassembly contributes 15 percent of the customer value but is 30 percent of the cost, there may be good opportunities for value engineering.

Instead of putting an X in the matrix as we did with the simplified QFD, we now put in a correlation factor which is multiplied with the weighting of the need and then summed for each subassembly or component.

We don't intend to go into great detail here because value analysis matrices are commonly used in value engineering and are well documented. But below is an example for the can opener. You will see that the "cutting wheel bearing and rivet" subassembly contributes 11.2 percent of customer value and is actually good value at a cost of £0.20 against a target of £0.22. The driving wheel and rivet, on the other hand, contribute 7.8 percent of customer value and are expensive compared to the value provided, with a cost of £0.40 against a target of £0.16.

The value analysis matrix doesn't give you any answers, but it does give insights into where value engineering activity can be best invested. Armed with these clues your team will more likely be doing the right work on the right things.

Concept Selection Strong ● 5 Moderate ▩ 3 Weak ▼ 1	Cutting wheel, bearing & rivet	Driving wheel & rivet	Gears & resistance weld	Spring & spacer	Shaft & bearing	Levers, rivets & covers	Crank & rivet	Stiffening plate	Safety guard	Importance
Open can	●	●	▼		●	●	●	▼		10
Open bottle								●		1
Safe						●	●	●	●	7
Doesn't rattle	●	▩		▩	●	●	▩		▼	7
Ease of use						●	●			5
Hardly any force to operate	●		●	●	●	●	●	▩		13
Smooth operation			●	●				▩		13
Comfortable/positive grip						●	●			8
Attractive appearance	▼	▼	▼			●	●	●	▩	10
Dishwasher safe	●	●	●	●	●	●	●	●	●	5
Easy to clean	●	●	●	▩	▩	●	●	●	●	5
Retains appearance	▼	▼	▼			●	●	●	▩	8
Durable – 10 years	●	●	●	▼	▩	▼	▼	▼		8
Value contribution	258	179	248	199	214	398	384	276	146	
Percent	11.2	7.8	10.8	8.6	9.3	17.3	16.7	12.0	6.3	
Target cost (2.00)	0.22	0.16	0.22	0.17	0.19	0.35	0.33	0.24	0.13	
Current cost	0.20	0.40	0.30	0.30	0.20	0.50	0.30	0.40	0.20	

Figure 6.46 Value analysis matrix for our can opener

6.4.8 Combining or Eliminating Parts

In the 1970s the automotive industry had an adage that "two cheap parts are more cost effective than a single more expensive one." Since then, though, this has been disproved in the vast majority of cases. Of course, newer materials and manufacturing techniques have helped, but we now know that

having fewer components in your designs leads to many other benefits that impact on overall costs, including:

- ☐ Reduced supply-chain logistics costs

- ☐ Reduced assembly costs

- ☐ Reduced inspection costs

- ☐ Reduced spare-part-stocking logistic costs

- ☐ Improved reliability

- ☐ Fewer suppliers to manage

On the project itself it can mean:

- ☐ Fewer drawings

- ☐ Less effort from purchasing and operations

- ☐ Fewer failure modes

- ☐ Less testing

Again, it is not our intention to make you an expert by presenting you with lots of information. However, the logic table in figure 6.47 is an excellent way of challenging engineers on the number of components in their product. Armed with these questions, you could start making a difference in achieving a simpler design from your very next design review.

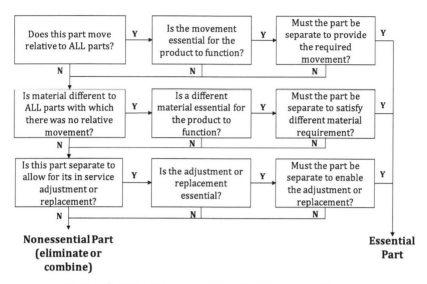

Figure 6.47 Part-count rationalization logic diagram

6.4.9 Value Engineering and TRIZ

We have mentioned TRIZ in many places throughout this book, and great inspiration for value engineering can come from TRIZ thinking. The Russians used it to great effect in the "space race" with the USA. They had only a fraction of the funding and resources of NASA, so they had to be as creative as possible. This same inventiveness is now being seen in Israeli engineering companies, as many Russian Jews fled there after the Second World War.

Some of our favorites from the Russian space program are:

☐ Don't put glass on outside lights—there's no need to hold a vacuum around the filament. NASA made their lights heavier by strengthening the glass to withstand take-off forces.

☐ Use a pencil instead of developing the "space pen."

☐ Use cork as heat-shield material on re-entry. It's very light, flexible, and damage tolerant. It then

221

turns to carbon in the heat of re-entry and forms the perfect thermal barrier. This idea might have saved NASA a lot of problems with the ceramic tiles on the space shuttle.

TRIZ thinking challenges the engineer to imagine how a function can be done differently and for a particular situation or trade-off gives suggestions of the best TRIZ principles to apply to increase the likelihood of success. With data from over four decades of inventive solutions, a TRIZ trade-off solutions matrix can literally put the equivalent of decades of experience at the fingertips of your teams.

6.5 Rapid Problem Solving, Learning, and Knowledge Capture

As we've said throughout this book, a major waste in new product development is caused by not learning fast enough and committing detailed work before fundamentals have been proven. Creating an organization that learns quickly and efficiently is an important element of this, and we will discuss ways to do that in this section. It is tremendously powerful if you can turn that learning into knowledge that means the next project can start from a higher knowledge base and less risk. If you do this well and accumulate knowledge project by project, you will continuously accelerate your time-to-market and drive your technical achievements ever higher. If you don't, you will have to learn the same things over and over again, you'll be held hostage by your experts, and your technical achievements will be limited by your short-term resource availability. An engineer we once met remarked, "We're a sixty-year-old company with 60 X 1 year of experience!"

Our clients often refer to their portfolio of patents when we mention intellectual property. These are important, of course, but the knowledge you have accumulated through many years of being in the business is much more valuable and is often a more effective barrier to market entry than patents, since getting that kind of experience represents a huge investment.

If every piece of learning had a price tag on it showing the cost of gaining it, we would keep them all in a company vault. Instead we don't record it, we throw it away and allow it to walk out of the door, all without a second thought.

6.5.1 Rapid Problem Solving and Learning

Putting an exact value on solving a problem or discovering new knowledge is difficult. But there are clear steps we can take to make it faster. Surprisingly perhaps, to most engineers at least, we can make use of the Lean manufacturing concept of having a Takt time.

Think about oil companies that need to keep discovering new oil resources or they will go out of business. If you were to ask any one company when they expect to find the next big field, they would tell you that it's not an exact science and that they have to look in more remote and hostile environments. It could be tomorrow or it could be years from now. This is all very vague, so how might a potential investor decide which oil company has the best chance of getting lucky? An answer might lie in the rate at which the companies are making test drillings and over how great a geographical spread of potential sites. A company making a test drilling every week may be a much better bet than one that drills every quarter. All else being equal, a Takt time of one week is better than a Takt time of three months.

This same principle can be applied to problem solving and learning. In the case study of the vehicle manufacturer presented in Chapter 3, we saw that it took them well over a year to do any learning from their first prototype. When problems arose and they needed to make changes, the new parts had to be ordered through production sources and it could take many months before a potential solution could be evaluated. The prototype manufacturing facility had been closed two years earlier. Their learning cycle had a Takt time of around three to four months and sometimes longer.

Most companies have even institutionalized this behavior into their NPD procedures. They create an "alpha" prototype which they evaluate and find hundreds of problems. They redesign it and produce a "beta" development machine six months later, which is their first chance to see if they've solved anything. They find more problems, and six months later they have a "gamma" preproduction machine and find more problems. There are only three learning cycles in the whole of the project.

For Lean thinkers, the pace of problem solving and the rate of learning are vital and what ultimately determine long-term performance. With Lean the idea is to first choose a very effective problem-solving approach—namely, the focus on and elimination of waste; second, ensure that it is being practiced widely by all using simple techniques, as opposed to a small elite corps with a set of very sophisticated tools and techniques.

Contrast this with a client of ours who has purposely created a fast learning and problem-solving capability (it's the same client who has the project room pictured earlier in this chapter). They have a manufacturing facility on site dedicated to the manufacture of prototypes and a very flexible test laboratory capable of a wide range of experiments and measurements. They also have a ring of suppliers around them that have been contracted to give a rapid response. They are "on account," and a sketch with the project leader's signature is as good as a purchase order. They cost more, but the client can have components to evaluate solutions and test theories within days and sometimes hours. Their learning cycle has a current maximum Takt time of a week. They focus on answering the missing knowledge on the QFD and DFMEA while steadily achieving integration points that show that more and more of the system can function together. Since investing in this capability, the company has delivered new products to market in half the time and at higher quality.

Team-based problem solving and learning can be chaotic and hard to share with others if you don't have some kind of structured process and a way of making it visible in a concise format. You need to be very careful that this does not create a

bureaucracy to slow down the speed of learning. Over the years we have gravitated to using Toyota's "A3" problem-solving and learning process. All of our clients use it proactively because it is intuitively correct, data based, peer reviewed, and gets results.

So what is Toyota's A3 process? There are some excellent texts on A3s, so we only seek to give you an overview of the technique here. The name comes from the A3 paper size used in Europe and Japan which is 297 mm by 420 mm. Toyota applies Lean principles to every element of their business, and they realized that if you couldn't describe a problem, what you knew about it, and what you were doing to solve it in a simple and concise way, it would be hard to share with others and you weren't thinking clearly enough! For this reason they insisted that everything concerning a single problem should be written on one side of a single piece of A3 paper. At the time it was the largest piece of paper that could be faxed, but soon it was realized that this size had major benefits, enabling teams to share it and work on it. The size created both a limit and a scale that seemed ideal to team-based problem solving. Additionally, working in pencils or erasable pens allowed the A3 to be walked around traditional politics and allowed many people to contribute to the content, thus distilling the ideas of many into a simple structure.

It is based on both the scientific method and W closed-loop problem solving. The A3 page is separated into boxes which are completed in a sequence. We still typically fill out the A3 by hand and in pencil because it is very much a human working document that is updated and reworked as you learn, concur, and solve problems as a team. Our preferred version of the A3 has nine boxes and contains elements vital to the solving of engineering problems. As with many techniques in our system, the power is greatest when it is used in a team. Think of the teams we referred to in the VVSMs and the decision flows we talked about earlier. Imagine each of them recording what is happening as they work via a series of A3s. In the literature you may also encounter A3s with fewer boxes, with the most common having seven. We prefer nine. See if you can see why.

Here is the nine-box template:

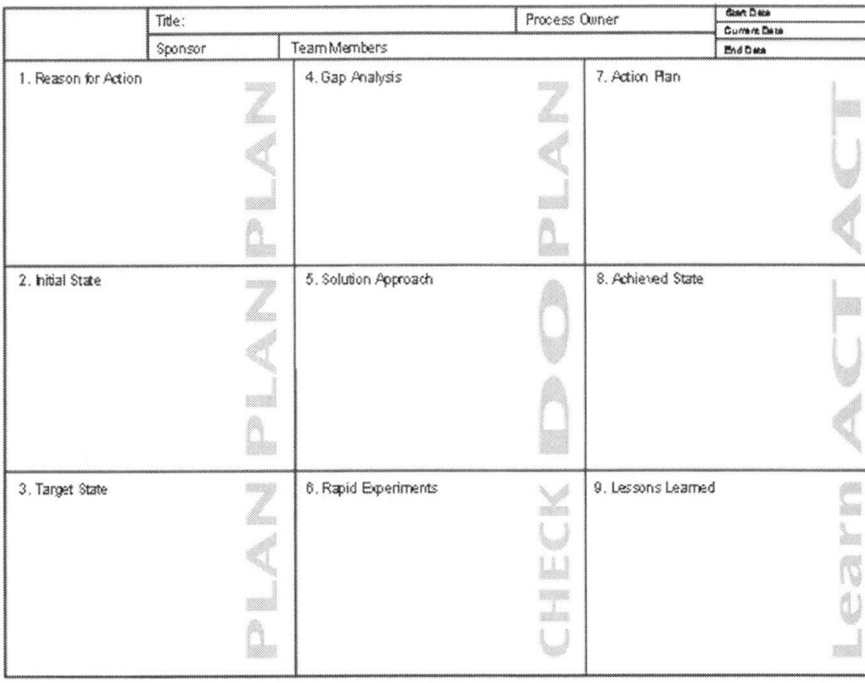

Title:			Process Owner	Start Date
				Current Date
Sponsor		Team Members		End Date

1. Reason for Action	4. Gap Analysis	7. Action Plan
2. Initial State	5. Solution Approach	8. Achieved State
3. Target State	6. Rapid Experiments	9. Lessons Learned

PLAN PLAN PLAN — DO PLAN — CHECK — Learn ACT ACT

Figure 6.48 Nine-Box A3 Problem-Solving Template

You can see that the cycle of problem solving is covered by the first eight boxes, with the ninth capturing what has been learned from solving the problem.

Let's have a quick look at the contents of each box.

Box 1 – Reason for Action

Here we define why we have to do anything at all. Sometimes this is clear and obvious, but there are many occasions when this simple step can help clarify our thoughts about the consequences of not solving this problem. Sometimes we might even decide to do something else instead.

Box 2 – Current State

This is where we write the directly observed facts (no assumptions) that describe the problem today. The box isn't that large and so we use numbers, graphs, and pictures if these are more concise than words. Being brutally honest is key to doing this well, and we need to be as quantitative as possible.

Box 3 – Future State

How will we know that we've solved the problem? Describe quantitatively what success is. Be realistic about what can be achieved in the required timescale rather than insisting on perfection. Box 3 is often expressed in similar descriptors to Box 2.

Box 4 – Gap Analysis

What is/are the root cause(s) of the problem or the observed symptoms? What are the things preventing us from achieving the performance described in Box 3? A gap analysis can take the form of an Ishikawa (fishbone) diagram or any other root cause analysis technique.

Box 5 – Solution Approach

Here we describe our solution(s) that addresses the root causes of our problem identified in Box 4. This may be in the form of sketches or a table like the one below that relates gaps (symptoms) to root causes and then to solutions. The gaps come from an Ishikawa diagram where they were identified with letters. You can see that groups of gaps have a common root cause which is identified in the second column. The solution to this root cause is given in the third column and the fourth column is where we are today relative to an implemented solution. Figure 6.49 is obviously describing an organizational problem but a table like this can just as easily be used to identify the solutions to a product reliability problem or any other issue for which you are choosing to use an A3. There is no right format as long as your problem solving is clear and concise and agreed upon by the team.

Gaps	Root Cause	Solution	Current State
A, B, T, K	"Preliminary Design" not recognised as an important phase in a project	Introduce "Adapted Lean PCP" Reorganisation of R&D to facilitate early risk reduction and system design	30% of PCP spend to Adapted PCP techniques Organisation does not support "Preliminary Design"
A, N	Assalm ment of system design knowledge not rewarded	Recognise System Designers and Preliminary Designers as job titles	System design is an "add-on" and Preliminary design does not exist
B, C, K, O	Early risk reduction not valued in favour of a "fight first time" approach in Design, Make & Test	Use A3 to instil the scientific method into our thinking	A3 is used in 3MLC
D, U	Lack of trust between Product Management and R&D because of a history of broken promises. Processes don't facilitate collaboration pre TG	Use the "Overlapped Double Diamond" model to get Product Management and System Design engaged with Preliminary Design	No formal process for overlapping this work
E	New project starts only a few times per year	Use HPM processes as a training ground for R&D by sampling	No cross-over between HPM and R&D
F, H, L	No knowledge management processes or coaching culture	Create a super group and knowledge management process	No formal support group or database
G, I, M	Focus on rework tasks overwhelms other considerations such as DFX and cost. Data and feedback of DFX performance is incomplete or non-existent (reliability, manufacturability, cost>)	Get projects approved on the merits of their NPV/PCP figure and Get base resources estimation and DFX prediction and target setting	NPV/PCP figure and being introduced. TDM Board needs to start managing this
J	Each project viewed as a single entity rather than part of a flow of projects that creates a even workload within our capacity	Introduce bottleneck and resource loading techniques	Bottlenecks managed by monthly P&D
P, R, T	Experiment, rapid prototype facilities allowed to disappear. Prototype outsource partners lost	Refurbishment of J building to provide prototype workshop Find local rapid prototype suppliers	J building refurbishment underway Not enough rapid prototype suppliers locally
O	Reliance on Clinical Applications rather than customer focus groups	Develop more relationship with hospitals that we trust not to leak information	Not enough trust with key user groups

Figure 6.49 Solution table

Box 6 – Rapid Experiments

For us this is the most important box on the A3 (with Box 9 in second place). It asks us to rapidly prove that the solution approach we've identified is actually going to work. Does it solve the problem, and what new problems does it introduce?

We are always amazed by the number of engineers who are convinced that their first idea of a redesign is going to work just because "it's different" and are happy to wait months to find out whether their assumptions are right or not! Our experience tells us that testing quickly and often is much better than waiting a long time for bad news.

Box 7 – Action Plan

Who is doing what and when? Actions may begin with learning more about the problem, then move on to rapid experiments of potential solutions, and finally integrating the solution into the product. Often A3-based work links to the team boards we described earlier.

Box 8 – Achieved State

How does the solution perform and how does it compare with the desired outcome in Box 3? Again, this is a time for brutal honesty. Has the problem really been adequately solved? If not, re-cycle around the A3, but don't forget to capture...

Box 9 – Lessons Learned

This is our second most important box, just behind Box 6, Rapid Experiments. We almost always learn something of significance when solving a problem.

- □   What works

- □   What doesn't work

- □   The best way of testing

- □   Materials to avoid

- □   The best suppliers

- □   Ways to measure performance

- □   Design formulas

Complete this box with information in a format most useful to the next person designing similar equipment or solving a similar problem.

You will appreciate that all of our clients soon view these A3s as very valuable intellectual property and would not be pleased if we published one of them in this book. The A3 shown below is over five years old and tracks a project completed shortly after we became consultants. We have sanitized it to take out any proprietary data. Here's a brief explanation of some of the information on the A3. In Box 1 you can see that there is a need to supply a piece of equipment for £200k when the previously designed version cost £750k. In Box 2 the shipping time from factory order to nuclear power

station is eighteen months. In Box 3 this must be reduced to four months. The pictures in Box 5 show, among other things, that we are going to put the hydraulics inside the gas storage system and we are increasing gas pressure from 330 bar, stored in a sphere, to 500 bar, stored in a cylinder. This reduced the cost of the pressure vessel and seals by over 80 percent. In Box 6 we can see the analysis and experimentation to make sure our solution is possible. They include finite element stress analysis and experiments to determine "gamma" (the adiabatic index) of nitrogen at very high pressures. The latter was found by partnering with a local university which had the right test equipment to determine the nonideal behavior of gases. In Box 9, the last learning point on the list refers to the fact that the adiabatic index of a gas actually changes when you reach high pressures like 500 bar. This simple tool works in the most complex of environments, and having been involved in hundreds of them, we recommend the method wholeheartedly.

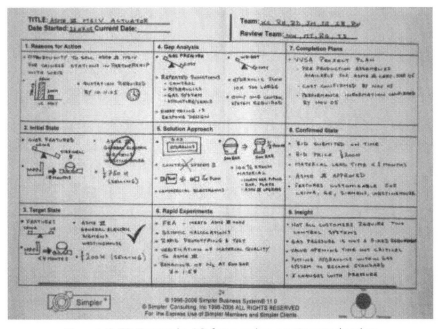

Figure 6.50 Example A3 for a value engineered valve

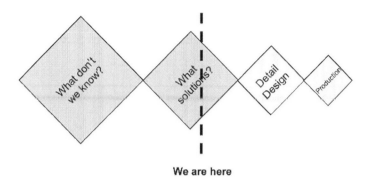

We are here

6.5.2 Knowledge Capture

Both of us worked in the aerospace sector within prime contractors. This was when the companies started buying and deploying the first IBM PC desktop computers.

This magical piece of technology opened the possibility for information stored on mainframe computers to be accessed by employees at their desks, so there were soon projects to enter all this data into the mainframes. In one company, filing cabinets were soon emptied, and every Friday afternoon all engineers stopped working on aeronautical work to read a pile of reports, wrote a brief synopsis of each one, and chose key words from a standard list. An army of secretaries then typed this information into the mainframe, together with the location of the paper report in case someone wanted to read it after finding the synopsis of interest. This was a huge effort that went on for months.

What was achieved through all this effort? An engineer could go and sit at one of the PCs and type in some key words. They would then get a list of report titles that could run into the hundreds. Hardly any of these report titles gave any indication of the learning that might be contained within. For example, a title might be "Thermal paint investigation of the RB211-524D4 LP Turbine," but a valuable piece of knowledge in the report might be the details on how to use and interpret a new thermal paint specification. If this happened to be what the

engineer was looking for, he or she would have to get copies of and read all the reports on the list because the synopses didn't mention the new paint either.

The key point to this story is that simple recording didn't create knowledge in the form most easily found and used by the people who needed to use it. The data remains just data that need to be researched to extract knowledge. Instead of doing the research once so that everyone else can get to the knowledge quickly, they created a database where everyone had to do his or her own research independently and repetitively.

Earlier, we saw how an A3 can capture the learning gained in solving a problem. This allows our skilled people to solve problems and to create better solutions more quickly. To speed this up we need to take the learning into a knowledge base that effectively makes our skilled people smarter.

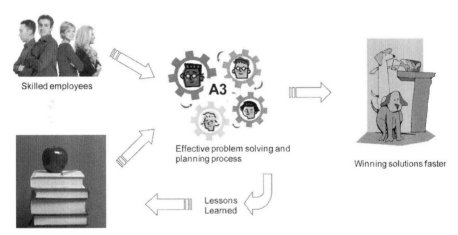

Figure 6.51 Turning skill and knowledge into winning solutions

So how can we capture the knowledge we need in a format that is most usable?

When we discussed technology demonstration earlier in the chapter, we saw how the learning can be presented as a trade-off graph that helped future projects to select the right ceramic-bearing material and choose a speed and load that works

at the operating temperature. The problem we have is that most A3s will not often have a graph like this in their lessons learned Box 9.

The A3 can be seen therefore as a "single point of learning" and is just enough to get a particular project completed or problem solved. If we were to ask the project to explore the design space beyond their own needs and write a thesis on the results, it would be very unlikely to be done because they have their own priorities of solving problems and getting a product to market. There are companies that understand that delivering a project and capturing knowledge work against each other when there are finite resources and deadlines to meet. To solve this they set up small groups of experts who actually have time set aside to look at individual A3 learning across all projects and to convert these into a usable knowledge bank.

For example, the handwritten A3 used as an example contained the knowledge that nitrogen gas has a compression factor 1.58 at 500 bar. This piece of information can be transferred to a knowledge document that contains everything the company knows about the use of nitrogen as an energy-storage medium. If other projects determine the compression factor of nitrogen at even higher pressures, the knowledge document can have a graph with the data points on it. The group of experts own the knowledge documents and make sure they are available to everyone who needs them.

In earlier times at GE these knowledge documents were known as "design guides," and you were awarded a GE pen if you made a contribution that the expert group thought was worthy of inclusion. Some engineers would have all the pens they'd "earned" in their shirt pockets as medals of honor! We have found that many cases such as the transition from paper drawings to CAD-based drawings led to the virtual loss of these documents, and every client we have worked with realizes that they need to be doing a lot more. We liken this essential retained knowledge to "key recipes." This analogy is useful for defining exactly how much should we retain and how should we keep it topical. Think of a family recipe that

has survived generations. How does that happen? How does it have to be maintained to stay topical?

What might a "knowledge document" look like? Some companies take the same approach used for A3 problem solving and take the view that if you can't explain all the knowledge on a piece of paper 297 mm by 420 mm. you have overcomplicated it and only a few will use it. This piece of paper is sometimes called a "K3," which is short for "knowledge A3."

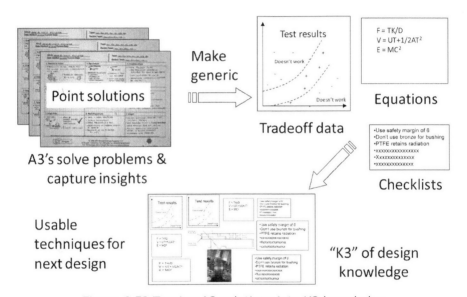

Figure 6.52 Turning A3 solutions into K3 knowledge

The data on a K3 may take the form of trade-off curves or equations, but just as useful are lists of what works and what doesn't. Toyota uses lists like this to great effect and publishes them in design notebooks. Let's be clear and consistent with what we said earlier. The use of K3s and checklists should not become part of the quality system, and there shouldn't be any bureaucracy of auditing whether checklists have been completed as a requirement of the NPD process. Good information is like a recipe. It is recommended and then used (pulled) because it is useful, not because someone is going to inspect whether it has been used or not.

There is no right and wrong here. You don't have to use a K3. Any format that fits your culture will be fine, provided you can find what you need and it is in the most useful form for you to do your work. The key is providing time and space for development. We once had a client who had merged two technical companies, each with a long and distinguished technical history. As you can imagine, each had its own team of highly opinionated technical staff in the field of tribology. Ultimately their opinions where driven by both the science of tribology and how their respective companies had applied this science over the years. What it took to unify the teams was two months of their being metaphorically locked in a room until not only was their knowledge captured for all to use, it was then amalgamated to create one body of unified knowledge. This act alone led to a leap in technical productivity as junior staff told us that capturing the knowledge had enabled them to stop negotiating the bottleneck of senior staff who had the most knowledge. We also found private stores of notes and "rules" that had previously been closely guarded and not shared with others. This sounds like a strange state of affairs, but in many organizations without a "career path" for technical staff. Knowledge literally is power.

Having made the case for the knowledge base, what data should you put into your base first? We're going to answer this with the very principle with which we started this book.

Look for the wasted time and effort in your projects caused by a lack of knowledge. Determine the knowledge that would reduce the waste the most and make it available to all.

6.6 A listing of all the techniques in this chapter and their difficulty

As we promised at the beginning of this chapter we've created a table of the techniques in this chapter. We've also indicated the extent to which we've modified the technique to suit our lean principles and how easy it is to apply them. Hopefully you will find this useful in your further study and in deciding if you

should seek assistance in applying these techniques until they become embedded in your business.

Section	Techniques	How Much Modified	Ease of Use
6.1 Product Planning	Product life cycle (S curves)	Unchanged	Easy
	Feature map & competitive comparison	Unchanged	Hard
	Systems thinking	Unchanged	Hard
6.2 Determine Customer Value	Environment of the Customer	Unchanged	Hard
	Kano Model	Unchanged	Moderate
	Data Collection Plan		Easy
	Voice of the Customer Table	Modified	Hard
	Analitic Hyrarchy Process (AHP)	Unchanged	Moderate
	Project Vision	Modified	Hard
	Quality Function Deployment	Heavily modified	Very Hard
	Taguchi Targets	Unchanged	Moderate
	Critical to Quality	Unchanged	Moderate
6.3 Managing Risk Early	Design FMEA	Modified	Very Hard
	Decision Flow	Unique	Hard
	Team Based Project Planning (VVSA)	Unchanged	Hard
	Team Board	Unchanged	Moderate
	Project Room	Unchanged	Moderate
	Set Based Thinking	Modified	Hard
	Pugh Selection	Unchanged	Moderate
6.4 Maximising Value	Function Mapping	Unchanged	Very Hard
	Combining Functions	Unchanged	Moderate
	Functional Worth	Unchanged	Hard
	Value Analysis Matrix	Unchanged	Moderate
	Combining or Eliminating Parts	Unchanged	Moderate
	TRIZ	Unchanged	Hard
6.5 Problem Solving, Learning and	A3	Modified	Moderate
	Knowledge Capture & K3	Modified	Moderate

Figure 6.53 The techniques in this chapter and their difficulty

Introduction to the Main Techniques of Execution

Introduction

You will have realized by now that the majority of this book is dedicated to the exploration phase of a project. This is because too often we see that a lack of exploration in a project is the cause of many problems and much wasted effort. Having said that, exploration itself needs to be focused and efficient, or otherwise it too will be wasteful, and we hope that the preceding chapter has shown how this can be achieved. We hope that we have also highlighted how existing "best practices" can in practice curtail exploration and drive the wrong behavior. But what of execution itself as a phase? In execution there will typically be a lot more resources committed, and surely the opportunity to create waste is even higher than in the exploration phase. This is true. However, much of the best practice in NPD published over the last half century has focused on how to execute projects more effectively and efficiently. What's more, many Lean techniques developed in manufacturing environments can, once a project moves into execution, be effectively applied by the NPD team. All of this best practice, however, falls apart when unknowns, uncertainty, and assumptions still exist and form the basis of the project at the start of execution. That's why we've dedicated most of this book to exploration. In this final chapter we don't intend to replicate the already published best practices. Instead we will outline the techniques and thinking that have served us well in getting a well-explored and thought-out design scheme to market more quickly.

As in all Lean thinking enterprises, the key to reducing waste, cost, and time is to create a flow of value-adding work and to see waste for what it really is. As we've already discovered,

knowing what should flow is a key insight, and in the case of exploration, the flow is one of knowledge and decisions. In execution, however, this focus changes to a flow of more tangible things like documents, components, tests, and tasks. There is a higher degree of repetitive work and in this environment it may be advantageous to create multipersonnel "flow cells" where needed, with "standard work" along similar principles to those used in Lean factories. However, there will almost certainly be some remaining unknowns that the exploration phase hasn't answered, as well as detail-design decisions. We have applied techniques such as decision flow and vertical value stream analysis (VVSA) and found them to be very effective early in the execution phase.

Before we go any further, we need to warn you that this chapter borrows heavily from some of the techniques described in Chapter 6. So it will be helpful if you are already familiar with QFD, decision flow, DFMEA, VVSA, team board, A3 problem solving, and knowledge management. If you have just dipped into this book at this chapter, you may wish to read about these techniques in the previous chapter before continuing.

7.1 When does the execution phase start?

The best way of answering this very important question is to remind ourselves of the deliverables from the exploration phase described in Chapter 6. The whole purpose of the exploration phase is to answer questions and risks identified in QFDs and DFMEAs. Therefore the outputs of the phase are completed QFDs and DFMEAs which define requirements (voice of the customer and voice of the engineer), test cases, critical to quality (CTQ) targets, and the beginnings of a maintenance strategy. In addition there will be a wealth of knowledge recorded in A3s, design rules, K3s, and test results.

Many of our clients already have good requirements management systems, and their NPD process usually has a stage gate at the point where a complete set of requirements has been developed and signed off on. Just before this stage gate there

is usually a planning activity to estimate the time and resources required for the next stage and to complete the project. Armed with this, it is now possible to create a business case for the project, since the requirements give us the customer value that is being created, and the planning estimates the project costs and timing.

The name or number of this stage gate varies from company to company, but it is usually easy to identify the stage gate that separates exploration from execution. In Robert G. Cooper's stage gate system, it is the gate between Stage 2, "Build Business Case," and Stage 3, "Development." In his system this is Gate 3, but for many of our clients the corresponding gate is usually number 2, since they launch the project at Gate 0.

7.2 Establishing flow in the execution phase

Just as in the exploration phase, a waste-free flow is only possible if uncertainties are managed and reduced before they can create waste and rework in the project. The uncertainties in execution are no longer ones of whether the technology works, whether there is a market for the product, or what it is that the customer actually wants. These risks and more have been removed in the exploration phase. However, there will be plenty of decisions which aren't "life or death" for the project but still have to be made nonetheless. These may include the choice of less critical suppliers, the selection of standard design features, and test methods, to name only a few.

7.2.1 Using a decision flow

We can again use a decision flow in the same way as in the exploration phase (see Chapter 6), but the starting point probably won't be unknowns generated by creating a QFD or DFMEA. These techniques were useful in identifying the "unknown unknowns" at the start of the project. By the time we

reach execution we should have "known unknowns." Instead, the design described by the QFD and DFMEA completed during exploration needs to be turned into a procurable product supported by all the supply chain, marketing, sales, service, regulatory, and distribution elements needed to bring it to market.

Because the work in the execution phase is more predictable, we have found that checklists of decisions are useful here as long as they are supplemented with limited brainstorms of the additional decisions required for the nuances of the project in question. It is worth noting, however, that if high-risk decisions are being identified, this is a serious indictment of how well the exploration phase has performed, and we need to identify why this has been allowed to occur and take corrective action. Just like in a Lean factory where a problem would and should stop the flow (after all, problems are best solved before they get any bigger, right?), we should take the same approach in NPD in the execution phase. Upon discovery of problems we can stop, track backward, and take corrective action at the point of cause rather than performing endless rework later. It sometimes feels like going in reverse as we often haul clients back to exploration, sometimes more than once, but to be clear, execution can only happen with low waste when you are truly ready.

7.2.2 Decision flow in "application engineering" environments

This book is primarily about new product development, but there are many companies that employ technical staff to take known design principles and apply them in different applications. For example, a valve and control company where Rob worked as the engineering director had a range of gate, ball, control, and butterfly valves which they supplied to the oil, gas, and power industries. Each valve came in a wide range of sizes, pressure classes, and materials together with an extensive variety of features and options. The majority of the possible specifications had never been designed because it was far more efficient to create designs only to meet a specific order, which was almost always for an application that required

a new combination of size, material, pressure, and features. This is what we call "application engineering" and it is a very common business model. The design rules for a valve are well understood and there is very little technical risk. However, decisions still have to be made during the configuration process. Even in this environment a decision flow can be very useful. For each type and class of valve there will be a sequence in which decisions should be made that minimizes the potential for creating waste, and this can be formalized as best practice since the decision flow can be reused each time that valve type is ordered. Also, the information or analysis required for each decision can be clearly shown. If a subsequent problem arises it is then easy to see where a decision, or the information to make a decision, was flawed and to update the best practice embodied in the decision flow. We have found with many clients in this kind of business that they get big increases in sales when their speed of response means that customers' requests are configured and quoted before their competitors have even acknowledged the request.

7.2.3 Project logic, vertical value stream analysis, and team boards

In the exploration phase of an NPD project, there is usually a small team with the common focus of learning as quickly as possible. In this environment a decision flow together with a vertical value stream analysis and a team board is usually enough to coordinate the team and keep it on track. In the execution phase, however, it is common that separate teams and suppliers can do their piece of the project without always needing to work together or even to communicate regularly with each other. These teams could be separated functionally or geographically, and in this modern world it is more and more common that design work is outsourced to suppliers who design, prototype, and test significant elements of the new product. Obviously they must all still deliver their work in a sequence and at agreed times, and so there is a need for a high-level plan that orchestrates all these elements of the projects. Each team, group, or supplier contributing to the

project will have their own sequence of milestones that they need to achieve. Although these milestones may all map to the project end date, there is also a clear need to align them to critical points throughout the project. As in all the techniques we've described in this book, this master plan must be visual, visible, easily understood, and team based. To achieve this we use what we call a "project logic," which is a form of master plan, and we've gone to great lengths to simplify our technique but still achieve the necessary alignment.

7.2.4 Creating a project logic

The construction of a project logic is quite simple. The example shown below is only about half complete but serves to illustrate the technique without compromising the company's development secrets.

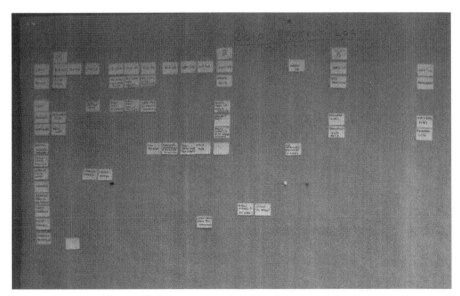

Figure 7.1 Example of a simple project logic

Time flows from left to right across the top, and there are "swim lanes" below that show when significant events or mile-

stones need to happen within different functions. For example, the illustration above has swim lanes for the following:

- ☐ Build— These are the different stages of prototype build from first prototype to preproduction. These have been named α (study prototype), β (test prototype), and γ (preproduction prototype).

- ☐ Test —These are descriptions of the various tests planned for each of the prototype builds.

- ☐ Processor—This is the standard of firmware needed on the prototypes.

- ☐ Software—This is the level of code required.

- ☐ Design freeze (hardware)—Many companies have a creeping permafrost, and this can be described as milestones on the project logic.

- ☐ Supplier long-lead tooling—It is often possible to finalize tooling such as casting or forging shapes well before the final detail is completed.

- ☐ Supplier long-lead items—These are long lead time items bought in parts.

- ☐ Manuals—These must be written, validated using hardware, and then translated into many languages.

- ☐ Special service equipment—The new product needs to be maintained, and some customers insist that all the support equipment be available before they will purchase the product.

- ☐ User interface—There were a few possible types, and the project logic captures when these should be selected and demonstrated.

- ☐ Cost model—This was rolled up continuously throughout the project, but a major milestone is the

cost analysis of all the development parts for the β build prototype.

☐ Market acceptance—This was a customer survey to verify that the basic principle of the new product was acceptable to the target market segments. This would then be followed up with events to solicit customer feedback as the design progresses.

The project logic plays a role similar to the conductor of an orchestra. Each musician has his own score that he has practiced, but the conductor keeps time and indicates the sequence of the individual parts, frequently making eye contact with a musician before his piece starts.

There are plenty of other "swim lanes" that could appear on a project logic, but it really depends on your business and what the project has to achieve. As we've said on a few occasions, all projects are different and you should not seek to prescribe the contents of these techniques. Instead they form an important part of right-sizing a project. Only include the work you have to do in the specific circumstances. Having said that, other swim lanes could be:

- Multiple modules—There is a time-to-market advantage in developing modules in parallel and somewhat independently, but there is a still a need to align key milestones in their development and integration into the whole product.

- Customer feedback sessions and evaluations

- Launch events such as shows or product reveals

- Regulatory compliance milestones

There are of course other ways of representing the master plan, and vertical value stream analysis is a good alternative. VVSA is described in detail in Chapter 6. To create the master plan we have functions across the top and time running downward. We then create a sequence of tasks or milestones,

placing them under the lead function. Just as before, there is one task or milestone per line. You can add lines and arrows showing the interdependencies of some of the activities.

Below is a picture of a section of an aerospace sector project plan. Although the team created it together, they had it printed and laminated so that everyone could have a copy of his or her own to refer to throughout the work.

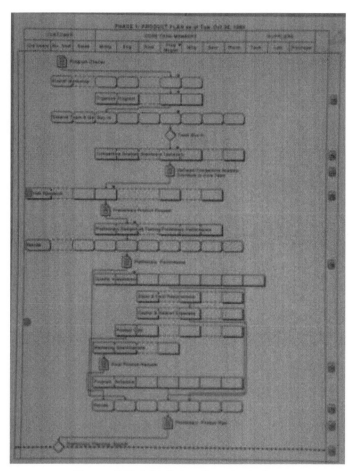

Figure 7.2 A high level project plan

As always, developing plans interactively as a team is a very powerful technique, as is making those plans constantly

visible and visual. If the plan is created without a team-based approach, then a huge opportunity has been missed. Even though we advocate low-tech approaches, we have lots of examples of how a little bit of technology can unite without disengaging teams. For example, a low-cost high-definition webcam can be trained on key documents in the obeya room for providing real-time information to share with other remote workers. We have more than once created obeyas in remote parts using multiple video-conferencing cameras and projectors. The key is to allow high-bandwidth face-to-face interactions to happen often and informally as well as formally. You need to be seeking to eliminate hundreds of emails and increase the flow of team-based working and decision making.

7.2.5 The need for project management

At this point it is worth saying a few words about project management as a distinct discipline, since many of our larger clients have professional project managers because their NPD projects are never on time. As we said earlier, a project manager, like the conductor of an orchestra, is useful if the activities of people who would never communicate with each other need to happen in a set sequence at set times. The construction industry was used as an example of one in which project managers are extremely useful. In many cases project managers have an engineering qualification but are not particularly expert in the technologies involved in their particular product. They have made a career of managing projects and are continually looking for bottlenecks, checking the critical paths, and communicating the key dates and milestones. They continually check task completion, spending, and resource levels, and fight for future budgets and manpower from functions across the business. Clearly, these skills can be useful if you have a large and complex business with many engineering and support functions with their own management structures. In a refreshing approach, BMW Rolls-Royce GmbH chose to develop their new gas turbine without professional project

managers and instead had a chief engineer who integrated the work of lead engineers who in turn led multifunction module design teams. At British Aerospace, Chris was one of the first of this new breed of engineers in the aerospace sector and was working directly for a group chief engineers staff who collaborated as a multidisciplinary team at the highest level. Because the "master plan" was visible to all and the eleven lead engineers met every two weeks to align activities, there was no need of a specific project management capability. In these business models the financial aspects and budgeting were the responsibility of the lead engineers but were facilitated by a small group of financial controllers assisting them.

A worrying trend for us is that professional project managers are being seen as a solution to the lack of flow and high levels of waste in NPD, even in smaller businesses. In the vast majority of situations, the use of project logic, decision flows, vertical value stream maps, and team boards would be more than enough to create teamwork, interfunction communication, keep a project on track, and make problems easily visible to management. Apart from the added cost of a relatively expensive professional project manager, PMs often have the effect of lessening teamwork and actually encouraging engineers to work in isolation. As we saw in Chapter 4, many engineers are introverts by nature and would love nothing better than to be left alone "to do their thing." The problem is that the professional project manager is often not expert in the technologies of the project and is not a good substitute for getting engineers and support functions working as a team and thrashing through problems. Many instinctively feel uncomfortable during exploration and often exhibit behavior traits that make things worse. This invariably leads to premature entry into the execution phase. We once witnessed a project manager say, "Can we take all this discussion and debate offline so we can actually get on with our plan?" Note this was while the team was discussing a basic configuration issue that had been unresolved at three previous design reviews because it had been "taken offline" then as well. "Taken offline" should be replaced with "who do we need so we can do it now!"

7.2.6 VVSA and team boards

Both vertical value stream analysis and team boards are described in detail in Chapter 6 and it is not our intention to repeat ourselves here. Both of these techniques are still extremely useful in the execution phase of a project. It is sometimes the case that the smaller team that concentrated on exploration has now been diluted by more technical staff and support functions joining the project, and it will no longer be practicable to have a single VVSA or team board. When this occurs, we have had success in creating smaller functional, module, or activity-based teams that are coordinated by project logic and systems thinking who run their own VVSA and team board. At times we have found that the frequency of team board updates can be varied. When there are large pieces of work to achieve, twice per week may be appropriate. In the run-up to a major milestone, when there are lots of things to close out, twice per day has been very effective. With team-based project planning working well, the chief engineer for the project can easily see the status of the project and dedicate his or her time to solving the more significant issues.

7.3 Managing non-co-located teams

With the ever-increasing trend toward globalization, it is not unusual to have NPD teams spread across multiple sites in different countries and time zones, but intuition tells us that dedicated and co-located teams must be faster than those that are not. However, Toyota, which is recognized as one of the fastest developers of new car models, has neither dedicated nor co-located teams. Instead they have a shusa (chief engineer) and integration engineers who make sure all the design elements are compatible, orchestrated, and sequenced together, with visual and visible information to keep everyone synchronized.

In our experience it is well worth the effort and cost of bringing the people working on the project together for the creation of the project logic, decision flow, and initial VVSA. Doing

team-based project planning together is essential to get the best thinking and a broad commitment. Once this has been completed, we have found that projects can be efficiently executed with dispersed teams by the use of "web-ex" type conference calls, internal web-based information-sharing sites, and by creating electronic versions of decision flows, VVSAs, etc. As we said before, even low-tech webcams trained on key charts during Skype calls can work well.

We have used Microsoft Excel effectively to create electronic decision flows and VVSAs. Cells can be colored in a similar way to using different-colored Post-it notes. You can also use Microsoft Project, but we have found that in reality it isn't as effective at visually spotting where people are overloaded because they are helping others with their tasks. It is also harder to see who is accountable, and resource leveling is fraught with problems. It tempts you to start playing with interdependencies and adding levels of detail beyond your ability to forecast accurately. For this reason we recommend keeping the information as simple and as clear as possible. We have to be clear, we are not anti-Microsoft, but its project management software is seen everywhere, and in a lot of cases we are turning around behavior and logic that Microsoft has encouraged.

One of our clients who develops significant amounts of software uses Atlassian JIRA for the same purpose. This is a software application designed to track the progress of software development tasks, test results, and corrective actions. It has easily configurable workflows and, most importantly, it supports multiple site usage.

We've even had a client have a web-ex meeting with a video cameras showing the Post-it-based decision flow, VVSA, and team board.

The most important thing is that you achieve effective teamwork, problem sharing, and milestone coordination as teams rather than sequential email-based baton passing. The method you use should be whatever best fits your employees, culture, and IT infrastructure. We are both excited about the possibility of social networking technology and its impact on the world of NPD.

7.4 Creating flow cells

As there are more repetitive work elements in the execution phase, these can be greatly improved by applying the flow cell approach as used in Lean manufacturing. These are usually pieces of work that require a sequence of tasks to be done by people from different functions that are dispersed across the business. In this situation a piece of work needs to criss-cross the organization, with multiple hand-offs between people. Each hand-off is an opportunity for the work to wait in a queue either physically in an in-tray or electronically in an inbox. Each hand-off is an opportunity for miscommunication and for errors to creep in without being detected until much later, which then drives long rework cycles. The waste caused by all this waiting and rework can bring the whole process to a standstill, collapsing under the weight of rework.

Here's a simple example. You decide to arrange an office night out and send an email to fifteen of your colleagues asking them when and where they would like to go out. Each of them replies to you and copies the message to the other fourteen colleagues. There are then a myriad of emails criss-crossing the office exchanging different views. You then try to estimate when the majority might be available and conclude that most would like to go out to a restaurant. You therefore propose a date and suggest a local French bistro. There is then another round of responses and suggestions, with the vegetarians noting that French cuisine is not particularly meat-free. Before you know it two weeks have elapsed and you are no nearer a decision.

Now let's look at an actual example. We worked with a major global engineering company that used a world-class engineering change management system. It had workflows built into it that allowed engineers to propose drawing changes and bills of material changes which then went through a series of impact assessments in supply chain, manufacturing, quality, service, regulatory compliance, etc. Once the changes had been approved, the system then managed the process of implementing the changes through supplier negotiation, obsolescence management, supplier quality assurance, and production

changeover. Below is a process map showing the elapsed time and touch times in the engineering change request (ECR) process. You can see that of the 258.4 days it takes a change to go through the part of the process depicted (process time), the ECR has only been worked on (value added time) for a mere 20.1 days! What's more, the error rate at each step means that only 4.6 percent of ECRs get through the process without the waste of rework. Even though the computer generated reports of where all the ECRs were in the process, the company was finding it impossible to speed up the process. Our investigations found that many functions did not have time to review the ECRs properly and so approved their piece with the thinking that any problems could be caught when the change was implemented. We found that one function in particular would clear thirty to forty ECRs in the space of an hour just to get them off their list. The problem was that errors found after the ECR was approved required further ECRs to correct them!

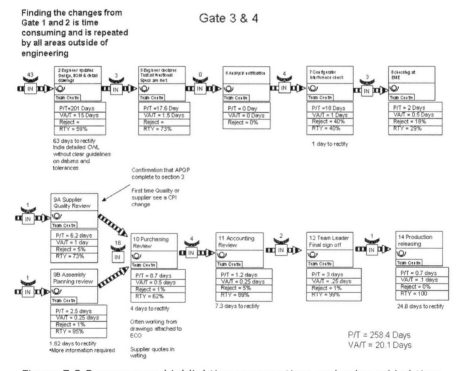

Figure 7.3 Process map highlighting process time and value added time

So how can a flow cell help? Well, in the case of the evening out for the office, it would be much quicker to get all your colleagues into a room and ask them what they would like to do. You then all get your calendars out and agree a number of possible dates. One of you calls the venue and makes sure they can take a booking for sixteen people on one of the chosen dates. All this could be done in only thirty minutes.

For the complex ECR process we can build a "flow cell" that might ideally look like this:

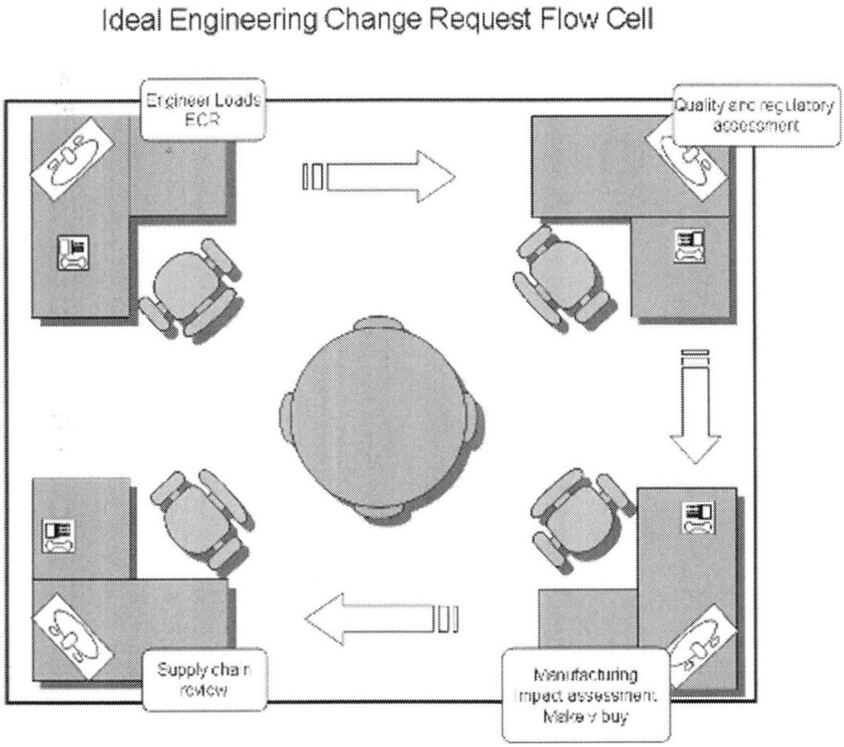

Ideal Engineering Change Request Flow Cell

Figure 7.4 Ideal Engineering Change Request Flow Cell

All it is is a space with four desks and four computers. On Tuesdays it is an ECR flow cell and the desks are occupied with the functional disciplines required to assess ECRs. Rather than shuffling pieces of paper between the desks, the self-same engineering change management software is used to progress

work through the system. The difference is that everyone is there at the same time. They can quickly confer with each other and clarify the information they have just received. Any possible errors can quickly be corrected without going through formal loopbacks. If, for example, there are on average four ECRs created per week, the Tuesday cell needs to process an ECR every two hours. If a backlog builds up, you can then choose to run the cell for an additional half-day when required.

The ideal in any flow cell is that only one item is in work at each of the "stations" in the flow. Like the old bucket brigades that firefighters used to use before hoses were developed, it is the fastest most efficient way for people to create flow between themselves. The benefit of this way of working is that the resulting low level of work in progress means that problems are not only more visible, they can be more manageable to solve as a team. Although this logic is sound and makes perfect sense and can be proven by the many demonstrations that have been devised, for many it actually goes against the habits of a lifetime. Setting things aside in order to "keep things moving" or "taking problems offline" all ultimately slow us down in the long run, but we all persist in many circumstances. Lean thinkers could be described as those who have become enlightened about the power of flow and the elimination of waste, but even those with decades of doing it have to have real discipline and a willingness to face problems head-on and solve them in real time. At first many flow cells seem crushingly slow, but speed soon develops. In short, it is a cultural change that will be instinctively (though not logically) resisted, but the results are always a step change in performance.

Because a desk with a phone and a computer is so versatile, this very same space can be a different type of flow cell on each day of the week. On Wednesday, for example, it can be a stress analysis cell. At Desk 1 an engineer retrieves a CAD model and applies a load case made up of force vectors, pressure areas, and constraints. At the second desk a finite-element expert applies her expertise to select the element types that will give the best combination of accuracy and computing speed. At the third desk the results are post-processed and an engineer checks

that they make sense. At the fourth desk an engineer creates a report of findings and recommendations for the design engineer at Desk 1 who originally commissioned the work. A work cell such as this could do ten stress cases in a day when it would normally take a whole week of everyone together to do the work together. On Thursday the space could be used for part-cost estimations, manual writing, creating factory work instructions, ordering prototype hardware, or any number of other activities where the waste of separation, waiting, miscommunication, and rework is overwhelming your current process.

In many instances you may not think you have the space for a dedicated flexible working cell like that described above, but remember, in execution, cellular-based working should be the norm, not the exception. There are many ways of creating flow cell–based working.

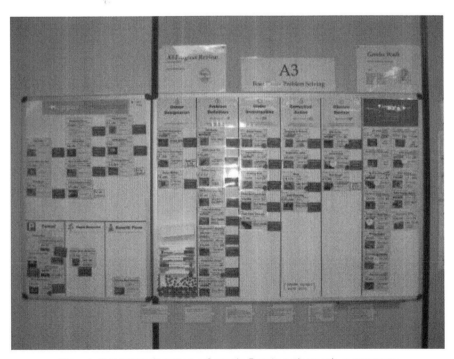

Figure 7.5 Visualization of work flowing through a process

The wall above, for example, has been dedicated to show the flow of work through a problem-solving process. The A3 has

been adopted as the problem-solving template so it is those which physically flow along the wall, so the wall shows the status of each of the problems according to the completed boxes. Weekly meetings are held during which the problems are worked on by a multifunctional group of manufacturing engineers, supplier quality assurance engineers, design engineers, and service engineers. At these meetings they share what has been done and agree what to do next on the problems in work. It is worth noting that the wall has a section for "problems evaluated but not started." These have A3s completed to Box 1, but further work will only start when there is capacity to do it. This means that the team has a collective in-tray, and problems in progress are kept to a manageable level.

In this instance, Box 1 has the calculation of the cost per year of not solving the problem. Not starting work until you have capacity to do so is an important point, because overloading the process just slows it all down to a crawl and very little actually gets completed. With a flow cell, any backlog in work is immediately apparent and management can make the decision to apply more people to problem solving or to expand hours of operation when needed.

7.5 Multiple projects through limited resources

As we've already discussed, there is a much larger involvement from support functions in the exploration phase and so there will be many more people who are not dedicated to a single project and thus have to share their time between projects and maybe other non-project work as well.

In passing it is worth noting that there is a trade-off between speed and efficiency when it comes to deciding whether to dedicate resources to a project or to share some of them across projects. Some businesses value speed to market more than efficiency because the value of being first to market far outweighs the cost of having additional people on the payroll. However, in the majority of situations the investment in new

products is significant and so there is a need to use resources as efficiently as possible.

As we've already seen, there is considerable waste when individuals stop and start work and wait for someone else to complete work upon which they are reliant. The effort of trying to orchestrate these activities through intense project management effort is also a wasteful activity, although many may see it as heroic firefighting. Clear prioritization, resource allocation boards, time slicing, and resource slicing are some simple techniques that can reduce the waste caused by sharing common resources among your projects. As long as the flow of learning and knowledge, decisions, and executions is being discharged as described, at least you know resources are being used efficiently.

7.5.1 Prioritization

If left to their own devices, people will naturally prioritize their own individual work with little regard to the big picture. This prioritization will almost always be inconsistent with that of others working on the same project. For example, I might pick what's fun to do first, then what I can complete quickly, then what is needed by a colleague who I'm friends with, and finally what is difficult and may take more than the day to complete. I will then work this list until the end of the day. Tomorrow I'll start again with a new prioritization, and the larger, more difficult task might be put off for yet another day until someone is shouting for it. This way of working means that we need to pay people to "shout," continually plan tasks and dates, and to keep asking for work to be completed and passed on to the next person in the current work sequence. When a worker is contributing to multiple projects, he will be forever putting jobs down and picking other jobs up depending on who is shouting loudest. He will attempt to work on things simultaneously, but the truth is that multitasking is inefficient, even though some of us are better at it than others.

To illustrate how clear prioritization can help this situation, let's take an example of a stress analyst who has four stress cases to analyze for four different projects. Each project should take one week of effort, and all of them are needed in one week from now. If the stress analyst tries to work on all four jobs at once, she will most likely finish all of them in five weeks' time. This situation is shown in the graphic below, which shows that all four jobs are four weeks late.

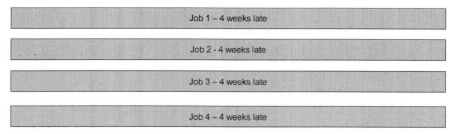

Figure 7.6 Work of unclear priority being done simultaneously

Let us now assume that there is a clear prioritization of the four jobs. The analyst starts Job 1 and finishes it in a week without distractions from other tasks and uninterrupted by project managers asking for the status of their jobs. She then starts the second job and completes that in the following week and so on.

The situation is shown below:

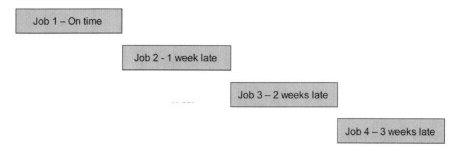

Figure 7.7 Work done in a sequence according to priority

As you can see, Job 1 is on time, Job 2 is a week late, Job 3 is two weeks late, and Job 4 is three weeks late. Just by simply

prioritizing all the projects you are better off, and you are better off even if you get the prioritization order wrong!

This effect is even more powerful if the same prioritization is given across the organization. The problem is that this may change for a particular resource as bottlenecks come and go and as a result of events on each project. A useful way of managing this without having project managers running around the organization is to use resource allocation boards.

7.5.2 Resource allocation boards

In a Lean factory it may not always be possible to have every piece of work "in flow," and an expensive machine tool may be shared between a number of flow lines. In this situation you may find *Heijunka* boards that look like a clothesline with a series of pigeonholes below. Pegged to the line is the job card for the current job, and in the pigeonholes are the waiting jobs in the time sequence needed by the flow lines on a "just in time" basis. Each morning a review of the waiting jobs is made to make sure that the sequence is still optimized. This review is made by the leaders of the project lines that share the machine tool.

This same principle can be effectively used in any situation in which multiple projects need to share the same resources. In its simplest form, this can be a board that is on the wall in the area with the shared resources. On the board is a list of all the people working in the area along the left, and all the projects that require those resources along the top.

Such a board is illustrated below and represents how four projects will share resources in the Safety Engineering Group in week 43.

Safety Group Resource allocation Board Week 43					
Name	Hours available this week	Project 1	Project 2	Project 3	Project 4
Fred	30	10	5	15	0
James	15	5	5		5
John	40	5	15	10	10
Michael	20	0	10	5	5
Michelle	10	0	0	0	10
Sally	25	15	5	0	5
William	35	25	0	0	10

Figure 7.8 A resource allocation board

The project managers meet with the safety group on Monday mornings. The safety group manager and his engineers have already updated the board with how many hours each engineer has available for project work in the upcoming week. The reason for engineers not being available for the whole week is that they have other non-project work to do in support of other areas of the business, e.g., knowledge capture and documentation.

The project managers then quickly discuss their needs and priorities and agree how the available hours should be split among their projects and what they expect to be achieved in the week. This gives clear direction to the safety group and manages the expectations across the projects. Resource-level issues become collectively evident on a weekly basis and problems can be identified and fixed much earlier than by individuals reacting to isolated priorities or missed milestones. This meeting should last around twenty minutes and certainly no more than half an hour.

The project managers then move to the next resource allocation board. Typically there are only a few shared resources between projects and so a tour of these boards will typically take between one and one and a half hours. However, the waste they can avoid is considerable.

The photograph below shows a weekly resource allocation meeting in the engineering department of a Swedish company. The department creates bespoke designs for client orders, and they typically have up to ten such projects running at any one time.

Figure 7.9 A weekly resource allocation meeting

7.5.3 Time and resource slicing

Another way of balancing the work between projects and other activities is to either "time slice" or "resource slice."

Time slicing is a method of getting people focused on a particular project activity at a particular time and can take many forms. For example, all the functions that need to work on Project A can agree to always work on that project on Monday and Tuesday. They then work on Project B on Wednesday and Project C on Thursday and Friday. We have found this to be practically a given if you want to have multidisciplinary team working in a multiproject environment.

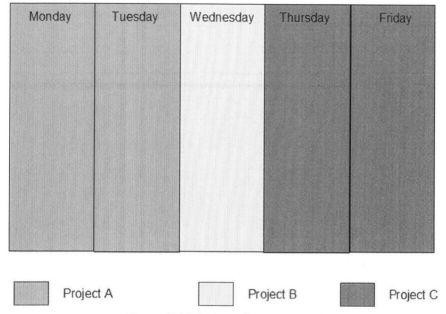

Monday	Tuesday	Wednesday	Thursday	Friday

Project A   Project B   Project C

Figure 7.10 A time slicing example

Alternatively, the service department may have to split its time between supporting customers and field engineers and supporting NPD projects. An example of time slicing would be that they do their customer and field engineer support work during the mornings and three afternoons a week. New product development work is then done during the two remaining afternoons and has the focus of the whole department. Other departments and planners also know that these are the hours available to them.

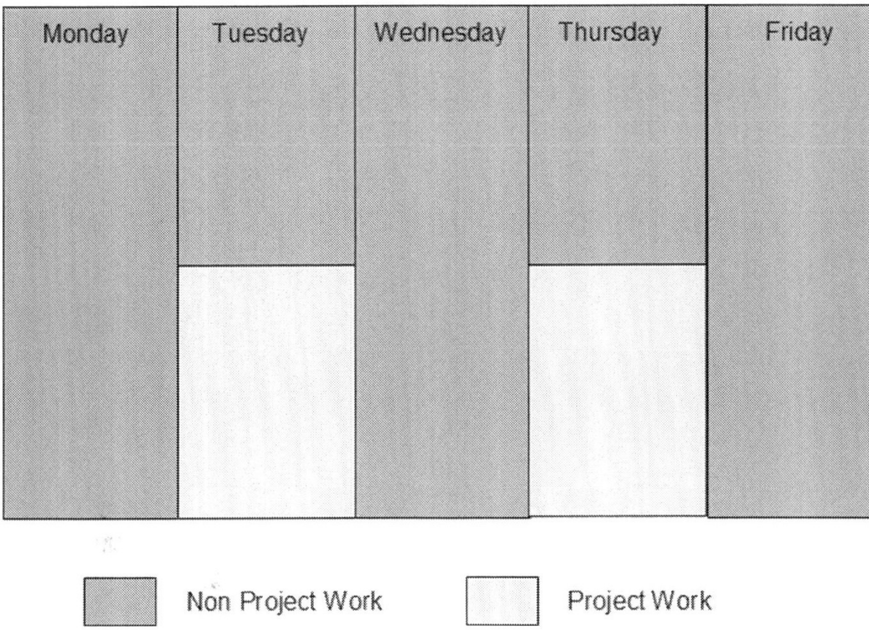

Monday	Tuesday	Wednesday	Thursday	Friday

Non Project Work   Project Work

Figure 7.11 Another example of time slicing

The example of the service department can also be used to illustrate "resource slicing." Instead of slicing the week into field support time and project time, the department could choose to split their people into the majority who support customers and field engineers full time, and the few who are needed to dedicate all their time to NPD projects. In this situation many companies choose to rotate their people between the roles.

A good example of resource slicing comes from a small engineering company we worked with in southern Sweden. They had recently merged with another manufacturing company and their designs were being produced on two sites, the second one unfamiliar with all the knowledge that couldn't be communicated by an engineering drawing. There were different manufacturing processes using different machine tools and equipment. Drawings had been created that were suited to one factory but weren't a good fit for the other. For this reason there was a high number of clarification questions and engineering change requests. These were hitting the small engineering team on an ad hoc basis and were constantly pulling

engineers away from their projects. The projects were to customize the company's products to a specific customer order, and without them there would be no new business. Tensions were running high because engineering was late with their projects *and* there were frequent stoppages in the factory as they waited for engineering information and decisions. Sales, engineering, quality, and manufacturing were all wasting time expediting work that was late. The engineering director questioned why his engineers should have to create "Donald Duck drawings" for manufacturing, who, he said, should be able to use the original drawings provided.

The solution to this problem was to recognize that manufacturing deserved to have timely information and decisions so that customers received their deliveries on time. We kept pointing out that "until you ship a product and collect the cash, *no one* gets paid." The means of providing this service to manufacturing was to resource slice the engineering department. Just one of the eight engineers was moved to an office in the factory close to the production lines with the role of preventing the manufacturing process from stopping due to a lack of engineering information. They called this the "rapid response" office and created a sign based cheekily on the Rolls-Royce emblem because they knew that Rob used to work there! The office was equipped with a CAD terminal and all the IT resources the engineer needed to do the job without travelling back to the office. When a problem was identified, an A3 was created and the time noted. The rapid response engineer then had sixty minutes to provide an answer that could allow work to continue. This could be in the form of a "marked-up" drawing with his signature. The rest of the engineering department were available to help but found they were now able to do their project work and support the rapid response engineer because they were no longer individually running to and from the factory with many of them getting involved in the same production issue because they were being chased by multiple departments trying to solve the same problem.

The Rapid Response engineer was in an ideal position for gaining an in-depth knowledge of manufacturing processes and their capabilities. This knowledge is invaluable for good

"design for manufacture," and so rotating the engineering team through the rapid response office is a hugely powerful training experience. In the Swedish company they planned to have an engineer in rapid response for a six-month term before being replaced. When Chris ran the engineering office we referred to earlier, he insisted the "shop engineer" role was one that all new hires shadowed as part of their induction.

The picture below shows the rapid response engineer updating his problem control board, and the rapid response emblem.

Figure 7.12 The Rapid Response engineer updating his problem control board

7.6 Knowledge management

Having read this far, you will not be surprised to learn that knowledge management is a vital factor throughout the entire NPD cycle, and the execution phase of the project is no exception. In this phase we are interested in "design for x" at a very detailed level. Remember we coined this term having realized that design-for-manufacturing or design-for-cost were not enough to take maximum advantage in team-based NPD. In the exploration phase the high-level architecture has been created and the team has explored elements of it in greater detail where there was insufficient knowledge to predict the system performance, reliability, or costs. During the execution

phase individual design features, tolerances, clearances, etc. are now being decided and the product must meet all the targets for performance, manufacturing, servicing, etc. As we made clear in the value engineering section of Chapter 6, the engineers need a good knowledge of the manufacturing processes that will produce and assemble the product and the way it will be serviced and supported in the field. Technical staff therefore need a broad appreciation of all stakeholder needs and trade-offs as well as purely technical trade-offs.

Again, it is important that information is readily available in a format that is instantly usable to the engineer doing her work, without the need for searching, compiling, analyzing, and interpreting data that has been stored in multiple formats for the convenience of those storing the information in the first place. We have recently found that a "wiki" style database edited by a few experts works very well. Any engineer can contribute information by creating a page and appending documents. The experts are automatically notified of newly created pages and have the power to edit them if they wish to. There is therefore no backlog of knowledge pages waiting for approval, and contributors see that their contribution is instantly available. To create consistency we've created templates for specific knowledge types, but we have also made the creation of new templates as easy as possible.

Just as in the exploration phase, checklists and design rules are useful, as are standard-feature libraries that match the capabilities of production processes and suppliers.

When creating a knowledge base and management system, keep asking yourself what knowledge is needed to improve the speed and accuracy of your projects and in what format this knowledge should be presented to technical staff. Keep it simple and easy to use, edit, and update. The bottom line is that if it is seen as value added then it will be used; if not, it will not be.

Figure 7.13 shows two wiki pages from the knowledge base of one of our client companies. They are the introductory page and one of the navigation pages. Of course we have

deliberately not shown the detailed knowledge since this is sensitive information now clearly understood to be vital competitive advantage.

Figure 7.13 One of our clients use InfoPoint for knowledge management

7.7 A3 problem solving

We have found that A3 problem solving is a powerful technique in every part of a business, and so it is of no surprise to find applications for it here in the execution phase. Lean thinking has taught us that wide-scale adoption of a simple problem-solving method will in the long term beat a limited elite with more esoteric tools. The execution phase of a project involves the creation and test of prototypes, and any problems identified here need to be resolved quickly. The A3 is ideal for managing this and encouraging teamwork to create solutions and the proof that the root causes have been addressed. We have created "A3 walls" where the status of all A3s can be seen and teams can easily determine where additional expertise or resources are needed to keep the process on track. A photograph of such a wall was shown earlier in this chapter in the section on flow cells.

7.8 Team-based project planning

In any situation requiring effective teamwork, the techniques described in Chapter 6 can be effectively employed. In the

execution phase, however, the number of people involved is much larger than in exploration and you need to keep in mind that large teams start becoming less effective. Our experience over the years shows us that eight to ten in a team is about the maximum for effective face-to-face teamwork on a regular basis.

Let's just explore that point for a minute. An engineer working on his own will eventually complete his project, but a second engineer added to the project would most likely enable the project to be completed in half the time. However, adding a third and fourth engineer is unlikely to complete the project in a third or a quarter of the time a single engineer would have taken. The reason for this is that the work needs to be divided into more parts, and the results of each engineer's work then needs to be integrated back into the whole. There also needs to be time for communication and coordination, and invariably there will be the occasional misunderstanding and time taken to make group decisions. This phenomenon is even more exaggerated in software development, where the task of writing a section of code is something that needs to be done alone and yet it all needs to be stitched back together and integration tested. So how large can a team become before it starts to sag under its own weight?

To answer this question, let's take a look at software development, since the problems of increasing team size are particularly acute there. A popular form of team-based project planning and execution in software development is the "scrum framework." Scrum is merely the term for a group of developers and testers. Scrum begins by estimating the hours required to complete tasks based on the complexity of the task relative to tasks already completed in the project. They then create a list of tasks that are to be completed with the available hours in the next "sprint." A sprint is usually a two- to four-week period, and the team works toward completing all the tasks by the end of the sprint. The advantage of this way of working is that problems are discovered quickly, as all the code created in a sprint must also be tested before the sprint ends. Over many years the software

community has realized that scrums larger than nine members slow down significantly and so they will create more scrums and have a "scrum of scrums" that keeps the work of each scrum aligned. It is not our intention to describe these software development techniques any further since there is a wealth of information readily available. However, the fact that they recognize that teams larger than nine begin to slow down significantly is noteworthy to us and in line with our experience

We have found that the situation with hardware design teams is slightly better than in the software world. This is because 3D CAD and physical parts allow for much better communication and coordination. However, we have observed that teams much larger than ten begin to struggle and it is best to seek ways of breaking down the work. The key is how to break down the work to keep multidisciplinary teams working at all levels, so it should be emphasized that creating smaller teams should not be done along functional lines. Having a design team, a service team, a marketing team, a test team, etc. will not achieve the teamwork needed to gain speed and eliminate waste. For this reason we always explore with clients exactly what they mean when they say teamwork. As in the exploration phase, the VVSA technique is very effective. In fact, the "sprint planning" used by software scrum teams is very similar.

7.9 Fix problems as you go

In the execution phase of projects there will of course be the need to verify and validate the new product designs. In many companies this phase is known as "design, make, and test." During the design stage there are usually a number of prototype builds which many companies designate with the Greek letters alpha, beta, and gamma. Each prototype is intended to be at an increasing level of maturity, with the gamma prototype being close to the production standard. The reason this is done is to recognize that only by building whole systems can

the performance truly be assessed and problems be identified. By "performance" we mean the design specifications, reliability, usability, serviceability, etc., etc.

Problems arise when the deadlines for alpha, beta, and gamma prototypes are fixed, and once the team has built the alpha prototype they are already under pressure to create the beta. The reason for creating the alpha is to learn as much as possible from it so that knowledge can be used in the beta. The team then needs to learn as much as possible from the beta before creating the gamma. All too often we see design teams crash through an aggressive schedule only to arrive at the final design reviews with an overwhelming number of unsolved issues which are then triaged into "must, should, and could" piles. This usually results in most of the "should and could" piles being left untouched, to be fixed as product changes after launch. Again, shaving time out of the project plan in the hope that it will be "right the first time" is very tempting, but the result is levels of waste as the backlog of open unresolved issues are continually being churned and worried about. It is much better to design tests that fully evaluate the prototypes and to allow the time and resources to solve the problems that are found.

In most companies the execution phase ends with validation tests of the production-ready version of the product, usually known as the "pre-build" standard. This testing involves all the tests needed for regulatory approval and qualifies production sources and processes. In some safety-critical industries with complex regulatory requirements, this testing can take many months. Because this is usually very close to the launch date, it is important that the rate of problem discovery is less than the rate of problem resolution. If the reverse is true then the product design is not maturing and the launch date is unlikely to be met.

Tracking the rates of problem discovery and problem resolution via the A3 flow and the accumulation of unresolved problems can be done on a daily basis, and resources can then be added to resolve problems if needed.

7.10 Allow for cost and weight to increase during verification testing

When Rob worked for a famous manufacturer of jet engines, the design teams knew that during the final testing stages of the program, it was as important to get a problem resolved quickly as it was to keep the cost of components low and the weight down. They looked at previous programs and found that during the development test phase, product cost would rise, on average, by around 5 percent and weight around 2 percent. They therefore planned for this in their project planning and drove the pre-validation test product cost to be 5 percent below their final target, together with a 2 percent lower weight target. Allowing for changes during the final "shakedown" is a great example of not planning for "right the first time," even in the final stages of your project.

We hope that you have found this book useful and applicable to your own organization and situation. We hope that the principles here, if not the exact examples, can help you see a better future for your NPD approach. We hope that this book ushers in a new era of awareness of NPD and nonrecurring projects in general, because we have seen that the potential performance that can be unlocked is amazing. For this to happen, our book has highlighted that technical staff and management must work together to use the knowledge we have advanced to find a new accord under which both go about developing and managing an NPD project.

The importance of recognizing the difference between exploration and execution phases and being respectful of the promise point is vital going forward. Technical staff working in isolation with walls either real or virtual should be something consigned to a previous era. We believe there is no place for the cubicle in our system. Multidisciplinary work should be the norm, not the exception, but the technique must be more than just throwing people in a room together. By using the techniques as we have described, we have seen teams come together to work with incredible efficiency and outcomes compared to the old approaches, and almost all would never want to go back to how it was before. In the coming decades we hope to see exploration-phase workers leaving their desks behind and moving to more studio-like work environments. We expect them to be joined by collaborators from many disciplines and to be led by people who understand the importance of learning as much as definition and completion of tasks. Similarly, we call on educators to start to break down the traditional divisions created in education and foster the talent it takes to be part of a high-performing team.

Above all we want more people to try our system and enjoy the benefits we have seen over and over so that this kind of

approach becomes the normal way of doing things in NPD. More than anything else, we cannot wait to see the better products and services you bring to the world as a result.

Rob and Chris

About the Authors

Rob Westrick

Rob Westrick is the Vice President of Research and Development for Elekta Oncology, a leading producer of radio therapy equipment. However, his career spans many industries including aerospace, construction vehicles, oil and gas equipment as well as complex medical devices. At General Electric Aircraft Engines Rob was trained in Edwards Deming's continuous improvement methods and Six Sigma. He spent four years as an aircraft mishap investigator which ignited his interest in design failures whether the cause was design error or a design that was unnecessarily hard to manufacture or service. He realized the decisions taken during the design process are all important but in many cases these decisions are made without realizing their true consequences.

As Rob moved to new sectors he took this knowledge with him and broadened his experience of transforming the process of creating new product designs. In 2005 he decided to start his own consultancy and in 2007 he joined Simpler Consulting where he met Chris Cooper, a kindred spirit, and together they created the Simpler Design System[SM].

Chris Cooper

Chris Cooper has over 20 years of leadership experience in the delivery of successful large-scale Lean transformations across a broad range of industries, companies and countries. His industry segment experience includes aerospace, defence, military, finance, marketing, health care, pharmaceutical, manufacturing, and maintenance, repair and overhaul (MRO).

Chris's Lean journey began in 1989 as a student of the Kawasaki Production System (KPS) while working for Europe's largest defence company, BAE Systems. During this time he became part of the leadership team that drove the company's Lean transformation of the defence division all the way to a value stream organized company winning a Queen's Award for Export. As a result, Chris was promoted to be the company's first Integrated Product Development Team Leader (IPT) position to introduce set-based-concurrent-engineering methods to Europe. During this period Chris was trained in six sigma and design six sigma by Motorola, Inc. As the IPT leader he won a Chairman's Award for Innovation and a McDonnell Douglas Supplier award for introducing Lean techniques beyond the shop floor. Directly before joining Simpler, Chris was the Lean Advisor to the Eurofighter Program, then the world's largest non-U.S. based military program, where he worked as a member of the Chief Engineer's staff team.

Chris's professional career in Lean and six sigma consulting began in 2002 when he joined Simpler in the early days of European expansion. As a member of the European leadership team, he has helped grow the business ten-fold since. Chris has been at the forefront of the Lean revolution speaking at conferences, working with executive teams, and as an assessor for the Shingo Prize. He has been the sensei for many significant and pioneering Lean transformations and has often introduced Lean concepts to new sectors and organizations in the commercial business and non-profit fields. As Vice President, Chris leads a multi-cultural team of consultants working in more than ten languages throughout Europe and Asia.

Chris also authored *The Little Book of Lean*. Chris is an Aeronautical Engineer through his formal apprenticeship program with BAE Systems, and has a Business and Technology (BTEC) Higher National Diploma (HND) from the University of Humberside.

36611982R00169

Made in the USA
Lexington, KY
28 October 2014